Lean Six Sigma Service Excellence

A Guide to Green Belt Certification and Bottom Line Improvement

Gerald M. Taylor

Library of Congress Cataloging-in-Publication Data

Taylor, Gerald M.
    Lean six sigma service excellence : a guide to green belt certification
and bottom line improvement / by Gerald M. Taylor.
        p. cm.
    Includes bibliographical references and index.
    ISBN 978-1-60427-006-8 (hardcover : alk. paper)
    1. Service industries—Management. 2. Six sigma (Quality control
standard) 3. Service industries—Quality control. 4. Production
management. I. Title.
    HD9980.5.T39 2008
    658.4'013—dc22   2008030940

Phone: (954) 727-9333
Fax: (561) 892-0700
Web: www.jrosspub.com

TABLE OF CONTENTS

PREFACE

Today, the U.S. economy is dominated by non-manufacturing service-oriented profit-seeking companies, government agencies, and not-for-profit organizations. Executives, middle managers, and individual contributors who work in service industries like health care, financial services, telecommunications, and call centers seek a user-friendly method for taking the applications of Lean Six Sigma and successfully translating them into a services environment.

This book is intended to be a source for the basic principles and applications of Lean Six Sigma as it relates to a services business context. It provides the tools and a simple step-by-step method for implementing a Lean Six Sigma performance excellence system in a non-manufacturing environment. The book is a 12-chapter resource and workbook that includes illustrations and practice exercises anyone can use to build their competence and confidence in the basic principles and applications of Lean Six Sigma. It functions as a manual in that it provides a solid road map to establish an operational excellence program within a services organization. It also is an excellent source for additional resources.

What makes this book different from other Six Sigma publications is that it not only is intended for service providers but also is written for the average business professional. You may have read about and heard how Six Sigma is heavily laden with and dependent on statistics. Many professionals believe that one has to have a high degree of competency in calculus and statistical analysis to be successful using the method. The truth is that Six Sigma is not difficult to apply. This book is a resource for the frontline supervisor as well as the executive who desires a user-friendly guide to service excellence and customer loyalty.

HOW THE BOOK IS ORGANIZED

Chapter 1 deals with what should be but isn't always the quest of all executives and managers in corporate America—improved productivity. The chapter defines productivity in measurable terms. It discusses why productivity is so vital to corporate America in general and why productivity growth is so important to the American economy. Given that this book is dedicated to managers of service and transactional organizations, this chapter emphasizes how the concept of productivity can be used as a distinctive competence to bring a competitive advantage to service companies.

Chapter 2 deals with the process. It defines the properties of a well-designed process management system, examines three basic methods for process development, discusses the qualities of a cross-functional organization, and outlines some basic process vocabulary and definitions. The objective of this chapter is to educate readers about service process design and all of the factors, activities, events, and requirements that make service processes work and work well.

It is true that even satisfied customers switch providers. Even though they are satisfied, they switch because they may be better off with another provider. Chapter 3 examines the concept of customer loyalty over customer satisfaction. It defines a loyal customer as one that operates with "extreme prejudice" toward a company's products and services. The idea behind this chapter is to encourage service companies to not only create value and customer satisfaction but to also acquire and maintain the largest loyal customer base in the marketplace.

An understanding of performance variation is essential to be effective at improving the processes by which a company delivers its services. As an outcome of reading Chapter 4, the reader will be better equipped to use his or her understanding of performance variation to make good business decisions with numerical facts and information, demonstrate how to display baseline process performance using a run chart, and take the right action to address each type of variation in performance.

The purpose of Chapter 5 is to provide a reference that explains how to construct and use the basic analytical tool kit employed by Six Sigma green belts and black belts around the world. The use of these tools and techniques is essential for achieving service excellence because they promote the use of facts and data as the basis for decision making and problem solving.

Chapter 6 covers the important topic of measuring performance. It defines and discusses the major categories of performance measurement for a service organization. It examines how a Six Sigma professional can define and structure a performance measurement system and how to use the tools described in earlier chapters to develop an effective dashboard of key performance indicators.

Chapter 7 is dedicated to the vital antecedent of a successful Six Sigma program: the Six Sigma project team. As a basic building block of a Six Sigma effort, the Six Sigma project team is the essential ingredient for an organization to eliminate those barriers to optimum productivity. This chapter discusses how a project team is structured and what its key roles and responsibilities are.

Chapter 8 focuses on key intra-team dynamics—how to work within a team to produce effective decisions and solve problems. This chapter also provides an overview of the basic elements for successfully facilitating change.

The practice of Six Sigma uses the vast experience of managers coupled with supporting facts and information to analyze problems at their root cause. Chapter 9 is devoted to defining the practice of Six Sigma. It discusses the prevailing definitions of Six Sigma and describes Six Sigma in terms of what it is and what it is not. It contrasts Six Sigma with other quality methods, explores key Six Sigma concepts, and provides an overview of how to manage a DMAIC project.

Chapter 10 lays out a brief overview and a step-by-step strategy to establish a performance excellence system in a service-oriented environment. The overview defines the attributes of a strong performance excellence system, and the chapter discusses how to focus on an organization's core processes, how to integrate a measurement system, how to eliminate non-value-added tasks, and how to move forward toward Six Sigma performance.

This book is not only dedicated to using Six Sigma as a means to achieve service excellence but is also devoted to employing Lean thinking to improve an organization's operating efficiencies. Earlier chapters alluded to the application of Lean tools without specific references to the practice of Lean. The purpose of Chapter 11 is to, in more explicit ways, define what Lean thinking is and how its principles are applied in a service environment. It provides an introduction to certain concepts of Lean production and their applicability in a non-manufacturing setting. The chapter focuses on the concepts of value, waste, value stream mapping, and the 5S of Lean thinking.

IN KEEPING

We are very excited about the fact that Lean Six Sigma is becoming very popular with retailers, utility companies, government agencies, finance and insurance companies, health care organizations, call centers, logistics companies, and shared services organizations. As you embark on using Lean Six Sigma, we would like to hear from you about how this book helps your efforts.

The Performance Management Group LLC
www.helpingmakeithappen.com
info@helpingmakeithapppen.com

ACKNOWLEDGMENTS

I read in a very good book that you should acknowledge the Lord in all that you do and he will direct your path. My first acknowledgment goes to my Lord and Savior Jesus Christ, without whom I would not have the strength, motivation, or courage to take this and many other steps in my life.

Second, I would like to thank Drew Gierman and everyone at J. Ross Publishing, Inc. for having the confidence and taking the time to consider the idea and manuscript that resulted in this publication. To be associated with such a professional organization that has such a commitment to quality and performance improvement is an honor.

I am grateful to all of the clients of The Performance Management Group with whom our training, certifications, and partnering have resonated and inspired me to write this book to further the good news about Six Sigma and performance improvement.

Finally, I would like to thank Dr. W. Edwards Deming—a man who was curious about "why some people have so many good things while others are sleeping on mats in rags, hungry."* I believe the following very true statement can be said about Deming and his cadre of statisticians: "Not since have so few done so much for so many."

---

* Walton, Mary (1986). *The Deming Management Method,* New York: Perigee Books/Putnam Publishing Group.

ABOUT THE AUTHOR

Gerald Taylor is Founder and President of The Performance Management Group LLC, a firm that specializes in performance improvement and leadership development. He has over 15 years of experience designing and implementing quality and Six Sigma solutions as an internal corporate consultant and as an external engagement manager. His past and present client list includes Dynegy Global Communications, HEB Grocery Stores, Logix Communications, The Oneok Corporation, PacWest Communications, and The University of Arizona.

Mr. Taylor is a certified Six Sigma black belt who trains and certifies Six Sigma professionals and quality practitioners to serve as technical experts in their working environments. He is a certified Malcolm Baldrige examiner through the Arizona Quality Alliance (2000 and 2001) and has participated as a two-time quality examiner for the Arizona Governor's Spirit of Excellence in Government Award.

In addition to his career as a business consultant, Mr. Taylor also was an associate professor of business administration at Western International University, where he taught supervision and leadership and human resource management. As a faculty member for Mesa College, he taught leadership and empowerment strategies. Currently, he serves as a board member for the Arizona Chapter of the Association for Strategic Planning. Mr. Taylor earned his undergraduate degree in management and his MBA from the W.P. Carey School of Business at Arizona State University.

Free value-added materials available from
the Download Resource Center at www.jrosspub.com

At J. Ross Publishing we are committed to providing today's professional with practical, hands-on tools that enhance the learning experience and give readers an opportunity to apply what they have learned. That is why we offer free ancillary materials available for download on this book and all participating Web Added Value™ publications. These online resources may include interactive versions of material that appears in the book or supplemental templates, worksheets, models, plans, case studies, proposals, spreadsheets and assessment tools, among other things. Whenever you see the WAV™ symbol in any of our publications, it means bonus materials accompany the book and are available from the Web Added Value Download Resource Center at www.jrosspub.com.

Downloads available for *Lean Six Sigma Service Excellence: A Guide to Green Belt Certification and Bottom Line Improvement* consist of project management and performance excellence system assessment tools, several Six Sigma planning and analysis templates, and control chart selection, construction, and analysis exercises.

THE QUEST FOR PRODUCTIVITY

Perhaps you should be more productive.

In a recent television commercial for an international seller of computers and business machines, an executive is talking to his psychiatrist. He is conveying the hellish nightmare he recently had and is looking for an interpretation of his dream. His dream consisted of a sword stuck in a stone and he couldn't get it out. It was his magic "cost-cutting" sword. He looks to his counselor for answers and receives, what he and many American executives would perceive to be, a very disturbing response: "Perhaps there are no more costs to cut." "What should I do?" the executive asks. And the counselor responds, "Perhaps you should be more *productive.*"

This book deals with what should be but isn't always the quest of all executives and managers in business today—improved productivity. In this chapter, productivity will be defined in measurable terms that are useful for managers at all levels. We will discuss not only why productivity is so important to business in general, but also why productivity growth is so essential to a strong national economy and a first-rate quality of life. Given that this book is dedicated to managers of service and transactional organizations, it will enhance your understanding of how the concept of productivity can be used as a distinctive competence to create a competitive advantage.

This chapter also will answer the "why" question regarding quality improvement in general and Six Sigma in particular. After reading it, you will know and understand why certain management practices like total quality management and the Baldrige National Quality Program Criteria for Performance Excellence have been embraced over the past decades and why Six Sigma and Lean thinking are now recognized as a means to deliver productivity improvements for successful companies worldwide.

WHAT IS PRODUCTIVITY?

In general, productivity is regarded as the key to economic prosperity and the essential component to a quality standard of living. For an organization, corporation, and nation, a solid and accurate measure of productivity can be an important tool in determining how to allocate time, energy, capital, and other resources.

There are a variety of ways to calculate productivity. Almost all of them involve some aspect of the following definition:

$$\text{Productivity} = \text{Output per unit of input}$$

Productivity also can be defined as the value produced for consumption in the marketplace divided by the factors required to produce the said value:

$$\frac{\text{Value produced}}{\text{Land} + \text{Labor} + \text{Energy} + \text{Capital} + \text{Machinery/Technology} + \text{etc.}}$$

A motorcycle plant could increase its productivity by increasing its output of motorcycles while keeping its factors of production fixed. Likewise, the same plant could increase its productivity by keeping its motorcycle output steady while decreasing its inputs of labor, energy, capital machinery, etc.

With respect to a service operation, a customer service department could increase its productivity by effectively responding to a greater volume of customer inquiries while keeping the number of its workstations, people, budgeted hours, etc. fixed. The same customer service center also can increase its productivity by responding effectively to a constant volume of customer inquiries while decreasing the number of people and workstations and the amount of time.

Whether you manage a manufacturing plant or a service operation, an effective metric of productivity should be an accurate measure of the value that is added to the basic resources that a company brings to bear in its *productive processes.* An effective metric of productivity also should accurately measure the wealth that is created at the end of that productive process. The deeper an activity goes into the process of manufacturing or service delivery, the more cost it creates because the activity taxes the factors of production and service provision. The object of each manager should be to create a situation where the value produced by the productive process far exceeds its cost. The difference will be returned to the company in the form of profit, shareholder value, and long-term employment. On a national scale, this difference is translated into quality of life, standard of living, and all of the economic virtues of capitalism.

In a *Wall Street Journal* article dated November 3, 2006, Mark Whitehouse and Tim Aeppel drove this point home. They commented on the fact that productivity growth is not only a key driver of a nation's prosperity but also is a crucial factor in controlling inflation, boosting profits, and improving living standards. In their words: "When companies can produce more for each hour their employees work, they can pay higher wages or reap bigger profits without having to raise prices. [A nation's] annual productivity growth of 2% would more than double inflation-adjusted wages over 40 years, all else being equal."

In a market economy driven by customer choice and competition, productivity growth not only is maintained through efficient management of the productive process but also is sustained by the quality of goods produced and services provided. The numerator in our definition of productivity—value produced (output)—takes into account that the products and services produced are marketable and in demand.

One of the best examples of the powerful impact that productivity can have on a company and an economy is the Ford Motor Company of the early 20th century. In the early 1900s, the Ford Motor Company was the birthplace of one of the greatest productivity breakthroughs in corporate history. Before Ford, cars were assembled by hand, one at a time, in what was called a job shop. In 1913, Henry Ford set up the first mass production assembly line. Through specialization of tasks, Ford's assembly line developed the capacity to produce a car every 10 seconds. This new capability and extraordinary output enabled Ford to cut prices to as low as $260 per car, while simultaneously doubling the minimum wage of its employees. The workforce prospered and the market of potential customers grew. Soon every manufacturer followed suit and the modern economy was born.

PRODUCTIVITY AND GLOBAL IMPLICATIONS: OUTSOURCING

In a global economy, improving productivity and prosperity is considered to be a "competition among nations." Corporations in developing countries like China, India, and Mexico can operate a manufacturing plant, a call center, or a back office operation and pay their workers a small percentage of what a company would pay an American worker. Economically speaking, these developing countries have a comparative advantage when accounting for productivity. It becomes nearly impossible for the company operating in America to compete globally on the basis of labor cost alone. According to a recent report from the Central Intelligence Agency's National Intelligence Council, the integration of China and India into the global economy is creating a huge, low-cost labor force. As more companies take advantage of this cheap labor, "the transition will not be painless and will hit the middle classes of the developed world in particular."* Simply put, global economics and competition are forcing international corporations to find a more favorable starting position with respect to productivity.

If the corporation operating in America cannot compete on the basis of labor cost, on what basis can it obtain a competitive advantage over its global rival in the newly developing world? Many theorize that the corporation operating in America has maintained, and can continue to maintain, an advantage in the area of knowledge and in the arena of *quality*.

QUALITY AND PRODUCTIVITY: A HISTORICAL PERSPECTIVE

In the early 1900s, the basis for measuring productivity was derived from time and motion studies. This basis dictated that the more total output that

---

* Dobbs, Lou (2005). "The Global Outlook on Outsourcing," CNN.com, January 31 (1927 GMT).

flowed from a production line, the more productive an operation was. Hence, management believed the faster the production line worked, the more productive the company was. As a consequence, American management viewed the function of quality control as an additional cost and a hindrance to increased productivity.

The problem with this concept of productivity was that it did not account for waste, scrap, rework, failures, and other costly outcomes of poor quality. It was never assumed that the faster the production line worked, the more waste it produced. The application of this concept resulted in not only more waste but also in many products being identified as junk and needing to be reworked. Any shoddy products missed by inspection were paid for by warranties. In the final analysis, the total cost of goods sold had to cover the cost of inspection, rework, scrap, rejected parts, and warranty returns. We also see similar results in service operations today, where the cost of providing service includes the cost of redundant inquiries into a call center, excessive rework in order management processes, and numerous customer credits rebated due to missed deadlines and broached service level agreements. These corporate management practices simply lacked, and currently lack, the understanding of how to effectively integrate the concept of quality with productivity.

Many of the ideas that helped integrate the concepts of quality and productivity were developed by engineers at Bell Laboratories during the early 20th century. Their principles were given wide expression and implementation when Dr. W. Edwards Deming, a statistician and Bell Labs engineer, was contracted as a consultant for Japanese companies shortly after World War II. Dr. Deming understood the substantial impact that improving quality can have on productivity. He introduced the Japanese to statistical quality control (a vital component of Six Sigma) and told them: "You can produce quality. You have a method for doing it. You've learned what quality is." He went on and instructed them to "...bring your process under control." As he would later relate in his seminars: "I told them they would capture markets the world over within five years. They beat that prediction. Within four years, buyers all over the world were screaming for Japanese products."* Buyers and customers the world over are still screaming for Japanese products today!

---

* Walton, Mary (1986). *The Deming Management Method*, New York: Perigee Books/Putnam Publishing Group, pp. 14 and 15.

THE COST OF POOR QUALITY

As discussed above, the traditional concept of productivity dictated that the faster you worked, the more productive you were. Also noted earlier, this concept of productivity failed to account for rework, failures, scrap, waste, and other costly outcomes of poor quality. American management failed to realize the financial impact these costs had on the value of companies. Deming, however, did not. He referred to these costs as the *cost of quality,* now known and perhaps more accurately described in the world of Six Sigma as the *cost of poor quality.*

What is the cost of poor quality? Simply put, the cost of poor quality is defined as the price a company pays for not being process perfect. If you account for the waste, scrap, loss of customer goodwill, lawsuits, fines, accidents, increased insurance premiums, customer credits, warranty returns, and damage to equipment, these mostly unbudgeted and unexpected costs can undermine the value of a company. The cost of poor quality can represent approximately 25% of all costs in a manufacturing company and almost 35% of a service company's cost of sales.

Failure cost is responsible for the lion's share of the cost of poor quality; it can be defined in two ways:

- **Internal failure cost**: Occurs before or during the delivery of a service to a customer. It is typically a negative by-product of the lack of quality in a service delivery operation. Examples of internal failures include process rework, redesigning networks, post-operation infections, longer hospital stays, incorrect billing, on-the-job accidents, etc.
- **External failure cost**: Occurs after the delivery of a service to a customer. Examples include patient returns, complaint investigations, increased warranty claims, fines and penalties, lawsuits, returned food, customer credits, lost customers, reprovision and redelivery of service, etc.

Deming understood and stated that the cost of poor quality, along with a loss of customer confidence, can "bring on a crisis that can threaten the very existence of a company."*

---

* Walton, Mary (1986). *The Deming Management Method,* New York: Perigee Books/Putnam Publishing Group, pp. 14 and 15.

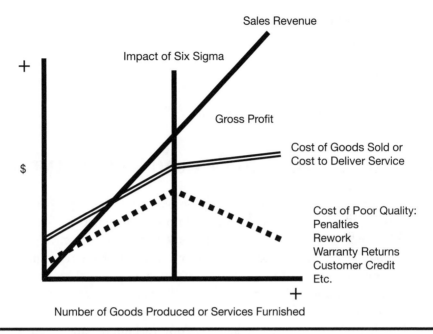

FIGURE 1.1. The Six Sigma Cost Curve

As illustrated in Figure 1.1, Six Sigma and other quality improvement methods strive to mitigate the effect the cost of poor quality can have by curtailing these costs and preventing them from developing. By eliminating and preventing the cost of poor quality, Six Sigma and other quality improvement methodologies have favorable impacts on the cost of selling goods and delivering services.

QUALITY IMPROVEMENT AND CORPORATE AMERICA

Deming and his contributions to Japanese companies laid the groundwork for the Six Sigma methodology effectively used worldwide today. Without Dr. Deming's contribution, corporate America would not have the practice of total quality management—the parent of Six Sigma. The practice of total quality management includes:

1. The Baldrige criteria (Malcolm Baldrige National Quality Award)
2. Statistical process control

3. Design of Experiments
4. Six Sigma
5. Kaizen
6. ISO
7. Process re-engineering
8. Continuous process improvement

THE VALUE PROPOSITION OF QUALITY IMPROVEMENT

The practice of quality improvement encompasses two main propositions: to increase corporate productivity and to improve customer loyalty. These theoretical models are illustrated in Figures 1.2 and 1.3, respectively.

Deming proved that improving quality creates a chain reaction that increases productivity and value. By experiencing a continual reduction in mistakes, delays, and errors, a company will experience less rework and waste and a more productive use of materials, employee time, and technology. The Deming Chain Reaction dictates a continual improvement in quality that translates into lower and lower costs. As costs go down, productivity goes up, along with better quality products and services. With better quality products and services at lower costs, a company will experience greater market penetration and more business. The result will lead to enhanced shareholder value and better paying jobs.

Figure 1.3 depicts how company X initiated a quality improvement program and increased its level of customer satisfaction, which led to a greater market share of loyal customers. Through *voice of the customer* assessments,

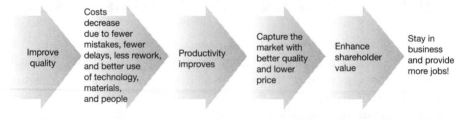

FIGURE 1.2. The Deming Value Chain. Proposition #1: An Operational Perspective—To Increase Corporate Productivity
Reprinted from Deming, W. Edwards, *Out of the Crisis*, p. 3, © 2000 Massachusetts Institute of Technology, by permission of The MIT Press.

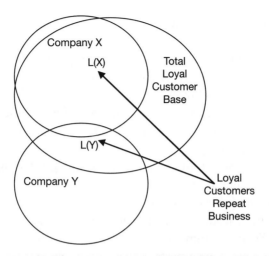

FIGURE 1.3. The Customer Loyalty Venn Diagram. Proposition #2: A Customer Perspective—To Improve Customer Loyalty

company X was able to ascertain its customers' needs, attitudes, and perceptions. Company X understands what its customers think is right and wrong about its products and services today. Company X's customers brag about its services and products. Its customers keep coming back! They are loyal and they do not require company X to expend any marketing or sales expenses on them. Due to customer loyalty, company X's fixed costs are already paid. It can now offer its products and services at a marginal discount, increase market share, and drive the marginal revenue directly to the bottom line!

THE BENEFITS OF THE QUALITY MOVEMENT IN CORPORATE AMERICA

We have discussed how companies can, by implementing quality improvement programs like Six Sigma, benefit from improved productivity. The following outline indicates additional positive by-products of implementing Six Sigma in the corporate situation.

- Benefits to the company
    1. Better financial position—due to improved operating efficiencies
    2. Greater share of loyal customers—less churn

    3. Reduced exposure to the downside effects of industry and economic downturns

    4. Great brand recognition and company reputation

    5. Better and more predictable environment in which to succeed

■ Benefits to its employees

    1. Reduction or elimination of the need for rework

    2. Improved communication and teamwork across functions and departments

    3. Greater assured company security and greater likelihood of employment security

    4. Increased job satisfaction

    5. Enhanced leadership and group dynamics skills

■ Benefits to its customers

    1. Customers have a partner they can count on

    2. Customers find it easy to do business

    3. Customers get great products and services repeatedly

    4. Customers feel good about their purchases—no regrets

    5. Customers get great value

THE QUALITY MOVEMENT IN AMERICA HAS DELIVERED ON ITS PROMISE

Malcolm Baldrige National Quality Program

For ten years, the U.S. Department of Commerce's National Institute of Standards and Technology (NIST) conducted a stock performance study of the Malcolm Baldrige National Quality Award winners. For eight of these ten, the investment study concluded that the Baldrige group stock outperformed the S&P 500.

The index included the publicly traded U.S. companies that won the Malcolm Baldrige National Quality Award between 1993 and 2002. NIST invested a hypothetical $1000 in each of the winners and also invested another hypothetical $1000 in the S&P 500. The investments were tracked from the first month following the award announcement through December 1, 2002. Adjustments were made in the case of stock splits. Results for the eight years from 1995 to 2002 are as follows:*

---

* NIST Web site at http://www.quality.nist.gov/Stock_Studies.

- **2002**: Baldrige outperforms S&P 500 3 to 1
- **2001**: Baldrige outperforms S&P 500 4.4 to 1
- **2000**: Baldrige outperforms S&P 500 almost 5 to 1
- **1999**: Baldrige outperforms S&P 500 2.6 to 1
- **1998**: Baldrige outperforms S&P 500 almost 3 to 1
- **1997**: Baldrige outperforms S&P 500 3.5 to 1
- **1996**: Baldrige outperforms S&P 500 4 to 1
- **1995**: Baldrige outperforms S&P 500 6.5 to 1

Other studies have indicated similar results. A joint study conducted by Vinod Singhal of the Georgia Institute of Technology and Kevin Hendricks of the University of Western Ontario showed a correlation between quality improvement and business results. The two conducted a five-year study of more than 600 recipients of various quality awards and found that quality award recipients experienced a 44% higher stock price return, a 48% higher growth in operating income, and a 37% higher growth in sales than a control group of similar size and industry standing. Other notable benefits included improvements in employee satisfaction, higher return on sales, and improved asset growth.

Six Sigma Quality Improvement

"According to the Six Sigma Academy, Six Sigma black belts save companies approximately $230,000 per project and can complete four to six projects per year. General Electric has estimated benefits on the order of $10 billion during the first five years of deployments."* GE initiated its Six Sigma program in 1995. To learn more about GE's Six Sigma program and accomplishments, go to http://www.ge.com/sixsigma/.

Companies of all types and sizes are in the midst of a Six Sigma revolution. The Depository Trust & Clearing Corporation, the largest financial services post-trade infrastructure organization in the world, identified annual savings of almost $2 million in its first year of Six Sigma implementations. The company experienced a 24% improvement in the number of inquiries resolved in one day, a 23% decrease in processing time per inquiry, and a 15% improvement in delivery order inquiries resolved in one day. In addition, an audit of both dividend and securities processing inquiries helped

---

* www.isixsigma.com/sixsigma/six_sigma.asp.

drop the company's already low error rate by 85%. To learn more about its accomplishments, go to www.dtcc.com/Publications/dtcc/dec01/6sigma.html.

At JP Morgan Chase, Six Sigma has been used to break down the opening of a new account into a series of measurable tasks. According to Charles P. Costa, an executive vice president and chief information officer for retail and middle-market banking, the changes have shortened the cycle time to open a new account at a branch by an average of 30%. "One sign that new-account problems are going away is that call volume from new customers has dropped 25%," Mr. Costa reported.* Additional gains experienced are in the form of reduced customer attrition and increased sales of existing products. He added that streamlined account openings and improved service processes are contributing "millions of dollars" to Morgan Chase's bottom line.

Kenneth D. Lewis, CEO and president of Bank of America, reported the following impacts of Six Sigma on the financial services giant:

> In the asset management group, associates are using Six Sigma to boost sales and revenue opportunities. Last year, for example, these efforts resulted in improvements in processing of 22% for same day payments and 35% for same day deposits. The bank's efficiency ratio—a measurement of how much it costs to make money— is 53.9% and continues to improve, thanks to Six Sigma troubleshooting.**

It is clear that a case has been made for Six Sigma and quality improvement methodologies as a winning operational strategy.

THE FOUNDATION OF THE QUALITY MOVEMENT IN AMERICA

The three experts who initiated and developed quality improvement as a management practice in America are Dr. W. Edwards Deming, Philip Crosby, and Joseph Juran. As gurus of the method, they adopted and taught the following principles:

---

*Costanzo, Chris (2002). "Bank Takes on Six Sigma: Service at Morgan, Processing at SunTrust," *American Banker,* June 5.

** From Bank of America's 2002 annual report, quarterly earnings reports, and various media.

1. Understand and satisfy what your customers demand, expect, and require of you.
2. Make quality everyone's job; be committed to it throughout your company.
3. Use statistical tools and metrics to analyze and measure your processes.
4. Understand your processes as a system of integrated elements consisting of people, procedures, methods, materials, information, and technology.
5. Promote teamwork within and across organizational boundaries.
6. Understand performance variation.
7. Eliminate waste and defects.
8. Never stop striving for continual improvement.

CONCLUSION

This chapter defined productivity in measurable terms useful for managers at all levels. It discussed why productivity is so important to business in general and why productivity growth is so essential to a strong national economy. The business case was made for the importance of quality improvement, Lean thinking, and Six Sigma. The chapter closed with some basic principles of quality. I now invite you to continue reading as the applications of Six Sigma and the fundamentals of Lean thinking for service companies are further defined.

2

IT'S THE PROCESS!

How many times during your work day do you say the word process?
—*Gerald Taylor*
Managing Consultant, TPMG

PAYING THE ULTIMATE PRICE FOR NOT BEING PROCESS PERFECT

In February 2003, the Associated Press reported that a 17-year-old girl, from a small town near Guadalajara, Mexico, temporarily moved to the United States with her family for a heart-lung transplant. The transplant was performed at Duke University Hospital, one of the nation's top medical centers. Three days after her February 7 surgery, the teenager lay in her hospital bed in critical condition after mistakenly receiving organs that did not match her type O-positive blood. The young girl was given organs from a donor with type A blood.

The AP reported that the hospital acknowledged making a tragic mistake—but at the time did not know how it happened. In a taped statement released by Duke, the operating surgeon reported that "unfortunately, in this case, human errors were made during the *process*" to match the organs with the patient. According to published AP reports, "In a letter to the United Network for Organ Sharing, which matches patients with donated organs, Duke officials said the surgeon and Carolina Donor Services, a procurement agency, failed to share information about her blood type." The donor organs were delivered to Durham, North Carolina from Boston, with the paperwork correctly listing the donor's type A blood, according to an official at the New England Organ Bank, which sent the organs. The hospital acknowledged making an unspecified mistake that led to the mix-up and has since modified its *process* and system to include double checks so the mistake will never occur again.

This is a tragic and regrettable event. The incident never needed to occur—it was preventable. Unfortunately, similar incidents occur every day in hospitals and health care systems across America. According to a recent study, more than 4000 children died in 2000 because of safety lapses in hospitals. In addition, more than $1 billion in hospital charges occur annually because of longer stays and follow-up care for the sick and injured. Post-operative infections, with infection rates as high as 11% for certain types of operations, account for a major cause of injuries and excess cost. According to the Centers for Medicare & Medicaid Services and the Centers for Disease Control and Prevention, many of these infections are preventable.

What does this have to do with Six Sigma? Whether you are delivering packages, responding to inquiries in a call center, or performing operations in a hospital, you are providing a service that requires you to be process perfect. The objective of this chapter is to teach about service process design and the factors that make processes perform well.

IT'S THE PROCESS!

One fundamental assumption of Six Sigma is that everyone in a *productive* organization contributes something of value. It is not always so, but the practice of Six Sigma works to accomplish that idea. Recall from Chapter 1 that as activities flow through work processes, they create operating costs because they tax the factors of production and service delivery. To be certain an operation is operating productively, a manager must be certain the value created by these activities by far exceeds the cost required to produce them.

Another driving assumption of Six Sigma is that everything, no matter how small or minor the task, is accomplished through a process. As illustrated in Figure 2.1, in everything we do there is an input, resources brought to bear on it, and an output. Likewise, for every process there is a supplier, a producer, and a customer.

In the practice of Six Sigma, process design and process management are not only concerned with what happens inside the black box but also inter-

FIGURE 2.1. The Black Box Theory

ested in the quality of work received from the supplier and the quality of the work product that is delivered to the customer. Six Sigma service excellence strives to answer the following questions:

1. How does a company manage its factors of production to deliver a service that is fit for its customers' use?
2. How does a company keep its cost to deliver that service far below the value that it creates?
3. How can a company deliver a service at a cost that drives a substantial return on its assets?

In this chapter, we will begin to explore some of the answers to these questions by starting with first things first—the process! Basic process vocabulary and definitions will be outlined, the properties of a well-designed process management system will be defined, three fundamental methods for process development will be examined, and the qualities of a *cross-functional* organization will be discussed.

PROCESS VOCABULARY: A COMMON LANGUAGE

To open this chapter, a brief list of process vocabulary is provided in Table 2.1. This list is provided to furnish a common language and terminology for Six Sigma professionals. Take a few minutes to read each word and definition.

PROPERTIES OF A WELL-DESIGNED PROCESS MANAGEMENT SYSTEM

As illustrated in Figure 2.2, processes generally involve combinations of people, technology, tools, procedures, and materials structured in a sequence

TABLE 2.1. Process Vocabulary

Term	Definition
Business context	The organizational structures, systems, circumstances, and expectations of a business enterprise.
Customer(s)	The receiver of an organization's or an individual's output(s)— the next in line. Customers may be either "internal" or "external" to a company. The ultimate customer is the end user, the recipient of the final product.
Input(s)	Work product of the supplier that meets the requirements of the customer.
Output(s)	The product of both the inputs and work process applied. Outputs become inputs to another process. Outputs may be either tangible products or intangible services.
Performance	To fulfill an obligation or requirement; to accomplish something as promised or expected.
Process	A series of requirements that must be satisfied in order to produce something of value. A process consists of steps, methods, and techniques applied to inputs that result in work products and outputs.
Process manager	The individual who is accountable for process results, who allocates resources, and who resolves or escalates process issues.
Process owner(s)	The people who actually produce the outputs. They are the "voice of the process" to the organization. They are also responsible for validating plans for changes in a work process, gathering performance data and information, and implementing changes.
Productivity	The output, or increase in output, of the department(s) for which a manager has accountability and of departments with which a manager has a significant working relationship.
Quality	Quality work is producing a product or service that conforms to customer wants, needs, and expectations as defined by "customer requirements." It means creating a product or a service that is "fit" for the customer's use.
Requirements	Customer wants, needs, and expectations of an output—also known as critical-to-quality requirements (CTQs). Requirements may be expressed as measures of quantity, timeliness, accuracy, and other characteristics.
Supplier	An individual or organization, whether internal or external to an organization, whose work products serve as inputs.

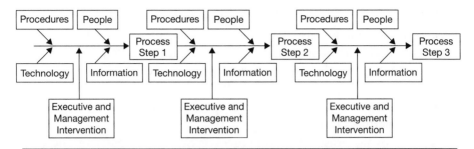

FIGURE 2.2. Elements of a Process: Inside the Black Box from a Services Perspective

of activities. These factors of production, or more appropriately named for this text, factors of service provision, are engineered to work as a *system* of variables designed to deliver a service. The expertise and staffing levels of a workforce, combined with clearly understood procedures, along with dependable technology and quality information flows, will dictate the effectiveness of a service delivery system. One more element deserves honorable mention. When and how executive intervention occurs in the fulfillment of services can have an extraordinary impact on service delivery performance.

In a manufacturing operation, strict adherence to a specific sequence of events with documented procedures and specifications is necessary and required. Many back office, order management, and service delivery operations also require strict adherence to a sequence of events and requirements. As noted in the opening example in this chapter, not understanding and reconciling process activities to strict requirements can create major performance failures. Service process designs need to include information which helps process owners fully comprehend and satisfy performance requirements. Furthermore, the design should help process owners follow a sequence of events useful in creating work products fit for a downstream customer's purpose.

For knowledge work such as product development, strategic planning, or research and development, not all process designs require formal sequences or steps. Rather, these types of process designs employ general guidelines such as timing, evaluation, reporting, etc. Such is the condition in a customer support or call center where a service center representative is a knowledge worker who creates *transactions* with customers. These transactions can range from simple answers to questions to major inter-departmental research in order to resolve complex customer issues.

Whether one is examining knowledge work or examining processes for back office operations, it is vital that certain principles be established as an organization embarks upon designing or re-engineering its core operating processes. Key principles of process management include:

- Establishing processes with direct linkages to suppliers, customers, and partners (internal or external)
- Employing measurements of process cycle time, output, efficiency, and quality
- Deploying a systematic method of evaluation
- Encouraging a culture committed to continuous improvement

Effective management of an organization's processes will require complete descriptions of key processes, their specific requirements, and how their performance relative to these requirements will be maintained. Effective process management also will include setting performance goals and work standards to guide resource allocations and management decisions. If variation in performance occurs and corrective action is needed, management can determine the proper mix of human and technical intervention for improvement.

Whatever the process design, the following properties always should be kept in mind:

- Integration of key process requirements, incorporating input from internal and external customers
- Adoption of key performance indicators to be used for process control and improvement
- Implementation of a systematic approach that includes a feedback loop designed to achieve better performance and keep processes current with business needs and customer expectations
- Establishment of a method to provide timely, actionable feedback to process owners and partners
- Use of an approach to minimize the overall cost associated with inspections, tests, and audits
- Adoption of policies to provide assistance or incentives to suppliers and partners to help them improve their overall performance
- Process designs that are flexible and adaptable to new product offerings and service changes

These principles and properties set the stage for effective process management and improvement. They are derived from the Performance Excellence Criteria utilized in the Malcolm Baldrige National Quality Award program. For more information regarding the Baldrige Performance Excellence Criteria, go to www.quality.nist.gov/ and click on "Getting Started with the Criteria for Performance Excellence: A Guide to Self-Assessment and Action."

PROCESS DESIGN

In this section, we will examine three methods of process design:

1. Traditional flowcharting
2. SIPOC diagramming
3. Requirements Based Process Design™

We will examine each method's definition of a process and the steps involved to create a process and will contrast the differences in each method's approach.

Flowcharting: A Traditional Process Mapping Method

In traditional flowcharting, a *process* is defined as a *series of steps* an operation performs to produce a work product or deliver a service. The flowchart itself is an illustration that depicts the sequence of actions and decision steps followed to make a process work. It is used to document and graphically display the various steps, events, and operations that constitute a workflow. A traditional flowchart diagrams a picture of how a process is working ("as is") or how it should work ("should be"). The elements of a traditional flowchart are displayed in Table 2.2, and Figure 2.3 shows a flowchart of a simple contract approval process.

Steps to Create a Traditional Flowchart

The flowchart is a very effective tool one can use to analyze a process and improve it. This kind of analysis is accomplished by first creating a process map based on how the process is actually functioning in its current state. The current state flowchart is generally referred to as an "as is" process map, as it indicates the current state of affairs. After the process is studied for

TABLE 2.2. Elements of a Flowchart

Symbol		Purpose
Oval	(oval)	Illustrates the scope of a process; the first and last steps or beginning and ending of a process
Rectangle	(rectangle)	Illustrates actions and steps of a process
Diamond	(diamond)	Used to illustrate decisions, which are depicted as a *yes* or *no* scenario or a choice between one or more options
Square	(square)	Used to show an inspection, verification, count, or any type of examination
Circle	(circle)	Used to illustrate an intentional work product modification of work in process (e.g., data entry, signature placement, order processing, etc.)
Semicircle	(semicircle)	Used to depict a delay, such as a stack of requisitions awaiting purchase order numbers or service orders and insurance claims awaiting processing
Connectors	(arrows)	Show direction and relationships

weaknesses and adjustments are made for improvements, a "should be" flowchart can be created to define and illustrate the new sequence of events and activities.

The steps to create a traditional flowchart are as follows:

1. Decide on the workflow to chart.
2. Define the "scope" of the process—its first and last steps.
3. Write the first event in an oval.
4. Identify the subsequent steps and illustrate them with their proper symbols.
5. When you reach an event that requires a decision, use the diamond to indicate the decision.
6. Proceed until finished; write the last step in an oval.

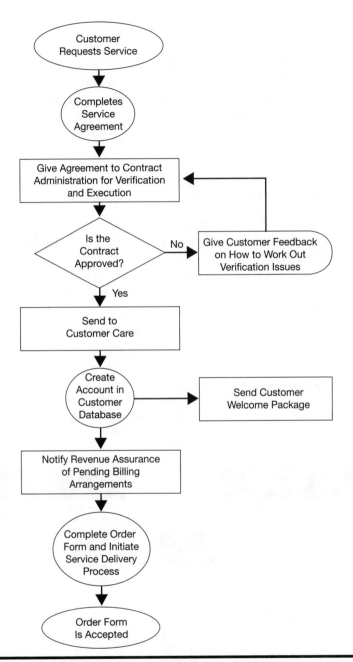

FIGURE 2.3. Flowchart of the Contract Approval Process

There are a number of ways to create a flowchart. A team can work together and construct it by consensus. A few team members can separately create a rough draft and then bring the team together to further develop it. Each team member can create a map individually and then the team comes together to discuss the creations as a group. What is commonly done is a team member separately interviews key process owners for each individual stage of the process and compiles the results of the interviews into a final work product.

SIPOC Process Mapping

The SIPOC process diagram, illustrated in Figure 2.4, is a tool used to *display process activities and information flows* designed to produce a tangible work product or deliver a service. The term SIPOC stands for a process's suppliers (S), its inputs (I), the process itself (P), its outputs (O), and the (C) customers who receive the process outputs. Even more than the traditional flowcharting method, the SIPOC diagram is a very good tool that can be used to scope activities in order to understand the nature of process interactions and interdependencies.

Steps to Create a SIPOC Diagram

SIPOC diagrams are usually created during consensus-building sessions where process owners come together and agree to either the method at hand or to

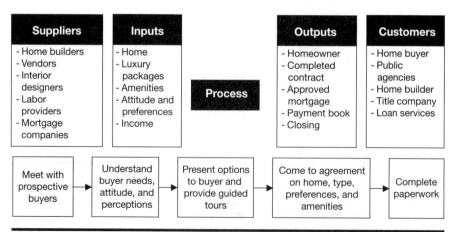

FIGURE 2.4. SIPOC Process Diagram for Purchasing a Home

an improved method for doing business. SIPOC construction steps are as follows:

1. **Select the right people**: The group that convenes should consist of those who are most knowledgeable about the day-to-day activities of the process. They are typically the frontline employees or supervisors with expertise in working in and around the current workflow. This group should also have a stake in and a sincere interest in seeing the process improved. *Caveat*: Ensure that all up- and downstream process owners and participants are involved in the consensus-building session.

2. **Prepare the meeting room, supplies, and agenda**: The agenda should allow for the appropriate amount of time for the consensus exercise. For processes with 10 steps or more, allow at least half a day to a full day for the session. Supplies should consist of butcher-block paper (60-inch), a large quantity of self-adhesive notes, felt-tip markers, and masking tape.

3. **Label the process map**: Post the butcher-block paper on the wall in front of the session participants. Label the map as illustrated in Figure 2.5. Document suppliers at the left and customers at the right. List process inputs at the left and process outputs at the right. Agree on the process scope and label its beginning at the left and label its ending at the right.

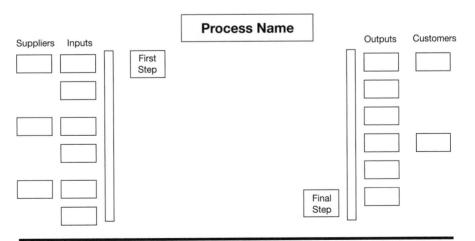

FIGURE 2.5. In-Process SIPOC Process Diagram

4. **Storyboard the process**: Each participant, according to his or her understanding, writes each process step on a separate self-adhesive note. The participants should not be concerned, at this stage, about the level of detail. On an individual basis, each participant posts his or her version of the process steps, in their perceived order, on the butcher-block paper without making any judgment about the wording. Each participant also uses his or her self-adhesive notes to identify and document suppliers, inputs, outputs, and related customer for each process step. Do not discuss the process steps in detail yet.

5. **Sequence the process steps**: After step 4, the meeting leader and participants work together to group the self-adhesive notes into "major" process steps. The groupings are reviewed in order to come to consensus regarding the level of detail to be reflected. Once all the process steps are agreed upon, write them directly on the butcher-block paper and draw arrows to indicate the process flow, as depicted in Figure 2.6.

6. **Code process steps**: Code each activity using symbols and/or colored self-adhesive notes. Be sure to include cycle time requirements for each step.

7. **Examine and validate the process**: Beta test the process by using an actual example activity. Change the diagram to reflect the result of the beta test:

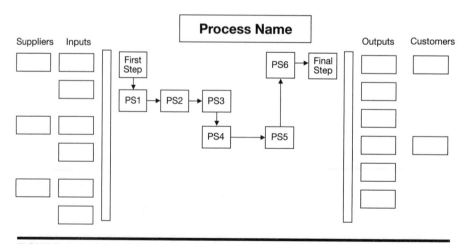

FIGURE 2.6. Complete SIPOC Process Diagram

- Find and eliminate non-value-added activities.
- Improve the modes and methods of communication.
- Confirm information flows.
- Seek process improvements.

Requirements Based Process Design™

Requirements Based Process Design™ (RBPD™) is another method used to systematically diagnose the activities, events, and information flows of a work process. It is used to analyze processes so all process stakeholders can improve their shared understanding, find improvement opportunities, and solve process-related problems. RBPD is particularly useful when one wants to understand:

- Who supplies inputs into a process
- What specifications are placed on process inputs
- Who the true customers of the process are
- What the requirements of the customers are

Whereas traditional flowcharting describes a process as a *series of steps* an organization performs in order to produce a work product and deliver a service and SIPOC diagramming views a process as a series of *activities* and *information flows* designed to produce a tangible work product and deliver a service, RBPD defines a process as a *collection of requirements* that must be satisfied in order to produce a work product and deliver a service that is fit for a customer's use. Customer utility of a work product is the chief concern of RBPD. The RBPD structure is illustrated in Figure 2.7.

The primary tools used to help depict the RBPD diagram are the work group swim lanes and the T-square. T-Squares help illustrate each process step in terms of its key elements. They create tangible descriptions of a process step's inputs, outputs, and interval requirements. The work group swim lanes enable the user to define departmental accountability for each task in a process. Fully mapped out, T-squares and work group swim lanes enable process owners to visualize key events and working relationships. At each step, one can analyze process requirements (inputs), process work products (outputs), and who is accountable for carrying out a task.

A third tool used in RBPD is the performance matrix. Depicted in Table 2.3, the performance matrix is a complement to the T-square map used to

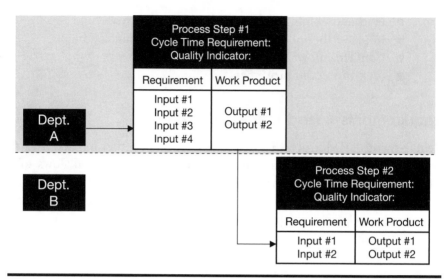

FIGURE 2.7. Steps 1 and 2 of Requirements Based Process Design

further detail process requirements. In addition, the performance matrix documents a process's key success factors, performance indicators, goals, and standards.

Together, the T-square map and the performance matrix serve to create a foundation for designing and improving work processes. Step 1 of a tele-communications service process is illustrated in Table 2.3.

Steps to Create a Requirements Based Process Design

1. **Select the right people:** The *right people* consist of those involved in and most knowledgeable about the day-to-day activities of the process. They are typically the frontline employees or supervisors. They also have a stake in and an interest in seeing the process improved. All upstream and downstream process owners should participate in requirements based process development.
2. **Prepare the materials, meeting room, and agenda:** Materials should include a large sheet of butcher-block paper (60-inch), felt-tip markers, masking tape, and blank performance matrix forms. Processing by consensus can be very involved for processes that exceed nine steps. At least one entire business day should be allocated for this type of consensus session.

TABLE 2.3. Step 1 of the Performance Matrix

Name of Work Group: _____

Name of Process: _____

Process Step	Requirements	Work Product	Key Success Factors	Measurements	Standards/Goals
Step 1 Initiate scope and network planning	Capacity requirements	Space & Power Request Form "Activity Service Request"	Accurate information	Acceptance ratio: # accepted # submitted	95% acceptance
	Address		Complete in the right format (Activity Service Request)		95% unconstrained
	Vendor information			% submitted with proper lead times	
	Tariff offerings		Appropriate lead time to vendor		
	Projected dates				
	Scope document				

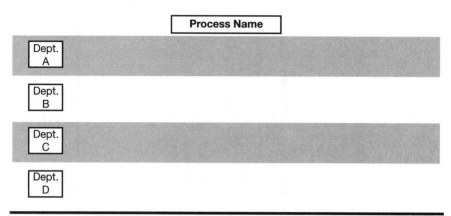

FIGURE 2.8. In-Process Requirements Based Process Design

3. **Label the process map:** Write the name of the process at the top of the butcher-block paper. Along the left side, vertically place blocks depicting the departments, work groups, or jobs that have input into the process. Label the blocks appropriately, as shown Figure 2.8.
4. **Storyboard the process:**
   a. As a group, determine the first process step. Construct the first T-square, label it accordingly, and then, as a group, determine the requirements that will serve as inputs to the first step. No matter how small, consider the upstream and downstream implications of each requirement (input) or lack thereof. The inputs are now the process specifications. Document them.
   b. After determining the inputs, define the output of that particular process step. Write a full description of the work product; the description should be considered in terms of the requirements and process specifications of the next process step. Document it.
   c. Define the step's key success factors. A key success factor is a factor that if undermined or not adhered to will compromise the ability of that step to produce the work product according to the specification outlined by the next step. Once defined, document it in your blank performance matrix form.
   d. Define the appropriate quality and cycle time measurements and performance indicators. Document them.
   e. Set a specific achievable target for the process step. Document it.

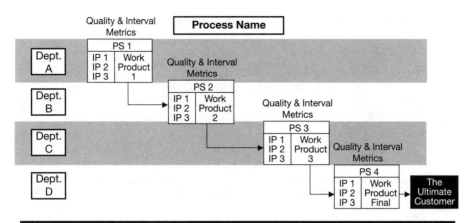

FIGURE 2.9. Completed Requirements Based Process Design

5. **Duplicate steps 1 to 4 for each process step until the process is completed.**

To accomplish a full flow diagram based on the RBPD methodology, it is essential that everyone begin to think of his or her work as producing a quality work product for a customer. Everyone must ask themselves: "Who is the person that receives my work? Whom must I satisfy? What do they need and expect from me?" Everyone has a customer, and everyone must know who that is and what they require. When your flowchart is complete, it should look similar to the one presented in Figure 2.9.

CREATING CROSS-FUNCTIONAL ORGANIZATIONS

In order to achieve service excellence, effective workflow design and process management must take into account all stakeholders in a process value chain. Those from whom a department receives its work products and to whom it provides work products are part of its value chain. For service organizations, cross-functional relationships must be characterized in this manner because a service delivery value chain is only as strong as its weakest link. In a service context, an operation has only one opportunity to impress a customer—its product is immediately perishable.

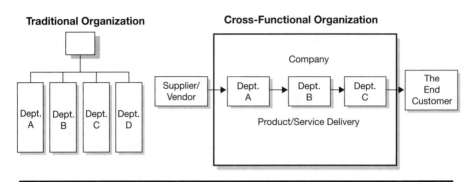

FIGURE 2.10. The Cross-Functional Organization vs. the Traditional Organization

Experience shows that *traditional organizations,* as depicted in Figure 2.10, often cannot see beyond their organizational boundaries or functions. They function as operational stovepipes, primarily concerned with their own job, their own efforts, and their own departmental accountabilities. As a consequence, the following performance issues usually arise within a company, limiting it from serving its customers effectively:

1. Inter-departmental competition that limit communication between functions
2. Defective work products, which pass between departments and create the need for seemingly never-ending rework
3. Unmanaged gaps between departments that interrupt the productive and efficient flow of work between work groups

An effective process design method should promote organizations that are *cross-functional.* A cross-functional organization, also illustrated in Figure 2.10, encourages relationships based not on a department's function but based on working relationships that cut across organizational boundaries. Especially for service companies, an effective process design method should encourage process requirements and actions based on customer expectations (internal and external) so the needs of the end customer can be articulated throughout the company. Companies that begin to see themselves in this fashion will improve their "shared" accountabilities and provide services as a true team, resulting in improved productivity and service delivery for both internal and external customers.

CONCLUSION

The objective of this chapter was to teach about service process design and the factors that make processes perform well. The properties of well-designed process management systems were defined, the three basic methods for process development were examined, and the qualities of *cross-functional* organizations were discussed. By following the basic elements and principles of process design, you will be empowered to define, analyze, and improve the service processes within your organization.

3

THE VOICE OF
THE CUSTOMER

What you need are customers that are more than happy. You need customers that boast about your product. That repeat customer! There's the gravy. Your fixed costs are all paid... *

—*W. Edwards Deming*

According to the General Electric Corporation, "Customers are the center of GE's universe: they define quality. They expect performance, reliability, competitive prices, on-time delivery, service, clear and correct transaction processing and more....Delighting our customers is a necessity, because if we don't do it, someone else will!"** GE perceives its customers to be more than just an important element of its business—GE's customers are its business. What could cause this kind of commitment?

This chapter will describe the fundamental Six Sigma philosophy that creates such a commitment—the *voice of the customer*. It will define what exactly the voice of the customer is, why a company should focus on customer loyalty, the properties of a well-designed customer loyalty model, and how to assess and interpret the voice of the customer.

---

*Walton, M. (1986). *The Deming Management Method,* New York: Perigee Books/Putnam Publishing Group, p. 30.

** www.ge.com/sixsigma/keyelements.html.

WHAT IS THE VOICE OF THE CUSTOMER?

The voice of the customer is a company's lifeblood. It has a specific meaning that largely determines a customer's purchase decision. Dr. Henry Assael, a professor of and chair of marketing at NYU's Stern School of Business, offers perhaps the most suitable definition of the voice of the customer. He defines it, and we apply it to our voice of the customer definition, as the positive or negative predisposition of the marketplace toward a company's product or service.* His definition implies that customers do not begin their purchasing process with a clean slate. Simply put, the voice of the customer is defined by the following terms:

- **Customer need**: The force that directs customers toward the achievement of certain goals
- **Customer attitude**: The customer's tendency to evaluate a company's product or service in a favorable or unfavorable way
- **Customer perception**: The way customers organize and interpret information about a company and its products and services

Service companies that hear the voice of the customer endeavor to influence customer purchase decisions by fulfilling service requirements that satisfy customer wants, needs, and expectations. They create and deliver service offerings that are *fit* for their customers' use. They develop:

- Product specifications that meet customer needs
- Service levels that favorably influence customer attitudes
- Advertising objectives that positively impact customer perceptions

Service companies that seek and understand the voice of the customer obtain greater market share, greater profitability, and develop a larger loyal customer base.

WHY FOCUS ON CUSTOMER LOYALTY?

The following matter-of-fact statements, made by W. Edwards Deming, go a long way in answering that question:

---

* Adapted from Assael's psychological set in Assael, H. (1990). *Marketing Principles and Strategy*, Chicago: The Dryden Press, p. 125.

- *"There's a production line. And [at the end of that line] there'll be a customer. It is very important to find out what he thinks is right or wrong about your product today. A satisfied customer may switch. Why not? He might come out better for the switch."*
- *"The customer—pretty important, isn't he? If nobody buys your product, the whole production line shuts down!"*
- *"The repeat customer, best part of any business. The one you don't have to argue with. He comes back...."*
- *"What you need are customers that are more than happy. You need customers that boast about your product. That return—repeat customers. There's the gravy. Your fixed costs are all paid..."*

Why focus on customer loyalty? Your customer may switch. In the telecommunications industry, industry churn (aka customer turnover) can exceed 40%.

Why focus on customer loyalty? You may lose your job. If fewer and fewer customers purchase your product or service, you will go out of business. Where is Montgomery Ward? In the past few years, what has happened to Kmart? Where are Eastern and Braniff Airlines? Where is TWA?

Why focus on customer loyalty? You may obtain the largest industry loyal customer base. How about Wal-Mart? Have you been to Target lately? How about the Washington Redskins? Despite only one post-season appearance in the past 10 years (at the time this book was written), each of the 80,116 seats in the Redskins' stadium, the largest stadium in the NFL, belongs to a season ticket owner. What about the Denver Broncos? At the time of this writing, there is an 8- to 10-year waiting list for season tickets, with 18,000 people on that list. Sold out!

The idea behind the voice of the customer is not only to value and create customer satisfaction, but to acquire and maintain the largest loyal customer base in the marketplace. A loyal customer can be defined as a customer that operates with extreme prejudice toward a company's services. The customer that operates with extreme prejudice will continue to use that company's services despite the many inducements and incentives offered by the competition. This customer brags about the company's business to others and will pay a premium to remain its customer.

---

* Walton, M. (1986). *The Deming Management Method,* New York: Perigee Books/Putnam Publishing Group, pp. 29–30.

PROPERTIES OF A WELL-DESIGNED CUSTOMER LOYALTY MODEL*

Deploying a well-defined customer loyalty model is the first step in acquiring a loyal customer base. A well-designed customer loyalty model has two major components:

- **Customer and market knowledge**: This component describes how a company determines its customers' short- and long-term requirements, expectations, and preferences to ensure the relevance of current product offerings and service levels.
- **Customer satisfaction and relationships**: This component describes not only how a company determines customer satisfaction but also how a company builds relationships to retain current business and develop new opportunities.

Customer and market knowledge properties are defined by how effectively a company will segment its customers, ascertain customer requirements, translate value assessments into service features, and listen for changing customer requirements. The following elements define these properties:

1. **Segmentation**: A service excellence company will effectively determine customer groups and market segments. For example, a company will know if its services are provided to end users via other businesses such as retail stores or dealers. Market segments can include size, industry, or region of a company's target market.
2. **Requirements assessment**: A service excellence company will effectively listen and ascertain the key requirements and drivers of purchase decisions for current, former, and potential customers. If determination methods differ for customer groups, the company will identify those key differences.
3. **Customer value assessment**: A service excellence company will determine key service features and their relative importance to customers for the purpose of current and future product market-

---

* Properties derived from the Baldrige National Quality Program Criteria for Performance Excellence.

ing and service delivery features. These features might include factors such as price, on-time delivery, responsiveness, courtesy, technical support, account relationship, etc.

4. **Feedback methods**: A service excellence company will keep its listening and learning methods current with business needs and directions.

Customer relationship is a property that describes how a company builds and enhances its associations with customers to retain current business and develop new opportunities. The elements of this property are as follows:

1. **Customer service**: A service excellence company will provide key access mechanisms to facilitate a customer's ability to conduct business, seek assistance or information, and make complaints. The access mechanism will be kept current with business needs and directions.

2. **Complaint system**: A service excellence company will provide an adequate complaint management process. The process ensures complaints are resolved effectively and promptly and all complaints are categorized and analyzed for patterns and improvement opportunities. Complaint measurements deployed may include handling effectiveness such as complaint response time, effectiveness of resolution, and percent of complaints resolved on first contact.

Customer satisfaction determination is a property that explains how a company determines the attitudes and perceptions customers share regarding its brand, products, and services. The elements of this property are as follows:

1. **Data collection**: A service excellence company will use a consistent measurement process to collect data and determine levels of customer satisfaction and dissatisfaction. Measurements might include both quantitative and qualitative data. Satisfaction data and measurements should provide reliable information about a company's service offerings and service quality and link their features to customers' likely future actions.

2. **Customer feedback loop**: A service excellence company will receive and follow up on actionable feedback from customers regarding service offerings and delivery for recent transactions.
3. **Benchmarking**: A service excellence company will obtain and use customer satisfaction information relative to competitors and benchmarks as appropriate.

Together, these properties set the fundamental stage for a company to adequately assess and react to the voice of the customer. Their effective deployment within a company's system of operation can ensure a proper and successful assessment of a customer base's needs, attitudes, and perceptions.

HOW TO ASSESS THE VOICE OF THE CUSTOMER

Clearly defining customer needs, attitudes, and perceptions is fundamental to achieving Six Sigma service excellence. Six Sigma drives the expression of customer needs, attitudes, and perceptions into explicit requirements. In Six Sigma language, these requirements are called *critical-to-quality* requirements or CTQs.

Customer requirements can range from general to very specific, but should relate directly to the customer's objectives. Generally speaking, CTQs fall into the following broad dimensions:

- Financial
- Quantity
- Timeliness
- Accuracy
- Responsiveness
- Functionality
- Thoroughness
- Product attributes

Examples of these attributes can be found in Table 3.1.

By clearly defining customer needs, attitudes, and perceptions up front, a company can begin to establish the desired level of operational performance for its customers.

TABLE 3.1. Critical-to-Quality Requirements

Dimension	Customer Requirements
Financial	"The round-trip ticket to Denver on your airline was 25% less than the other carriers."
Quantity	"I need to receive at least 20 completed loan verifications from you each week." (internal customer)
Timeliness	"I need the reports by 9:00 a.m. every Monday morning." (internal customer)
Accuracy	"Before forwarding the report to me, each and every item has to be 100% correct according to the customer's file." (cross-functional customer)
Responsiveness	"When our circuit goes down, we begin to lose data integrity within three hours; we need service restoration within two hours."
Functionality	"Every time I turn on the system, I want it to automatically boot up and display the menu screen."
Thoroughness	"We can't start processing the order until we have all of the information sheets in our hands."
Product attributes	"If the computer is more than 20 inches deep, it won't fit on my desk."

Voice of the Customer Assessment Techniques

There are two basic approaches used to ascertain the voice of the customer: qualitative research and quantitative research. *Qualitative research,* also known as exploratory research, is research that asks customers to respond to questions in a "semi-structured" manner. Qualitative research is often used as a precursor to survey research in order to gather primary data, themes, and anecdotes regarding customer requirements. The main goal of this method, however, is to gain greater clarity and understanding of a broad, vague, or complex customer issue. *Quantitative research,* also known as survey research, is the most commonly used method of collecting customer data. It is referred to as quantitative research because it seeks to quantify the attitudes, perceptions, and opinions of a customer population. Survey research involves developing a questionnaire; conducting telephone surveys, mail surveys, or personal interviews with a representative sample of respondents from a customer population; and then analyzing the results. Often, hundreds and even thousands of customers are assessed using this method. Survey research often is conducted after qualitative research has improved clarity around a particular customer issue.

Qualitative Research Methods

Focus Groups

Focus groups are one of the most effective and most frequently used methods for collecting qualitative data about customer attitudes and perceptions. Focus groups are informal loosely structured customer interviews with groups of roughly 8 to 12 participants. A trained moderator asks a group to focus on a particular topic and facilitates an open-ended, free-flowing discussion regarding an existing or proposed service offering. The strength of conducting focus groups is that they are an excellent method for gathering in-depth information about customer attitudes and opinions regarding the use of a company's product or service. The weakness of conducting focus groups is that they use a statistically small sample size population and the attitudes and opinions expressed by a single or a few focus groups may not be representative of the population as a whole. The way to mitigate the risk of using a focus group is to conduct a large enough number of sessions to develop your survey instrument. Additional strengths and weaknesses of focus groups are listed in Table 3.2.

Personal Interviews

Personal interviews are much like focus groups, but they are conducted on a one-on-one basis. Personal interviewing is an excellent method for gathering in-depth opinions of how customers use and view a company's products and services. However, with personal interviews, the positive aspects of group interaction are lost and it takes much longer to accumulate enough responses to have any confidence in the results. In addition, you can expect to learn only what a given person is willing to tell you and only to the extent he or she is willing to talk.

TABLE 3.2. Strengths and Weaknesses of Focus Groups

Strengths	Weaknesses
■ Excellent for gathering information regarding customer attitudes and opinions and learning exactly how internal and external customers use your work products and services	■ A focus group is a statistically small sample size of a population, the attitudes and opinions of which may not be representative of the population as a whole
■ Provide fast turnaround time for acquiring knowledge	■ Management often can be unduly influenced by the opinions of a few live customers
■ Relatively inexpensive to conduct	■ Often do not produce numerical values
■ Can generate a great deal of customer information	■ Participants sometimes can make it difficult to consider more than one major topic at a time
■ Can uncover unsuspected problems and solutions	

Quantitative Research: Surveys

Surveys are a quantitative form of information gathering and data collection that provide a company a way to express its customers' needs, attitudes, and perceptions numerically. Surveying is the method most often used to collect primary data on customer opinion. It involves selecting a representative sample of respondents from a population, developing a questionnaire, asking the respondents questions, and then analyzing the results. A well-done survey can be inferential in that the results can provide reliable information not only about the customers surveyed but also about most of the segment being surveyed. One can survey hundreds of customers in a segment and their responses can be projected, with a level of confidence, to a total population of thousands. The researcher has his or her choice of how to conduct a survey. It can be conducted in person, by telephone, by mail, or over the Internet. Each approach has its strengths and weaknesses.

The Use of Customer Surveys

Customer surveys are used to ascertain the extent to which customers will remain loyal to a product or a brand. Surveys are also used to assess customer perception of certain service intangibles such as:

- Company reputation
- Knowledge of employees
- Ease of communication
- Courtesy of employees
- Overall experience and interaction
- Quality

Surveys often are used to assess consumer attitudes about value, price, ease of product use, and the value of certain service features. Quantitative research also is very a good method of ascertaining the importance customers ascribe to service attributes such as timeliness, responsiveness, service delivery, and overall service quality. Overall, survey research can provide a company with a means to quantify its customers' willingness to repurchase the use of its services and their willingness to recommend its products and services to others.

Developing a Survey: What to Ask

When developing a questionnaire or designing a survey, one must account for the characteristics of a company's service offerings. Most service and transactional encounters are "high-touch" experiences. Service companies like hotels, hospitals, banks, and retail outlets will want to measure the quality of customer contacts and interactions. Other companies like telecommunications companies, on-line retailers, airlines, and shipping companies may want to measure ease of use of their Web sites as well as the timeliness and overall reliability of their service delivery performance.

Whatever the business context, the design of a survey should consider at least the following three elements:

- **Importance:** The service attribute being assessed should be germane to the idea of satisfying the customer—a satisfaction driver.
- **Relevance:** The service attribute being assessed should be recognized and understood by customers and help them reach their goals.
- **Controllable:** The service attribute being assessed should be within the company's ability to manage and change.

When to Conduct a Survey

When is the right time to conduct a survey? The Performance Management Group recommends a company conduct surveys on two different occasions: immediately following a focus group and soon after a customer service experience.

A company can deliver a survey while conducting primary research through focus groups. Through focus groups, a company can obtain an understanding of how its customers rely on its services. Once a company gains a deeper understanding of its customers' desires, it can translate that understanding into specific service attributes and CTQs. These attributes may reflect the customers' desire for on-time delivery, service reliability, or employee knowledge and expertise. At the end of a focus group, a company can distribute a simple survey for customers to rate the level of importance of each CTQ uncovered. This process will be discussed in further detail later.

A company also can deliver a survey soon after a customer purchase or service experience. Restaurants often ask their customers to complete a concise questionnaire soon after a meal. Hotels may contact their customers soon after a stay. Telecommunications (business-to-business) customers may be surveyed soon after service installation. In these cases, an assessment of customer satisfaction is completed after customers have had time to form a considered opinion of a provider's performance.

Who to Survey

Not all customers are the same. A company must segment its customers. Segmentation is a technique that separates survey respondents into groups by interests or needs. For example, frequent flyers and business travelers may have different needs than the occasional traveler. Individual mobile phone consumers may have different needs and weigh service attributes differently than business users. Furthermore, the type of industry and the size of a customer may drive different customer requirements for the business banker. In addition, it is important to understand that in most business-to-business relationships, the buyer of a company's services may not be the end user of the services. The surveyor must make this distinction for business-to-business surveys. The surveyor may have two interests to assess: that of the user and that of the purchaser.

It is vital, in this type of circumstance, that the surveyor uses an instrument that uncovers situations where the dissatisfaction of one respondent can be hidden by the high satisfaction of the other. For example, suppose a telecommunications network provider surveys its largest Internet service provider (ISP) customers and asks the buyers to rate their overall satisfaction with its services and the business relationship on a scale of 1 to 4, where 4 = very satisfied, 3 = satisfied, 2 = somewhat dissatisfied, and 1 = very dissatisfied. The respondents' average score is 3.6, which the company is pleased with—until it learns that the average score of the operational users in the same customer base is 1.8.

As you can see, these two interests can compete with one another and may drive the use of two different focus groups and survey instruments. One instrument may focus on *cost of service,* which may satisfy the purchasing department, while the other considers the operational users and their emphasis on *quality of service.*

In order to conduct an effective analysis of importance and satisfaction, the surveyor will need to question customers twice. One query will question the *importance* of service requirements, and the second will question how *satisfied* customers are with the company's performance to the stated requirements.

As mentioned earlier, The Performance Management Group recommends using a survey after first conducting primary research through focus groups. Through focus groups, a surveyor will ascertain a general understanding of how customers rely on company services to help them achieve their goals and meet their needs. During a focus group, a surveyor also may realize that customers do not consider all service features equally important.

The focus group can be an effective tool to uncover general and consistent themes of a customer segment which can be translated into specific customer requirements (CTQs). At the end of the focus group, a customer survey can then be used as an effective tool to quantify the relative weight and importance the customer segment places on each attribute/requirement. Once this survey is completed, the surveyor is in position to perform the second query needed for an effective analysis of importance and satisfaction.

Caveat: In order to avoid *response bias,* it is a good idea to let some time pass between the two queries. Some survey experts believe that one response can unduly influence the other.

ASSESSING THE VOICE OF THE CUSTOMER: AN ANALYSIS OF CUSTOMER IMPORTANCE AND SATISFACTION

Expanding on the example above, suppose the telecommunications company focus grouped the customers (operational users) in its ISP segment and uncovered the following service attributes (CTQs) from the sessions:

1. Service delivery effectiveness
2. Customer service call center response
3. Network operations center access
4. Network availability and quality
5. Courtesy of employees
6. Operational expertise
7. Billing accuracy

Before the customers leave the focus group, moderators have them rate these attributes in terms of their degree of importance. The instrument used is shown in Table 3.3.

TABLE 3.3. Importance Survey Instrument

Please tell us how important the following service quality features are to you. Circle your answer.

Service	Not Important	Somewhat Unimportant	Important	Very Important
A. Service delivery dates met	1	2	3	4
B. Network operations center access	1	2	3	4
C. Customer call center access	1	2	3	4
D. Network quality (service level agreements)	1	2	3	4
E. Price	1	2	3	4
F. Courtesy of employees	1	2	3	4
G. Operational expertise	1	2	3	4
H. Billing accuracy	1	2	3	4

TABLE 3.4. Satisfaction Survey Instrument

Over the past three months, how satisfied were you with the quality of our service and the support you received from our company? Circle your answer.

Service	Very Dissatisfied	Somewhat Dissatisfied	Satisfied	Very Satisfied
A. Service delivery dates met	1	2	3	4
B. Network operations center access	1	2	3	4
C. Customer call center access	1	2	3	4
D. Network quality (service level agreements)	1	2	3	4
E. Price	1	2	3	4
F. Courtesy of employees	1	2	3	4
G. Operational expertise	1	2	3	4
H. Billing accuracy	1	2	3	4

The company determines that it wants to ascertain the levels of customer satisfaction for these attributes once every quarter of transactions. After one quarter, the survey instrument in Table 3.4 is sent to a large group of its ISP customer base.

Once the surveys are completed and returned, the company is able to measure how this particular customer segment feels about its performance with respect to the service attributes that matter. Averaging the ratings of the respondents produces two numbers for each requirement: one number represents the mean score for importance and the other represents the mean score for satisfaction. The results are shown in Table 3.5.

TABLE 3.5. Importance and Satisfaction Survey Results

Service Requirement (CTQ)	Importance	Satisfaction
A. Service delivery dates met	3.8	2.6
B. Network operations center access	4.0	3.6
C. Customer call center access	2.3	3.9
D. Network quality (service level agreements)	4.0	3.8
E. Price	2.0	2
F. Courtesy of employees	3.1	2.3
G. Operational expertise	3.8	2.4
H. Billing accuracy	3.0	3.0
Grand average	**3.25**	**2.95**

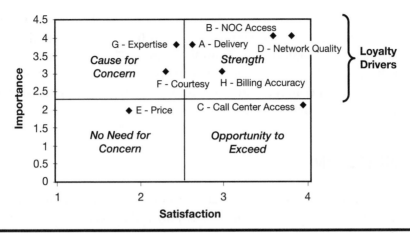

FIGURE 3.1. Service Quality Matrix

After the company acquires the results, the data are plotted on a service quality matrix, as shown in Figure 3.1. The matrix illustrates customer *satisfaction* represented on the horizontal axis and customer *importance* represented on the vertical axis.

A quick examination of the matrix reveals the company's opportunities to satisfy its customers. The attributes with a rating a little higher than 2 in terms of importance are where the company needs to invest its time, resources, and efforts. These attributes are called *loyalty drivers,* and as the name implies, positive results relating to these requirements can engender customer confidence and long-term customer loyalty.

Customer characteristics and requirements clustered in the upper half of the matrix are those that are important to the ISP customer base. The analysis reveals that the telecommunications company is performing well with respect to the important CTQs. It can consider network quality, NOC access, billing accuracy, and call center access to be company strengths in the opinion of the operational users of its ISP customer segment.

Customer characteristics and requirements clustered in the upper left quadrant of the matrix are important to the ISP customer base but the company is not doing such a good job satisfying them. Not satisfying these requirements should give the company some cause for concern. The company should reassess its service delivery performance, along with the expertise and courtesy of its employees.

Customer characteristics and requirements clustered in the lower right quadrant of the matrix are not important to the ISP customer base but the company is doing a good job satisfying them. Because these requirements may be considered less important to a customer base, some companies may consider shifting resources away from those areas. The Performance Management Group refers to this quadrant as an opportunity to exceed customer expectations; even doing the little things over a period of time adds up to service quality "intangibles" for which customers often will pay a premium.

CONCLUSION

This chapter described a fundamental aspect of the Six Sigma philosophy— the *voice of the customer*. It defined exactly what the voice of the customer is and why a company should focus on customer loyalty. The properties of a well-designed customer loyalty model were documented and an example of how to assess and interpret the voice of the customer was provided. By following the basic elements and principles of this chapter, you will be empowered to analyze and improve the relationship your company has with its customers and, by doing so, create long-term value for your stakeholders.

ANALYZING PERFORMANCE VARIATION

Our Customers Feel the Variance, Not the Mean

Customers don't judge us on averages, they feel the variance in each transaction, each product we ship. Customers value consistent, predictable business processes that deliver world-class levels of quality. This is what Six Sigma strives to produce.

—*General Electric Web site*
(www.ge.com/sixsigma/sixsigstrategy.html)

ANALYZING PERFORMANCE VARIATION

Six Sigma is best supported when managers and employees back decision making with numerical facts and information. This concept is called *management by fact.* Whether a company is manufacturing a product or delivering a service, it must manage by fact in order to satisfy customer requirements and operate productively.

Understanding performance variation is a Six Sigma concept that serves as a basis for making good decisions and managing by fact. A sound analysis of performance variation is essential to improving the processes by which a company delivers its services. As an outcome of reading this chapter, you will be able to:

- Recognize the importance of evaluating performance variation in the delivery of services
- Use this understanding of performance variation to make good business decisions with numerical facts and information
- Demonstrate how to display baseline process performance metrics using a run chart
- Analyze process performance with special cause rules
- Take the right action to address each type of performance variation in a service delivery operation

THE SCIENTIFIC BASIS FOR PERFORMANCE VARIATION*

In 1840, while studying the position and area of the earth, Carl Frederick Gauss established the basis for statistics. Gauss discovered, through thousands of observations and sightings, that his measurements often produced similar results. When he plotted his measurements on a chart, he discovered that his graph repeatedly resulted in a bell-shaped curve, as illustrated in Figure 4.1. Half of his measurements consistently fell to the left of the center and half fell to the right. He believed that these observations fell in a well-

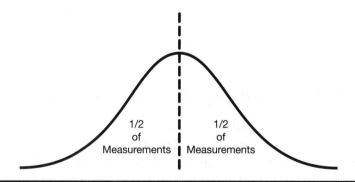

FIGURE 4.1. The Bell Curve: Gaussian Distribution

---

* Adapted from Brewer, R.F. (1996). *Design of Experiments for Process Improvement and Quality Assurance,* Engineering & Management Press.

defined pattern too frequently to occur by chance. After additional analysis, Gauss discovered that this pattern happened with great frequency and could be mathematically estimated in advance. What he happened upon was the law of large numbers which happens to occur throughout nature. This law of large numbers, now referred to as the Gaussian law of *normal distribution,* is understood to be one of the most basic of all natural laws. This normal distribution is evident in the height of people, the speed of runners, the diameter of trees, etc.

Werner Heisenberg, a 1932 Nobel Prize–winning atomic physicist, coined what is commonly known in quantum mechanics as the *uncertainty principle.* This principle asserts that it is impossible to establish the exact position and momentum of a particle at the same time with unlimited accuracy. The principle also states that there is a *small disturbance* in nature that creates an uncertainty in all measurements.

When the law of normal distribution and the uncertainty principle are combined and translated into industrial terms, they state that whenever measurements of operational performance are taken, they will not—in general—be identical to each other. They will vary, and if nothing disturbs the operation, they will *naturally* vary within definite limits. Measurements of operational performance will form a predictable normal distribution.

WHAT IS PERFORMANCE VARIATION?

Performance variation refers to the way operational performance changes over time. The concept of performance variation is familiar to all of us because it is part of our daily lives. In nature's process of growing similar trees, growth rates may vary. The time it takes for us to drive to work will vary every day. There is variation in the time we stand in line at a bank and the time it takes us to speak to a customer service representative over the phone. Likewise, the average handling time in a call center will vary from call to call, minute by minute, hour by hour, and shift by shift. In fact, there is no process in existence that performs exactly the same over time.

In business, there will always be performance variation. There will be variation in the performance of people, the productivity of processes, and the quality of services delivered. Generally speaking, the less variation an operation experiences, the more effective management can be at planning, allocating resources, and predicting outcomes. The key is to understand what causes performance variation so management can respond appropriately to reduce variation. To that end, the first thing to know about performance variation is that it is always caused.

Six Sigma defines two types of performance variation based on its cause: common cause variation and special cause variation. *Common cause variation* is a *natural* consequence of production factors coming together in the performance of a process. For example, the average speed of answering a call at a call center is a natural consequence of factors like call volume, the number of representatives working, call mix, and the expertise of call center representatives all working together during an interval of time. The important thing to understand about common cause variation is that it is an inherent and natural outcome of every process. An operation with only common cause variation is considered to be stable, and its measured results are predictable and considered to be in statistical control.

Special cause variation, however, is performance variation that can be attributed to an extraordinary factor or set of factors acting on an operation. Special cause variation is not a normal or inherent part of an operation's performance. It develops from some unusual event or circumstance. For example, the time it takes someone to drive to work may be greatly influenced by a major traffic accident, construction delays, or a flat tire. These special causes make daily commutes frustrating and arrival times hard to predict.

Operations with a combination of common cause and special cause variation are considered to be unstable and their measured results out of statistical control. In a corporate context, it is vital for managers to distinguish between common and special cause variation so they can take the right actions to resolve performance issues.

ANALYZING BASELINE PERFORMANCE: THE RUN CHART

In a service organization, measures of operational performance typically are based on cost effectiveness and customer expectations. Managers typically look at customer requirements (critical-to-quality requirements) that relate to timeliness, accuracy, and quality. With respect to cost effectiveness, managers will measure productivity and cost. These attributes can be translated into measurable quantities (metrics) and tracked on charts in order to get a visual representation of operational performance over time. A graphical display can empower management by showing baseline performance and variation from a broad perspective.

A tool management can use to evaluate operational performance is a run chart. Run charts, also known as line graphs and trend charts, are graphs of performance data captured over time. They provide a display of how performance can change from shift to shift, day to day, week to week, and month to month. A sample run chart is shown in Figure 4.2.

A run chart is one of the simplest statistical tools in the Six Sigma tool kit and is an effective chart for detecting the presence or absence of special cause variation in operational performance. A run chart:

- Tracks time or sequence of occurrences on the horizontal (x) axis
- Displays measurements on the vertical (y) axis
- Graphically represents operational performance over time
- Is used to visually detect and display performance variation
- Shows how operational performance can change as a result of an adjustment

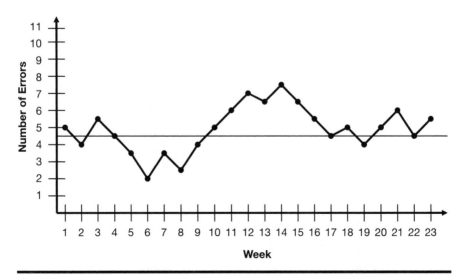

FIGURE 4.2. Run Chart

How to Construct a Run Chart

IMPORTANT   There are a number of software applications on the market that can easily manipulate data to construct a run chart. The application this author suggests is *QI Macros*; it is the application of choice for this text and is fully compatible with Microsoft Excel®. QI Macros is provided at a discounted price for *ship to* orders for all purchasers of this text. You can order the application on-line at The Performance Management Group Web site at www.helpingmakeithapppen.com or download it at http://www.qimacros.com/products.php?PARTNER=tpmgllc.

Construction with QI Macros

1. Enter your data and labels in a spreadsheet. (Sample data and labels are provided in Table 4.1.)
2. Highlight the data set and labels in the spreadsheet.
3. Select **QI Macros > Run Chart**.
4. Title the chart and click **OK**.
5. Label the vertical axis and click **OK**.
6. Label the horizontal axis and click **OK**.
7. Label the run chart according to your preference.

TABLE 4.1. Run Chart Labels and Data

Labels	Data	Labels	Data
Week 1	51	Week 16	103
Week 2	72	Week 17	70
Week 3	45	Week 18	114
Week 4	80	Week 19	91
Week 5	91	Week 20	82
Week 6	95	Week 21	120
Week 7	120	Week 22	99
Week 8	105	Week 23	50
Week 9	61	Week 24	112
Week 10	80	Week 25	115
Week 11	119	Week 26	60
Week 12	119	Week 27	98
Week 13	70	Week 28	89
Week 14	93	Week 29	114
Week 15	102	Week 30	111

TABLE 4.2. Data for Run Chart Construction Exercise

Hour of the Day	Average Speed of Answer (Seconds)	Hour of the Day	Average Speed of Answer (Seconds)
100	11	1300	10
200	9	1400	15
300	10	1500	9
400	9	1600	14
500	10	1700	16
600	11	1800	19
700	9	1900	14
800	12	2000	10
900	10	2100	11
1000	14	2200	11
1100	10	2300	15
1200	9	2400	17

Run Chart Construction Exercise: Call Center Response Times

A regional bank's 24-hour customer service call center strives to answer customer calls within 10 seconds of customer contact. Every hour, the call center tracks the average time it takes to answer a customer's call in the queue. The data in Table 4.2 represent the call center's average speed of answering calls (in seconds) for each hour of the day (in military time). Using these data and the QI Macros application, construct a run chart. Once you are finished, compare your results with the completed run chart in Appendix A.

Analyzing Run Charts

As mentioned earlier, a run chart can empower a manager by showing baseline performance as well as variation. It provides a graphical display of changes in performance and is also a very effective tool for detecting the presence or absence of special cause variation in operational performance.

For the Six Sigma professional, the object of analyzing run charts is to determine whether or not special cause variation is present in operational performance. The Six Sigma professional uses three basic rules in run chart analysis to make that determination. These basic rules are called special cause rules and are outlined below.

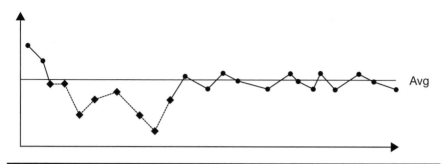

FIGURE 4.3. Shift Rule Violation

Special Cause Rules

Shift Rule: The shift rule relates to any significant change or movement in a performance average. The shift rule dictates that if eight or more *consecutive* points fall above or below the process average, special cause variation may be present in an operation's performance. An example of a shift rule violation is illustrated in Figure 4.3.

The shift rule has its basis in the laws of probability. The chance of eight or more consecutive points falling above or below the performance average is the same as flipping a coin eight times and the coin coming up heads eight times in a row—which is expressed mathematically as 0.5^8 or 0.00396. Violation of the shift rule means that if only common cause variation exists in a process, the chance of eight points falling above or below the centerline is less than 0.4%—a highly unlikely consequence. If a shift rule violation is found, the odds are in favor of the existence of special cause variation in the operation.

Trend Rule: The trend rule relates to an out-of-the-ordinary long series of consecutive increases or decreases in operational performance. The trend rule dictates that if seven consecutive points move in the same direction, special cause variation is present in operational performance. As depicted in Figure 4.4, a trend may move in an upward or downward direction.

Trends often present themselves after some change has been made. They inform us if adjustments have had a positive or negative impact on operational performance. A trend also may be part of a learning curve associated with some form of training.

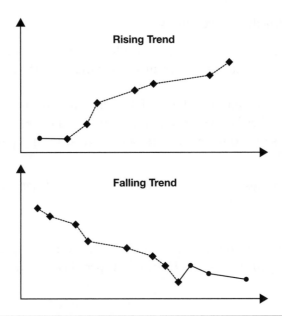

FIGURE 4.4. Trend Rule Violation

Cycle Rule: The cycle rule is used for identifying any non-random pattern. The cycle rule suggests that any non-random pattern discovered is an indication of special cause variation. The cycle rule dictates that when any pattern recurs eight or more consecutive times, as depicted in Figure 4.5, the odds are in favor of the existence of special cause variation. Note that the cycle in Figure 4.5 is two points above the centerline followed by one point below.

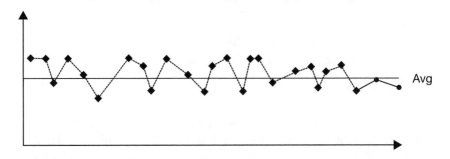

FIGURE 4.5. Cycle Rule Violation

Run Chart Analysis Exercises

Purpose: To apply and use run chart analysis rules and discern whether or not special cause variation is present in operational performance.

Action: Analyze the run charts for the following three exercises and determine whether or not special cause variation is present. Explain the rationale for your conclusion. Answers to these exercises can be found in Appendix A.

Run Chart Analysis Exercise 1: Number of Application Errors

Analyze Figure 4.6:

- What is your conclusion? Is special cause variation present?
- What is your rationale? (*Hint*: What special cause rule is violated, if any?)

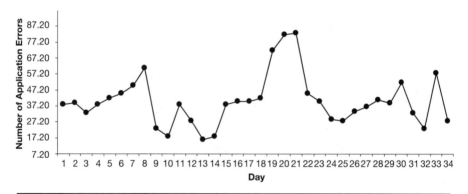

FIGURE 4.6. Run Chart Analysis Exercise 1: Number of Application Errors

Run Chart Analysis Exercise 2: Monthly Cost of Telecommunications Network Services

Analyze Figure 4.7:

- What is your conclusion? Is special cause variation present?
- What is your rationale? (*Hint*: What special cause rule is violated, if any?)

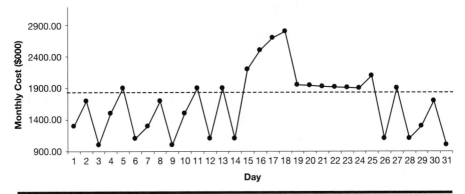

FIGURE 4.7. Run Chart Analysis Exercise 2: Monthly Cost of Telecommunications Network Services

Run Chart Analysis Exercise 3: Total Defects

Analyze Figure 4.8:

- What is your conclusion? Is special cause variation present?
- What is your rationale? (*Hint*: What special cause rule is violated, if any?)

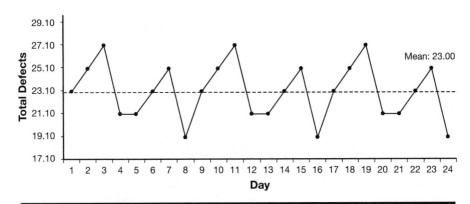

FIGURE 4.8. Run Chart Analysis Exercise 3: Total Defects

COMMON CAUSE AND SPECIAL CAUSE MANAGEMENT ACTIONS

Special cause variation is not an inherent part or naturally occurring part of an operation. Operations that have a combination of common cause and special cause variation are considered to be out of statistical control. An operation out of statistical control lends itself to crisis management.

If you find special cause variation within a process, you should conduct root cause analysis and determine its source. If the special cause has a negative impact on performance, root out the cause and take preventive measures so it does not recur. If the special cause has a positive impact, if feasible, try to standardize it and make it part of your operation.

Common cause variation is a naturally occurring part of every process. It is a result of the inherent natural interactions of an operation's factors of production. All processes have common cause variation. Those processes which have only common cause variation are considered to be in statistical control.

When analyzing process performance, it can be tempting to react to common cause variation as if it were special cause variation, but that would be considered tampering. Tampering with common cause variation can cause management to inadvertently introduce special cause variation into process performance, which can increase performance variation and aggravate operational performance. If dissatisfied with overall performance, management can work to continuously improve operational effectiveness and reduce common cause variation.

CONCLUSION

In this chapter, we discussed the importance of understanding and studying performance variation in the delivery of services, demonstrated how to display baseline operational performance using a run chart, analyzed process performance using special cause rules, and discussed the right actions to take in order to address both common and special cause variation in operational performance.

5

THE BASIC
SIX SIGMA TOOL KIT

An apprentice carpenter may want only a hammer and saw,
but a master craftsman employs many precision tools.
—*Robert L. Kruse*
Data Structures and Program Design

A vital part of Six Sigma implementations is the use of statistical quality control tools. In addition to the methods discussed in previous chapters, the analytical tools presented in this chapter are commonly used to improve productivity and service quality. Table 5.1 outlines the Six Sigma improvement process (DMAIC) and the set of statistical tools that are commonly used at each stage.

THE SIX SIGMA ANALYTICAL TOOL KIT

The use of Six Sigma tools is essential to achieving service excellence because they promote the use of facts and data in decision making and problem solving. Six Sigma tools provide decision makers with a means to solve problems with objectivity and clarity. The tools also enable decision makers to manage by fact instead of basing decisions on opinion and intuition alone.

TABLE 5.1. The Basic Six Sigma Tool Kit

Six Sigma Tool	1 DEFINE Establish business case Identify problem Set project goal	2 MEASURE Plan data collection Collect data Measure process defects Quantify gaps	3 ANALYZE Root cause analysis Stratify causes Prioritize causes Identify and verify root cause(s)	4 IMPROVE Generate solutions Test alternatives Select best solution Implement solution	5 CONTROL Define control system Determine process capability Select control chart Develop SOPs
Cause and effect diagram			✓		
Control chart	✓				✓
Data sheet	✓		✓		
Flowchart	✓	✓			
Histogram	✓		✓		
Pareto analysis	✓	✓	✓		
Process capability analysis	✓	✓	✓		✓
Run chart	✓	✓	✓		
Scatter diagram				✓	✓
Statistical process control	✓	✓			✓

Decision makers are empowered to manage by fact when:

- They can track performance with data that can be analyzed over time.
- They understand process requirements, activities, and work products.
- They use numerical facts to describe issues objectively.

The purpose of this chapter is to provide a reference that explains how to use the basic analytical tool kit employed by Six Sigma professionals around the world. Each of the tools will be described in the following manner:

- **Definition**: Description and purpose of the tool and technique
- **Example**: An illustration of how the tool is used
- **Construction**: The process followed for using the tool
- **Exercise**: An opportunity to practice the use of the tool and technique

Data Sheet

Definition

A data sheet is used to collect, record, and inventory data for evaluation. Data usually are collected and recorded in real time, but data sheets often are used to record past events. Data sheets can be housed in spreadsheets in many popular software applications.

The following is a list of the many types of data collected and recorded in data sheets:

- The frequency of an occurrence
- Interval and cycle time analysis
- The quality of work products
- The cost of a process activity over a period of time
- The quantity of work products produced

Example

The sample data sheet shown in Table 5.2 is a collection of call center data. The data represent the number and types of trouble calls processed during a four-week period by a customer service center.

TABLE 5.2. Sample Data Sheet

	Data Sheet Call Mix			
Type	Week 1	Week 2	Week 3	Week 4
Service orders	1,975	2,335	2,965	7,432
Collections	2,004	2,464	2,475	6,087
Billing information	1,776	1,965	2,932	5,652
Trouble tickets	259	983	800	2,075
Technical	472	865	400	1,943
Other	1,472	1,865	2,075	5,075
Totals	7,958	10,477	11,647	28,264

Dates: November 3–7, 10–14, 17–21, 24–28, 2008
Place: Austin Customer Service Operations
Scope: All customer service agents
What: All service calls

Construction

1. Determine what data you want to collect and why.
2. Decide the best and most reliable way to collect the data.
3. Create a data sheet in a format with simple categories.
4. Collect the data.
5. Input the data into the worksheet.

Histogram

Definition

A histogram is a special kind of bar chart that enables a decision maker to display operational performance in a graphical representation. This graphical representation, a distribution of performance data, empowers managers to review their business results with greater objectivity and provides them with a context in which to evaluate their business results.

Example

Suppose you are a new graduate student and you want to determine the amount of time, on average, you should allow yourself to drive to school each day. On your best day, you can make it to class in 15 minutes. On bad days, you encounter traffic and it takes you almost 45 minutes. You want

TABLE 5.3. Commute Time Data Sheet

25	26	30	25	28	27	30	18	27	29
38	16	32	35	27	26	29	19	28	27
26	15	28	27	27	26	19	28	29	20
18	22	32	28	17	28	29	27	31	24
42	32	28	30	31	29	30	34	26	27
33	30	31	31	26	35	27	31	27	27
35	28	26	27	27	26	25	32	30	27
34	37	37	29	32	36	28	31	30	34
28	25	29	30	33	32	29	28	27	31
28	30	32	30	30	29	28	25	29	30

to know what your *normal* travel time is. A histogram is a tool you can use to visually display your travel time and provide an answer to your question.

You collect data by logging your drive time to class in a data sheet for 100 days (see Table 5.3). From the commute time histogram shown in Figure 5.1, you find a distinct pattern or distribution of your drive time results. The data show that your longest drive time was almost 45 minutes and your

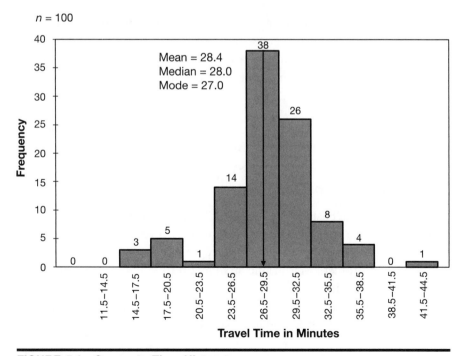

FIGURE 5.1. Commute Time Histogram

shortest drive time was just under 15 minutes. All but five of the trips fell between 15 and 35 minutes. However, you still want to know your normal drive time.

What is considered to be your normal drive time is referred to, in statistical terms, as a *central tendency*. Central tendency refers to the location of the middle or center of a distribution of data. Statisticians use central tendency for any statistic that can be quoted as *representative* of an entire data set (population). In business, managers use central tendency to determine how an operation is performing; for example, "on average our cycle time is x hours."

There are three measures of central tendency used in statistics: the mean, the median, and the mode. They are defined as follows:

- **Mean**: The simple average of a set of values. It is a measure of central tendency that is determined by adding all the values in a data set and dividing them by the total number of values. In our commute time example, the *mean drive time* is 28.4 minutes.
- **Median**: The halfway point in a set of data. The median is the number where half the values are greater than or equal to it and half are less than or equal to it. In our commute time example, the *median drive time* is 28 minutes.
- **Mode**: The most frequently occurring value in an array or range of data. In our commute time example, the *mode drive time* is 27 minutes.

As a result of your analysis, you can safely conclude that, under normal conditions, your drive time to class will be anywhere from 27 to 29 minutes.

Manual Construction

1. Collect the data. Histograms require at least 30 observations. A good data collection plan for a histogram will include 70 to 100 data points. The data in the data sheet in Table 5.4 represent the amount of time (in minutes) customers wait in line at a bank during the lunch hour. There are 132 data points ($N = 132$).
2. Calculate the range (R) of the data set. Subtract the smallest value from the largest value. From the data set in Table 5.4, the range is calculated as follows:

$$11.0 - 9.0 = 2.0$$

TABLE 5.4. Customer Wait Time Data Sheet

9.3	9.3	9.4	9.7	10.0	10.0	9.4	9.6	9.7	9.8	9.5
9.3	9.6	9.7	9.7	9.7	9.8	9.9	10.2	10.2	10.7	9.6
9.5	9.6	10.0	10.0	9.2	10.4	9.7	9.9	9.8	9.7	10.7
9.6	9.6	10.1	9.5	10.1	9.3	9.8	9.5	9.4	10.2	9.3
9.6	9.6	10.4	10.1	9.9	9.8	10.2	10.1	9.8	10.0	9.6
9.8	9.8	9.9	9.8	9.7	9.4	9.6	9.7	9.9	10.0	9.3
9.9	9.8	9.6	10.1	9.4	9.8	10.1	9.8	10.2	9.9	9.4
9.9	9.8	9.3	9.9	9.5	9.7	9.2	9.9	10.3	10.2	9.5
9.9	9.8	9.5	9.0	9.4	9.8	9.7	9.8	9.5	9.7	10.0
10.1	10.0	10.7	9.8	10.2	10.3	10.7	9.3	10.0	9.9	10.1
10.3	10.1	9.8	10.1	9.7	9.5	10.0	10.0	9.7	9.7	10.5
10.3	10.3	9.5	10.6	9.7	10.1	10.0	9.8	9.5	10.1	11.0

3. Based on the number of observations (N), use the guideline in Table 5.5 to determine the number of classes (K) or bars for the histogram. The guideline allows us to use 7 to 12 classes in this example. We will use 10 classes.

4. Calculate the class width (H) by dividing the range by the number of classes determined in the prior step:

$$H = R/K = 2.0/10 = 0.20$$

5. Calculate the class bands and limits. The smallest number of observations is the lower limit for the first class of data points. In our example, the smallest number is 9, which becomes the lower limit of the first class. Next take this lower limit number and add it to the class width (H):

$$9 + 0.20 = 9.20$$

TABLE 5.5. Class Number Guideline

Number of Data Points (N)	Number of Classes (K)
$N < 50$	5–7
$51 < N < 100$	6–10
$101 < N < 250$	7–12
$250 < N$	10–20

TABLE 5.6. Frequency Distribution Table

Class Number	Class Limits	Tally	Frequency
1	9.0–9.19	/	1
2	9.2–9.39	///// /////	10
3	9.4–9.59	///// ///// ///// ///	18
4	9.6–9.79	///// ///// ///// ///// ///// //	27
5	9.8–9.99	///// ///// ///// ///// ///// ///// /	31
6	10.0–10.19	///// ///// ///// ///// ////	24
7	10.2–10.39	///// ///// //	12
8	10.4–10.59	///	3
9	10.6–10.79	/////	5
10	10.8–11.00	/	1
Total			**132**

The lower limit of the second class is 9.20. The first class limit will range from 9.0 to 9.19, but will not include 9.20; 9.20 will be the first data point for the next class bandwidth. Follow through with this procedure until all class bands and limits are determined.

6. Create a frequency distribution table based on the customer wait time data, as illustrated in Table 5.6.
7. Construct the histogram (see Figure 5.2) based on the frequency distribution information in Table 5.6. The y-axis is the frequency of each class. The largest measurement on the scale should be greater than the largest

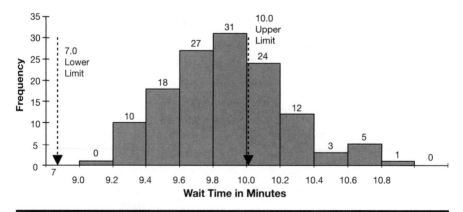

FIGURE 5.2. Wait Time Histogram

observation of the class frequency. The x-axis will correspond to the metric under observation. Draw the bar graph such that the bars are touching. Make the height of each bar graph correspond to the number of observations in the frequency distribution table.

8. Review and analyze your histogram. In our example, the specification for the customer wait time critical-to-quality requirement is 7 to 10 minutes, with a target of 9 minutes. The histogram shown in Figure 5.2 indicates the process performance is over-queued.

Construction with QI Macros

1. Enter the data in a spreadsheet.
2. Highlight the data set in the spreadsheet.
3. Select **QI Macros > Frequency Histogram**.
4. Input the upper specification/tolerance limit and click **OK**.
5. Input the lower specification/tolerance limit and click **OK**.
If you have no tolerance or specification limit (i.e., goal), then press cancel.
6. Title the chart and click **OK**.
7. Label the vertical and horizontal axes and click **OK**.
8. Label the histogram according to your preference.

Histogram Exercise: Understanding Call Center Efficiencies

Purpose: To construct and analyze data in a histogram.

Action: A data table of average handling times for a 24-hour call center is shown in Table 5.7; 120 observations are recorded. The call center's standard for handling service calls is between 3.25 and 3.5 minutes. Use the data in the table to construct a histogram and determine the call center's ability to meet its efficiency standard. Once you are finished, compare your results with the completed histogram in Appendix B.

Cause and Effect Diagram

Definition

The cause and effect diagram, also known as the *fishbone* diagram because of its shape, is a tool used during brainstorming sessions to study the factors

TABLE 5.7. Call Center Average Handling Time Data Sheet

193	193	194	197	210	210	194	196	197	198
193	196	197	197	197	198	199	202	202	207
195	196	210	210	192	204	197	199	198	197
196	196	201	195	201	193	198	195	194	202
196	196	204	201	199	198	202	201	198	210
198	198	199	198	197	194	196	197	199	210
199	198	196	201	194	198	201	198	202	199
199	198	193	199	195	197	192	199	203	202
199	198	195	199	194	198	197	198	195	197
211	210	217	198	212	213	207	193	210	199
213	211	198	211	197	195	215	213	197	197
213	213	195	216	197	211	210	198	195	211

that may have some bearing on a given situation. In the practice of Six Sigma, the *effect* is the problem in a process produced by a system of causes. In a manufacturing environment, the system of causes is grouped around four basic categories: materials, methods, manpower, and machines. For a service environment, however, a system of causes is organized around the following categories: people, methods, (management) policies, information, and technology (see Figure 5.3).

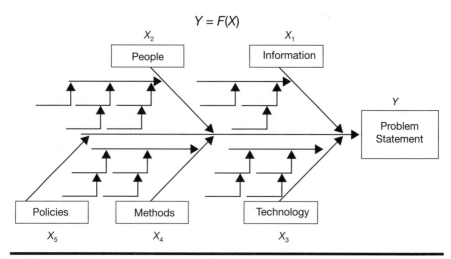

FIGURE 5.3. Cause and Effect (Fishbone) Diagram

Example

The elements of the fishbone diagram are remarkably similar to the productive system outlined in Chapter 1. This structure is by design. Logic dictates that productively and efficiently produced work products (Y) are a function of the factors of production $F(X)$ engineered into an operation. Likewise, problems and barriers to quality and productivity are a function of malfunctioning factors of production engineered into an operation. In both cases, $Y = F(X)$.

The components of the fishbone diagram are:

- A problem statement box (the fish's head) in which the effect is written
- A long horizontal line (the fish's backbone) extending from the problem statement box
- A series of diagonal lines (the fish's ribs) connected to the backbone, which represent the major categories for the "system of causes" that has produced the undesirable situation being studied
- A series of potential causes which branch out from the major categories

Construction

As mentioned earlier, the fishbone diagram is used during brainstorming sessions to study the possible factors that could have a bearing on a problem. In order to use this tool correctly, key people who work in the operation must participate in the brainstorming session. The session should include those people with intimate knowledge of the operation and experience with the problem. The brainstormers also should include frontline (hourly) employees as well as people from those departments whose work products directly and indirectly affect the operation's input requirements.

The steps to construct a fishbone diagram are as follows:

1. Write the problem/effect in the problem statement box (the fish's head).
2. Draw a horizontal line (the fish's backbone) extending from the problem statement.

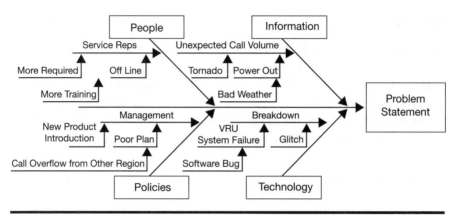

FIGURE 5.4. Completed Cause and Effect (Fishbone) Diagram for Slow Call Center Response Times

3. Use brainstorming to identify the major categories/factors of causes for the problem being examined.
4. Draw diagonal lines (the fish's ribs) above and below the backbone and label the categories on the diagram.
5. Generate a list of possible causes for each major category. Go around the room until ideas are exhausted.
6. Improve the list of possible causes by asking why five times or until a useful level of detail is reached.

The objective of the brainstorming session is to produce a large list of possible causes that could be affecting the operation. Once that task is completed, initiate a second round of brainstorming. Use consensus to select the top six or seven causes that are most likely to be at the root of the problem and then investigate those possible root causes firsthand. An example of a completed fishbone diagram is illustrated in Figure 5.4.

Cause and Effect Diagram Exercise: A Hot Time in the City

Purpose: To use the fishbone diagram as part of a brainstorming exercise.

Action: Use the following exercise to practice cause and effect diagramming with a group. You may want to include individuals who have some familiarity with auto maintenance.

Scenario: You live in Phoenix, Arizona. It is a hot July day (120 degrees Fahrenheit) and you are driving in rush hour traffic. As you glance at the dashboard indicators, you notice that the engine temperature is rising. As the seconds go by, it rises faster and faster. Suddenly, the air-conditioning automatically shuts off and the temperature gauge runs past the halfway mark, then past three-quarters, and finally is in the red. You pull off the road as your car overheats. You become angry because you recently had your radiator flushed. What could be wrong?

Directions:
- Break out into teams of three or five.
- Construct your fishbone diagram.
- Choose your categories.
- Begin filling in the fishbone diagram.
- Brainstorm and try to produce more than 35 reasons why your car would overheat.
- At the end of 25 minutes, bring the list of causes into group discussion.
- Analyze your list and eliminate those reasons that most likely are not at the root of the problem.

For this exercise, there is one root cause. Once you have completed this exercise, turn to Appendix B to see if the root cause is among your list of causes generated by brainstorming.

Scatter Diagram

Definition

The scatter diagram, also known as a scatter plot, is a tool used to graphically illustrate the possible relationship between two quantitative variables.

There are three main components of a scatter diagram: the y-axis, the x-axis, and the plane. The *y-axis* is the place on the diagram where the response variable is plotted. The *response variable,* also known as the *dependent variable,* is the variable in the relationship that is acted upon. The *x-axis* is the place on the diagram where the explanatory variable is plotted. The *explanatory variable,* also known as the *independent variable,* is the variable that impacts the dependent variable and helps explain the response that is plotted. The *plane* is where the plots of the observations are made.

Six Sigma professionals often use scatter diagrams to examine a situation for possible *cause* and *effect* relationships. There are several types of cause and effect relationships. The ones we will be concerned with are illustrated in Figure 5.5.

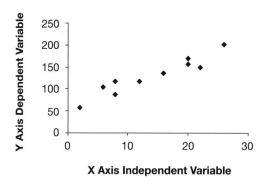

Positive Correlation:
Is determined when an increase in *Y* can be explained by an increase in *X*. If *X* is controlled, *Y* will be naturally controlled.

Some examples include:
- Height vs. weight
- Training vs. performance
- Speed vs. distance

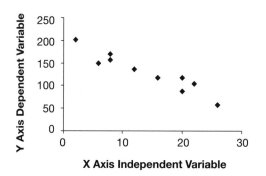

Negative Correlation:
Is determined when an increase in *X* can explain a decrease in *Y*.

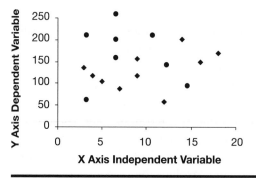

No Correlation:
No apparent correlation exists between *X* and *Y*.

FIGURE 5.5. Scatter Diagrams

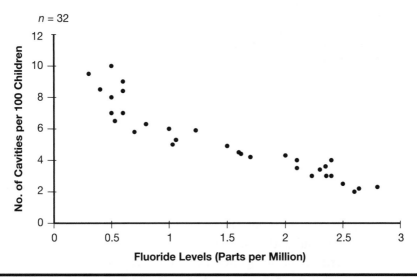

FIGURE 5.6. Scatter Diagram for Fluoride Levels in 32 Cities

Example

Figure 5.6 is an example of a scatter diagram for fluoride levels in 32 cities. The scatter plot shows that children with fewer cavities reside in cities that added more fluoride to their water. This type of relationship is defined as a *negative correlation,* where the increase in fluoride levels (X) explains the decrease in the number of cavities per 100 children (Y).

Manual Construction

1. Collect data in paired samples. Create a data sheet as shown in Table 5.8.
2. Draw both the vertical and horizontal axes of the scatter diagram. Plot the explanatory (independent) variable on the horizontal (x) axis and the response (dependent variable) on the vertical (y) axis.
3. Plot the data on the plane of the scatter diagram.

Construction with QI Macros

1. Highlight the labels and data in two columns (explanatory and response variables).

TABLE 5.8. Sample Scatter Diagram Data Sheet

Number of Observations	Fluoride Levels (Parts per Million)	Number of Cavities per 100 Children
1	0.5	10.0
2	0.3	9.5
3	0.6	9.0
4	0.5	8.0
5	0.4	8.5
⋮		
32	2.8	2.3

2. Select **QI Macros > Scatter Diagram**.
3. Title the chart and click **OK**.
4. Label the vertical and horizontal axes and click **OK**.
5. Label the scatter diagram according to your preference.

Caveat: Correlation Does Not Necessarily Mean Causation

Effective use of scatter plots can make it clear whether cause and effect relationships exist. It is important to understand, however, that a graphical representation of a correlation does not necessarily mean that a real correlation (causation) exists. Case in point: The scatter plot in Figure 5.7 examines the possible correlation between ice cream sales and murders in a major U.S. city. It is unlikely that increased ice cream sales explain the up tick in murders over those months. As a caveat, this plot underscores the concept that scatter plots test for *possible* correlations between two variables. The use

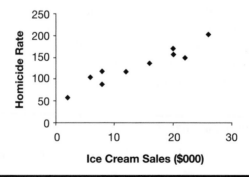

FIGURE 5.7. Scatter Diagram of Murders vs. Ice Cream Sales in June, July, and August

of the scatter plot is merely a beginning to understanding the nature of relationships that may exist between two variables.

Scatter Diagram Exercise: Field Operations Supervisor

Purpose: To construct, analyze, and interpret a scatter diagram.

Action: Use the following exercise to practice scatter diagramming.

Scenario: Suppose you are a supervisor for a cable company's field operations. You suspect there is some relationship between the level of experience of an installation technician and the total number of installations he or she can perform in a week. You collect data on 20 of your technicians for 4 months and document it accordingly. Your aim is to adjust your staffing in order to improve the overall install productivity. You record the data as shown in Table 5.9. Construct a scatter diagram and analyze it. What conclusions can you draw from it? Compare your results to the answer in Appendix B.

Pareto Analysis

Definition

Pareto analysis is a method used to clarify the most significant factors that can have bearing on a given situation. Many quality experts define the outcome of Pareto analysis as separating the *vital few* causes from the *trivial many*. There are three main goals of Pareto analysis:

1. Prioritize issues and problems
2. Separate the significant issues from the insignificant ones
3. Define issues based on methods of comparison

For a Six Sigma professional, it is important to determine the most important opportunities for improvement in order to get the largest return from the effort put into a project. Pareto analysis can help achieve that end.

Example

A Pareto diagram is a bar chart that organizes data according to significance. A Pareto chart is somewhat like a histogram. Whereas a histogram is a

TABLE 5.9. Scatter Diagram Data Sheet for Experience vs. Production

Employee	Years on the Job	Average Weekly Production	Production Certification
Frank	14	12	None
John	7	10	Certification
Matthew	3	3	None
Mark	15	10	None
Reggie	11	9	None
Fred	10	6	None
Arnold	12	10	None
Vivian	14	10	None
Amy	7	5	None
Judd	10	8	None
Gordon	16	11	None
James	12	9	None
Sid	8	6	None
Homer	9	7	None
Franklin	13	10	None
Jessie	9	7	None
Jennifer	8	12	Certification
Robin	7	5	None
Kathy	8	10	Certification
Clarence	9	6	None

frequency bar chart used for quantitative data grouped into classes, a Pareto diagram is a frequency bar chart used to quantify data by qualitative characteristics. An example of a Pareto chart can be found in Figure 5.8.

The Pareto diagram consists of two major components:

1. **Bar chart**: Shows the impact of the individual categories on the overall effect
2. **Cumulative line**: Shows how the individual categories add up to the total overall effect

Analysis and Conclusion

The Pareto chart in Figure 5.8 illustrates the major types of document errors in an order management process. It also shows that the most frequently occurring errors are missing SIC codes and incorrect pricing. Missing SIC codes account for almost half of the processing errors, and when combined

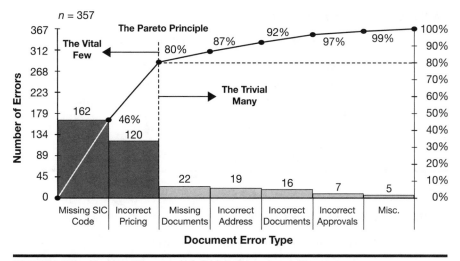

FIGURE 5.8. Pareto Diagram of Order Document Errors

with incorrect pricing, both error types account for 80% of all the document errors. The vital few are separated from the trivial many. From the analysis, it can safely be concluded that conducting root cause analysis and implementing solutions for missing SIC codes and incorrect pricing will substantially improve the productivity of the order management process.

Manual Construction

1. Determine what you want to know. Decide whether the outcome of the analysis is to measure the cost of certain error types, the frequency of certain error types, the adverse impact certain error types have on productivity, or all three.
2. Decide how you want to categorize your data.
3. Collect your data.
4. Create the Pareto diagram(s).
5. Analyze the diagram(s) and decide if the Pareto principle appears. The Pareto principle, also known as the 80/20 rule, states that 80% of a problem is caused by 20% of its contributors. This principle seeks to separate the vital few issues from the trivial many. If the Pareto principle appears, move forward in resolving your issue. If it does not appear, categorize your data from a different perspective and repeat steps 3 through 5.

TABLE 5.10. Pareto Analysis Data Table

Document Errors	Number of Errors
Missing SIC code	162
Incorrect pricing	120
Missing documents	22
Miscellaneous	19
Incorrect documents	16
Incorrect approvals	7
Incorrect address	5

Construction with QI Macros

1. List the items in the category in the first column.
2. In the second column, to the immediate right of the first column, list the data that match the items in the first column (see Table 5.10).
3. Highlight the labels and data in both columns.
4. Select **QI Macros > Pareto Chart**.
5. Title the chart and click **OK**.
6. Label the vertical and horizontal axes and click **OK**.
7. Label the Pareto chart according to your preference.

Pareto Analysis Exercise: Cost Due to Poor Health Care Quality

Purpose: To construct, analyze, and interpret Pareto diagrams.

Action: Use the following exercise to practice Pareto analysis.

Scenario: A hospital group consisting of three hospitals is experiencing an extreme amount of unbudgeted excess cost due to poor quality of care issues. The company decides to conduct an analysis of the types of problems it is experiencing and the cost associated with them. During the six-month study, five major problems were found to occur most frequently. A data sheet was created to record each problem type by hospital by month. The five problem types and related average cost for each occurrence were recorded as follows:

Error 1: Deadly infections in the bloodstream $6935.00
Error 2: Wound reopening after surgery due to infection $5325.00
Error 3: Accidentally leaving an instrument or sponge in
         a patient's body $1300.00
Error 4: Dispensing the wrong medication $500.00
Error 5: Excess overtime due to correcting invoicing errors $25.50

The six-month study revealed the frequency of occurrence of each problem type. The results are recorded in Table 5.11.

Your task is to:

1. Determine at least three ways these data can be categorized.
2. Create a Pareto chart for each categorization.
3. Analyze the charts and draw conclusions.
4. Determine your next steps.

Compare your results with the findings in Appendix B.

TABLE 5.11. Pareto Analysis Data Sheet

January						February					
Hospital	**E1**	**E2**	**E3**	**E4**	**E5**	**Hospital**	**E1**	**E2**	**E3**	**E4**	**E5**
West	10	0	10	0	30	West	10	10	10	10	30
North	0	10	10	10	20	North	0	0	0	20	30
South	10	0	10	20	40	South	0	10	10	10	30

March						April					
Hospital	**E1**	**E2**	**E3**	**E4**	**E5**	**Hospital**	**E1**	**E2**	**E3**	**E4**	**E5**
West	10	0	20	10	40	West	0	10	0	20	20
North	10	0	0	10	20	North	0	10	10	20	30
South	0	10	10	10	50	South	0	10	0	10	20

May						June					
Hospital	**E1**	**E2**	**E3**	**E4**	**E5**	**Hospital**	**E1**	**E2**	**E3**	**E4**	**E5**
West	0	20	10	10	20	West	0	10	10	10	40
North	10	0	10	0	40	North	0	20	0	10	30
South	0	0	10	20	30	South	0	0	10	10	40

STATISTICAL PROCESS CONTROL FOR SERVICE EXCELLENCE

Statistical process control (SPC) is a method of analyzing operational performance by taking samples of operational results, at specified time intervals, and charting the outcomes in a graphical summary. Three reasons why Six Sigma professionals use SPC are:

1. **Process assessment**: SPC provides management with the means to ascertain whether the performance of an operation is free of special cause variation. If an operation is free of special cause variation, management is empowered to predict, within certain limits, how the operation will perform and what results can be expected in the future. If an operation is not free of special cause variation, it becomes unstable and difficult to manage. SPC enables management to detect when special cause variation is present and take corrective action to eliminate it at its source.
2. **Process comparison**: SPC provides management with a means to compare operational results of similar operations within a company and benchmark similar processes between companies. Making such comparisons can empower management to engineer the proper mix of a process's factors of production to obtain the highest levels of productivity.
3. **Process verification**: SPC provides management with a metric to verify whether a change to a process has had a favorable impact on performance. SPC enables everyone to competently answer the questions: "What is the impact of a solution on an operation?" and "Has performance improved?"

The main tool used in SPC is the control chart. The control chart, illustrated in Figure 5.9, is a measurement tool used to measure the quality, productivity, and cost effectiveness of an operation's performance. The three elements of a control chart are as follows:

1. **Critical-to-quality requirement (CTQ)**: The CTQ being measured.
2. **Centerline (CL)**: Measures the central tendency of the performance data (i.e., mean, median, or mode).

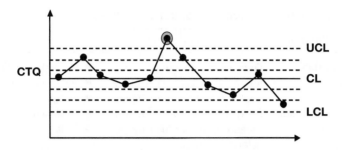

FIGURE 5.9. Sample Control Chart

3. **Upper (UCL) and lower (LCL) control limits:** Used to determine whether special cause variation is present in an operation. The control limits are set at plus and minus 3 standard deviations from the mean.

Control Chart Selection

Several types of control charts exist. The type of control chart used in a situation depends on the type of data collected. The type of data collected depends on what the user wants to know. For the purpose of SPC, data can be classified into two major categories:

1. **Continuous data:** The type of data that yields a measurement or number for each unit measured. Continuous data most often are used to measure an operation's productivity, efficiency, or cost effectiveness.
2. **Discrete data:** The type of data that is categorical or where the attributes measured relate to defects or defective units. Discrete data most often are used to measure the quality of an operation's work product.

Table 5.12 describes each classification in more detail.

As mentioned earlier, there are several types of control charts. The types that are effective for continuous data include:

1. **XmR chart:** Individual measurement with moving range chart
2. **$\overline{X}$,R chart:** Average and range chart
3. **$\overline{X}$,S chart:** Average and standard deviation chart

TABLE 5.12. Statistical Process Control Data Classification

Data Classification	Definition	Examples
Continuous data Also known as: ■ Variable data ■ Measurement data ■ Analog data	Data which account for performance or a specification for each unit observed. Typical performance data include measures of productivity, efficiency, and cost.	■ Average handling time ■ Average response time ■ Length ■ Cycle time ■ Cost
Discrete data Also known as: ■ Attribute data ■ Count data ■ Digital data	Data that are categorical and measure a conformance or non-conformance to a specification or requirement. Typical performance data include quality measures defined by the presence or absence of an error or fault, as well as counts of defects or defectives.	■ First-call resolution ■ Order form error rate ■ Percent misdirected calls ■ Rejection rate ■ Acceptance rate ■ Invoice error rate

The types of control charts that are effective for discrete data include:

1. **np chart**: Number of defectives chart
2. **p chart**: Proportion of defectives chart
3. **c chart**: Number of defects chart
4. **u chart**: Average number of defects per unit chart

The use of a specific type of control chart is suitable only when certain conditions are met. Figure 5.10 is a decision tree that can be used as a guide in the selection of an appropriate control chart for a given situation.

Making the distinction between a defect and a defective is essential in selecting the right control chart for the right situation. What separates a defective from a defect is:

■ **Defective:** A defective work product is a non-conforming/non-performing *item* that in some way fails to conform to one or more requirements.
■ **Defect:** A defect, or non-conformity, is the lack of conformance to a specification of a single portion of a work product.

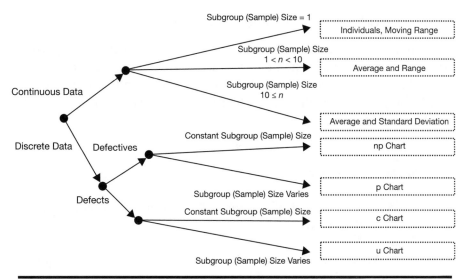

FIGURE 5.10. Control Chart Decision Tree

A non-conforming/non-performing work product is defective and will have one or more non-conformities (defects). When a customer service call does not achieve first-call resolution, the call itself is defective because it fails to satisfy the customer need. The reasons that lead to the defective call are considered defects.

Control Chart Selection Exercises

Purpose: To use the control chart decision tree to select the right control chart.

Action: Read the following four scenarios and use the control chart decision tree to determine the most appropriate control chart to use for each scenario. Specifically:

- Identify the appropriate control chart.
- Explain your reasoning for using it.

When finished, compare your responses to the answers in Appendix B.

Control Chart Selection Example Exercise

A telecommunications company wants to reduce the number of billing errors on invoices sent to its customers. The accounting department decides to track the number of invoices sent out every month and account for the *number of incorrect bills* adjusted. The total number of invoices mailed monthly is relatively constant.

Answer
Type of Data: Discrete data.

CTQ Tracked: The number of defective bills sent out every month out of the total number of invoices.

Sample Size Vary?: Total number of invoices remains relatively constant on a month-to-month basis.

Control Chart: The suitable chart is the np chart.

Reasoning: The company has decided to account for the total number of incorrect bills sent out, which implies a non-conforming/non-performing type of data or defective data. The standard of incorrectness is applied to the entire invoice—one error creates a defective bill.

Control Chart Selection Exercise 1: Filling Job Vacancies

A company's human resources director wants to track the percentage of jobs filled by external candidates. The company's objective is to leverage more internal candidates to fill company vacancies. The number of job openings varies significantly from one month to the next.

Type of Data:

CTQ Tracked:

Subgroup Size Vary?:

Control Chart:

Rationale:

Control Chart Selection Exercise 2: Reworked Orders

The number of new service orders signed by a company's sales force remains relatively *constant* from week to week. However, the sales manager believes too many orders have to be reworked before the service can be delivered. A Six Sigma team has been formed to reduce the number of reworked orders.

Type of Data:

CTQ Tracked:

Subgroup Size Vary?:

Control Chart:

Rationale:

Control Chart Selection Exercise 3: Call Center Response Times

A call center director wants to improve the center's response times. The call center describes its response time indicator as the average time, in seconds, it takes to answer a customer's call—the average speed of answer. The call center operates 24 hours a day and response times are taken at the end of every hour.

Type of Data:

CTQ Tracked:

Subgroup Size Vary?:

Control Chart:

Rationale:

Control Chart Selection Exercise 4: Monthly Revenue

A company's chief financial officer would like to look at monthly revenue for the past two fiscal years. He would like to know how month-to-month revenue varied over that time period.

Type of Data:

CTQ Tracked:

Subgroup Size Vary?:

Control Chart:

Rationale:

Control Chart Descriptions

The purpose of this section is to provide you with the knowledge and skills to use SPC in your Six Sigma efforts. The following instruction and exercises will facilitate your learning and comprehension of SPC. The section also will give you the competence and confidence to apply SPC for practical use within your company. First, the method and calculations required to produce and utilize control charts are provided. Second, additional rules are presented for analyzing control charts for special cause variation.

Control charts can be very tedious to construct manually. This section explains the mechanics and calculations to construct and draft control charts manually. It also covers construction of control charts with the QI Macros software application.

XmR Chart: Individual Measurement with Moving Range Chart

An XmR chart, illustrated in Figure 5.11, is used as a metric to measure and graphically display operational performance for continuous data. As the name implies, XmR charts track individual measures and serve a very useful purpose of measuring process output in low-volume operations.

Manual Construction

1. Collect your data. For this example we will use the data captured in the XmR chart shown in Figure 5.11. These data represent the average wait time for bank customers for one month. Record each data point in the

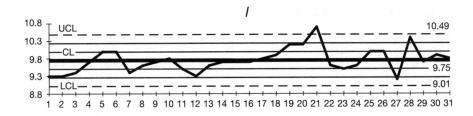

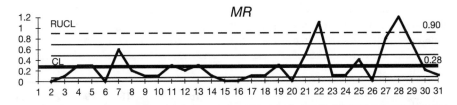

FIGURE 5.11. XmR Chart: Individual Measurement (Top) with Moving Range (Bottom) Chart

individual measurement row, as shown in Table 5.13, in the order it was collected.

2. Calculate the moving range (MR) values. The moving range is the absolute value of the difference between the consecutively recorded measurements.

$$R_2 = (X_2 - X_1) = (9.3 - 9.3) = 0.0$$

$$R_3 = (X_3 - X_2) = (9.4 - 9.3) = 0.1$$

$$R_4 = (X_4 - X_3) = (9.7 - 9.4) = 0.3$$

Record the results of your calculations as shown in Table 5.14.

3. Determine the average $(\overline{R})$ of the moving ranges by adding all of the range values and dividing the result by the total number of range values:

$$\overline{R} = \frac{R_1 + R_2 + R_3 + \dots + R_k}{k - 1} = \frac{0.0 + 0.1 + 0.3 + \dots + 0.1}{31 - 1} = 0.28$$

where $\overline{R}$ = average range and k = number of values.

TABLE 5.13. Individual Measurement with Moving Range Data Sheet

Operation: Branch Teller Operations

Function: Teller Service		Measurement: Average Wait Time (in Minutes)	

	Day										
	1	2	3	4	5	6	7	8	9	10	11
Observation (X)	9.3	9.3	9.4	9.7	10.0	10.0	9.4	9.6	9.7	9.8	9.5
Difference (MR)		0.0	0.1	0.3	0.3	0.0	0.6	0.2	0.1	0.1	0.3

	Day									
	12	13	14	15	16	17	18	19	20	21
Observation (X)	9.3	9.6	9.7	9.7	9.7	9.8	9.9	10.2	10.2	10.7
Difference (MR)	0.2	0.3	0.1	0.0	0.0	0.1	0.1	0.3	0.0	0.5

	Day									
	22	23	24	25	26	27	28	29	30	31
Observation (X)	9.6	9.5	9.6	10.0	10.0	9.2	10.4	9.7	9.9	9.8
Difference (MR)	1.1	0.1	0.1	0.4	0.0	0.8	1.2	0.7	0.2	0.1

TABLE 5.14. Moving Range Data Sheet

Moving range (MR)	0.0	0.1	0.3	0.3	0.0	■	0.0	0.8	1.2	0.7	0.2	0.1

4. Calculate the upper control limit (UCL_R) for the range chart:

$$UCL_R = 3.267 \times \overline{R} = 3.267 \times 0.028 = 0.90$$

where $\overline{R}$ = average range and UCL_R = upper control limit for the range chart.

5. Draft your range chart. Draw the average range as a solid line and the UCL as a dashed line.

6. Determine the mean for the individual measurements ($\overline{X}$) by adding the X values and dividing by the total number of X values:

$$\overline{X} = \frac{X_1 + X_2 + X_3 + \ldots + X_k}{k} = \frac{9.3 + 9.3 + 9.4 + \ldots + 9.8}{31} = 9.75$$

where $\overline{X}$ = average of values and k = number of X values.

7. Calculate upper (UCL$_X$) and lower (LCL$_X$) control limits for the individual observations:

$$\text{UCL}_X = \overline{X} + (2.66 \times \overline{R}) = 9.75 + (2.66 \times 0.28) = 10.49$$

$$\text{LCL}_X = \overline{X} - (2.66 \times \overline{R}) = 9.75 - (2.66 \times 0.28) = 9.01$$

where UCL$_X$ = upper control limit for the X chart, LCL$_X$ = lower control limit for the X chart, $\overline{R}$ = average range, $\overline{X}$ = average of the values, and 2.66 = a constant for individual measurements.

8. Draft the control chart for individual observations. Plot your data. Draw the average as a solid line and the control limits as dashed lines. Label the average and control limits and note their values on the chart.

Note: The number of observations required to calculate reliable control limits for an XmR chart is 25. It is important to resist the temptation to analyze operational performance before 25 observations are charted. However, if the data are obtained slowly, preliminary calculation of control limits can be made with only 10 observations, but be careful not to draw any conclusions regarding process stability until a threshold of at least 25 measurements is reached.

Construction with QI Macros

1. Plot your text and data in a spreadsheet.
2. Highlight the text and data.
3. Select **QI Macros > Control Charts > XmR Chart (Individuals)**.
4. Label the range chart.
5. Label the X chart.

Note: Each measurement represents a data point. Each data point is categorized by some unit. In this example, each measurement is categorized by day. This is your text. Be sure to highlight the data (numbers) and text (day 1…day 31). Doing so will enable the software package to distinguish between the size of the sample (subgroup) and how many samples (subgroups) there are. In this example, there are 31 samples (subgroups), but the sample size (subgroup size) is 1.

$\overline{X}$,R Chart: Average and Range Chart

The average and range chart, commonly referred to as the $\overline{X}$,R chart, is used as a metric to measure and graphically display operational performance for continuous data. It often is used to track productivity, efficiency, and cost effectiveness of an operation. An $\overline{X}$,R chart is shown in Figure 5.12. The average chart (the upper chart) is used to evaluate the central tendency of operational performance by measuring the process average over time. It is also used to measure and evaluate performance variation between subgroups. The range chart (the lower chart) is used to evaluate the dispersion or process variation within subgroups over time.

The basis of control charting is the *rational subgroup.* Rational subgroups are samples of work products that are produced under the same circumstances. Each subgroup represents a snapshot of an operation's performance at a point in time. The average chart examines between-subgroup variation (σ_b), which is the difference in subgroup averages, whereas the range chart evaluates within-subgroup variation (σ_w), which is the variation that occurs within a subgroup.

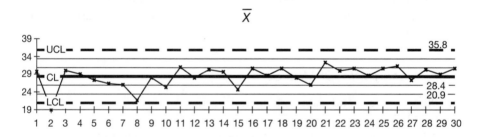

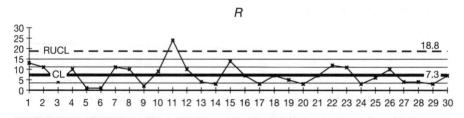

FIGURE 5.12. $\overline{X}$,R Chart: Average (Top) and Range (Bottom) Chart

Manual Construction

1. Collect your data. Decide what you want to know and then determine your subgrouping strategy (by shift, by day, weekly, etc.). It is important to draw samples produced under the same conditions. In our example, a midsized local telecommunications company's business-to-business service delivery project team selects three service orders every day for one month to evaluate the average number of days it takes a service order to complete its service delivery process. The data are shown in Table 5.15.

   Subgroup Size: $\overline{X}$,R chart subgroup sizes are limited to $1 < n < 10$; typically a sample (subgroup) size of 4 to 5 observations is used. If at all possible, use a constant subgroup size; $\overline{X}$,R charts can be used with varying subgroup sizes, but varying sample size tends to complicate matters. In our example, the constant subgroup size equals 3.

TABLE 5.15. $\overline{X}$,R Chart Data Sheet

Operation: New Order Process

Customer: Installation Customers							Measurement: Order Origination to Acceptance (in Days)							

	Day														
	1	**2**	**3**	**4**	**5**	**6**	**7**	**8**	**9**	**10**	**11**	**12**	**13**	**14**	**15**
Sample	25	26	30	25	28	27	30	18	27	29	18	22	32	28	17
size	38	16	32	35	27	26	29	19	28	27	42	32	28	30	31
	26	15	28	27	27	26	19	28	29	20	33	30	31	31	26
Average	30	19	30	29	27	26	26	22	28	25	31	28	30	30	25
Range	13	11	4	10	1	1	11	10	2	9	24	10	4	3	14

	Day														
	16	**17**	**18**	**19**	**20**	**21**	**22**	**23**	**24**	**25**	**26**	**27**	**28**	**29**	**30**
Sample	28	29	27	31	24	35	28	26	27	27	26	25	32	30	27
size	29	30	34	26	27	34	37	37	29	32	36	28	31	30	34
	35	27	31	27	27	28	25	29	30	33	32	29	28	27	31
Average	31	29	31	28	26	32	30	31	29	31	31	27	30	29	31
Range	7	3	7	5	3	7	12	11	3	6	10	4	4	3	7

Number of Subgroups: For reliable and ongoing control limits, the recommended number of subgroups is 25. In our example, the number of subgroups equals 30.

2. Determine the within-group variation by calculating the ranges for each subgroup. This is done by subtracting the smallest value within a subgroup from the largest value:

$$R = X_{max} - X_{min} \text{ (for each subgroup)}$$

$$R_1 = 38 - 25 = 13$$

$$R_2 = 26 - 15 = 11$$

$$R_3 = 32 - 28 = 4$$

Record these ranges in the bottom row of the table, as shown in Table 5.16.

3. Determine the average of the ranges $(\overline{R})$ by adding all the subgroup ranges and dividing them by the number of subgroups:

$$\overline{R} = \frac{R_1 + R_2 + R_3 + \ldots + R_k}{k} = \frac{13 + 11 + 4 + \ldots + 7}{30} = 7.3$$

where $\overline{R}$ = average range and k = number of subgroups.

TABLE 5.16. Average and Range Chart Data Sheet

	Day											
	1	2	3	4	5	6		26	27	28	29	30
Sample size	25	26	30	25	28	27	...	26	25	32	30	27
	38	16	32	35	27	26	...	36	28	31	30	34
	26	15	28	27	27	26	...	32	29	28	27	31
Sum	89	57	90	87	82	79	...	94	82	91	87	92
Average	30	19	30	29	27	26	...	31	27	30	29	31
Range	13	11	4	10	1	1	...	10	4	4	3	7

4. Determine the upper (UCL_R) and lower (LCL_R) control limits for the range chart:

$$\text{UCL}_R = \bar{R} \times D_4 = 7.3 \times 2.574 = 18.8$$

$$\text{LCL}_R = \bar{R} \times D_3 = 7.3 \times 0 = 0$$

where $\bar{R}$ = average range, UCL_R = upper control limit for the range chart, LCL_R = lower control limit for the range chart, D_4 = range UCL constant, and D_3 = range LCL constant. The values for D_3 and D_4 can be found in the table of factors for the average and range chart in Table 5.17.
5. Draft your range chart. Draw the average range as a solid line and the control limits as dashed lines.
6. Determine the mean for each subgroup:

$$\bar{X} = \frac{X_1 + X_2 + X_3 + \dots + X_n}{n}$$

$$\bar{X}_1 = \frac{25 + 38 + 26}{3} = 30$$

TABLE 5.17. Factors for the Average and Range Chart

Subgroup/Sample Size (n)	Averages (A_2)	Range (D_3)	Range (D_4)	Sigma (d_2)
2	1.880	0.0	3.267	1.128
3	1.023	0.0	2.574	1.693
4	0.729	0.0	2.282	2.059
5	0.577	0.0	2.114	2.326
6	0.483	0.0	2.004	2.534
7	0.419	0.076	1.924	2.704
8	0.373	0.136	1.864	2.847
9	0.337	0.184	1.816	2.970
10	0.308	0.223	1.777	3.078
11	0.285	0.256	1.744	3.173
12	0.266	0.284	1.717	3.258
13	0.249	0.308	1.692	3.336
14	0.235	0.329	1.671	3.407
15	0.223	0.348	1.652	3.472

$$\overline{X}_2 = \frac{26 + 16 + 15}{3} = 19$$

$$\overline{X}_3 = \frac{30 + 32 + 28}{3} = 30$$

where $\overline{X}$ = average or mean for the subgroup and n = size of the subgroup. Log the results in the subgroup average row as shown in Table 5.16.

7. Determine the "grand average" for the data set. The grand average $(\overline{\overline{X}})$ is the mean for all of the subgroup averages:

$$\overline{\overline{X}} = \frac{\overline{X}_1 + \overline{X}_2 + \overline{X}_3 + \ldots + \overline{X}_k}{k} = \frac{30 + 19 + 30 + \ldots + 31}{30} = 28.4$$

8. Determine the upper and lower control limits for the $\overline{X}$ chart:

$$\text{UCL}_{\overline{X}} = \overline{\overline{X}} + (R \times A_2) = 28.4 + (7.3 \times 1.023) = 35.8$$

$$\text{LCL}_{\overline{X}} = \overline{\overline{X}} - (\overline{R} \times A_2) = 28.4 - (7.3 \times 1.023) = 20.9$$

9. Draft your $\overline{X}$ chart. Plot your data. Draw the central tendency (grand average) as a solid line and the control limits as dashed lines.

Construction with QI Macros

1. Plot your text and data in a spreadsheet.
2. Highlight the text and data.
3. Select **QI Macros** > **Control Charts** > **XbarR Chart**.
4. Label the range chart.
5. Label the $\overline{X}$ chart.

Note: The average of each subgroup represents a data point. Each subgroup is categorized by some unit. In this example, each subgroup is categorized by day. The day is your text. Be sure to highlight the data (numbers) and text (day 1…day 30). Doing so will enable the software package to distinguish between the size of the sample (subgroup) and how many samples (subgroups) there are. In this example, there are 30 samples (subgroups), but the sample size (subgroup size) is 3.

$\overline{X}$,S Chart: Average and Standard Deviation Chart

Average and standard deviation control charts often are used to track productivity, efficiency, and cost effectiveness of an operation. $\overline{X}$,S charts are similar to average and range charts in all but one respect: the subgroup standard deviation is used to measure within-group variation rather than the subgroup range. Like $\overline{X}$,R charts, $\overline{X}$,S charts also are used as a metric to measure and graphically display operational performance for continuous data. They should be used in situations where subgroup size is large ($n \geq 10$). An example of an $\overline{X}$,S chart is shown in Figure 5.13.

Manual Construction

1. Collect your data. Decide what you want to know and then determine your subgrouping strategy (by shift, by day, weekly, etc.). Draw samples that are produced under the same conditions.

    Subgroup Size: $\overline{X}$,S chart subgroup (sample) sizes are limited to $n \geq 10$. Use a constant subgroup size; $\overline{X}$,S charts can be constructed with varying subgroup (sample) sizes, but varying sample size tends to complicate matters.

    Number of Subgroups: For reliable and ongoing control limits, the recommended number of subgroups (samples) is 25.

    In this example, the same midsized local telecommunications company's customer service call center management team selects collected data related

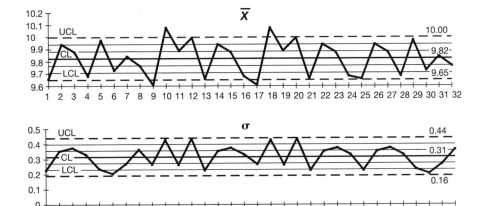

FIGURE 5.13. $\overline{X}$,S Chart: Average (Top) and Standard Deviation (Bottom) Chart

to the center's answer response time. Since it is a high-volume call center, the center's average speed of answer is collected every 15 minutes during the midday shift (8 hours). The results are categorized for 32 consecutive days. There are 32 subgroups and the subgroup size is 32. The response times are recorded in seconds. A sample data sheet is illustrated in Table 5.18.

2. Determine the mean for each subgroup:

$$\overline{X} = \frac{\text{Sum of subgroup measurements}}{\text{Subgroup size}}$$

$$\overline{X}_1 = \frac{9.3 + 9.3 + 9.5 + 9.6 + \dots + 9.9}{32} = 9.7$$

$$\overline{X}_2 = \frac{9.6 + 9.6 + 9.6 + 9.6 + \dots + 9.8}{32} = 9.7$$

Log the results in the subgroup average row as shown in the Table 5.18.

3. Determine the variance (s^2) and standard deviation (s) for each subgroup:

$$s = \sqrt{\frac{\sum_{i=1}^{n} (x_i - \overline{X})^2}{n - 1}}$$

$$s_1^2 = \frac{(9.3 - 9.7)^2 + (9.3 - 9.7)^2 + \dots + (9.9 - 9.7)^2}{32 - 1}$$

$$s_1^2 = 0.1$$

$$s_1 = \sqrt{0.1} = 0.3$$

$$s_2^2 = \frac{(9.6 - 9.7)^2 + (9.6 - 9.7)^2 + \dots + (9.8 - 9.7)^2}{9}$$

$$s_2^2 = 0.1$$

$$s_2 = \sqrt{0.1} = 0.3$$

TABLE 5.18. Average and Standard Deviation Chart Data Sheet

Date	Day									
	1	2	3	4	5		29	30	31	32
1	9.3	9.3	9.4	9.7	10.0	...	9.6	9.7	9.8	9.5
2	9.3	9.6	9.7	9.7	9.7	...	10.2	10.2	10.7	9.6
3	9.5	9.6	10.0	10.0	9.2	...	9.9	9.8	9.7	10.7
4	9.6	9.6	10.1	9.5	10.1	...	9.5	9.4	10.2	9.3
5	9.6	9.6	10.4	10.1	9.9	...	10.1	9.8	10.0	9.6
6	9.8	9.8	9.9	9.8	9.7	...	9.7	9.9	10.0	9.3
7	9.9	9.8	9.6	10.1	9.4	...	9.8	10.2	9.9	9.4
8	9.9	9.8	9.3	9.9	9.5	...	9.9	10.3	10.2	9.5
9	9.9	9.8	9.5	9.0	9.4	...	9.8	9.5	9.7	10.0
10	10.1	10.0	10.7	9.8	10.2	...	9.3	10.0	9.9	10.1
11	10.3	10.1	9.8	10.1	9.7	...	10.0	9.7	9.7	10.5
12	10.3	10.3	9.5	10.6	9.7	...	9.8	9.5	10.1	11.0
13	9.3	9.3	9.4	9.7	10.0	...	9.6	9.7	9.8	9.5
14	9.3	9.6	9.7	9.7	9.7	...	10.2	10.2	10.7	9.6
15	9.5	9.6	10.0	10.0	9.2	...	9.9	9.8	9.7	10.7
16	9.6	9.6	10.1	9.5	10.1	...	9.5	9.4	10.2	9.3
17	9.9	9.8	9.5	9.0	9.4	...	9.8	9.5	9.7	10.0
18	10.1	10.0	10.7	9.8	10.2	...	9.3	10.0	9.9	10.1
19	10.3	10.1	9.8	10.1	9.7	...	10.0	9.7	9.7	10.5
20	10.3	10.3	9.5	10.6	9.7	...	9.8	9.5	10.1	11.0
21	9.3	9.3	9.4	9.7	10.0	...	9.6	9.7	9.8	9.5
22	9.3	9.6	9.7	9.7	9.7	...	10.2	10.2	10.7	9.6
23	9.5	9.6	10.0	10.0	9.2	...	9.9	9.8	9.7	10.7
24	9.6	9.6	10.1	9.5	10.1	...	9.5	9.4	10.2	9.3
25	9.3	9.3	9.4	9.7	10.0	...	9.6	9.7	9.8	9.5
26	9.3	9.6	9.7	9.7	9.7	...	10.2	10.2	10.7	9.6
27	9.5	9.6	10.0	10.0	9.2	...	9.9	9.8	9.7	10.7
28	9.6	9.6	10.1	9.5	10.1	...	9.5	9.4	10.2	9.3
29	9.6	9.6	10.4	10.1	9.9	...	10.1	9.8	10.0	9.6
30	9.8	9.8	9.9	9.8	9.7	...	9.7	9.9	10.0	9.3
31	9.9	9.8	9.6	10.1	9.4	...	9.8	10.2	9.9	9.4
32	9.9	9.8	9.3	9.9	9.5	...	9.9	10.3	10.2	9.5
Average	9.7	9.7	9.8	9.8	9.7	...	9.8	9.8	9.8	9.8
Standard deviation	0.3	0.3	0.4	0.3	0.3	...	0.3	0.4	0.3	0.3

4. Determine the average standard deviation:

$$\bar{s} = \frac{\text{Sum of subgroup sigmas}}{\text{Number of subgroups}}$$

$$\bar{s} = \frac{0.3 + 0.3 + 0.4 + \ldots + 0.3}{32} = 0.31$$

5. Determine the upper (UCL) and lower (LCL) control limits for the S chart. For subgroup sizes less than 25, use Table 5.19 along with the following formula:

$$LCL_S = B_3 \bar{s}$$

$$UCL_S = B_4 \bar{s}$$

Note: Table 5.19 represents approximations of the following (UCL, LCL) calculation. For subgroup sizes larger than 25, use the following formula:

$$LCL_S = \bar{s} - \frac{3\bar{s}}{\sqrt{2\bar{n}}} = 0.3 - \frac{3(0.3)}{\sqrt{2(10)}} = 0.16$$

$$UCL_S = \bar{s} + \frac{3\bar{s}}{\sqrt{2\bar{n}}} = 0.3 + \frac{3(0.3)}{\sqrt{2(10)}} = 0.44$$

6. Draft your standard deviation chart. Draw the average sigma as a solid line and the UCL and LCL as dashed lines.
7. Determine the grand average ($\bar{\bar{X}}$):

$$\bar{\bar{X}} = \frac{\text{Sum of subgroup averages}}{\text{Number of subgroups}}$$

$$\bar{\bar{X}} = \frac{9.7 + 9.7 + 9.8 + 9.8 + \ldots + 9.8}{32}$$

$$\bar{\bar{X}} = 9.82$$

TABLE 5.19. Control Chart Constants: Factors for Control Limits

Subgroup Size (n)	Chart for Averages			Chart for Standard Deviations			
	A	**A_2**	**A_3**	**B_3**	**B_4**	**B_5**	**B_6**
2	2.121	1.880	2.659	0	3.267	0	2.606
3	1.732	1.023	1.954	0	2.568	0	2.276
4	1.500	0.729	1.628	0	2.266	0	2.088
5	1.342	0.577	1.427	0	2.089	0	1.964
6	1.225	0.483	1.287	0.030	1.970	0.029	1.874
7	1.134	0.419	1.182	0.118	1.882	0.113	1.806
8	1.061	0.373	1.099	0.185	1.815	0.179	1.751
9	1.000	0.337	1.032	0.239	1.761	0.232	1.707
10	0.949	0.308	0.975	0.284	1.716	0.276	1.669
11	0.905	0.285	0.927	0.321	1.679	0.313	1.637
12	0.866	0.266	0.886	0.354	1.646	0.346	1.610
13	0.832	0.249	0.850	0.382	1.618	0.374	1.585
14	0.802	0.235	0.817	0.406	1.594	0.399	1.563
15	0.775	0.223	0.789	0.428	1.572	0.421	1.544
16	0.750	0.212	0.763	0.448	1.552	0.440	1.526
17	0.728	0.203	0.739	0.466	1.534	0.458	1.511
18	0.707	0.194	0.718	0.482	1.518	0.475	1.496
19	0.688	0.187	0.698	0.497	1.503	0.490	1.483
20	0.671	0.180	0.680	0.510	1.490	0.504	1.470
21	0.655	0.173	0.663	0.523	1.477	0.516	1.459
22	0.640	0.167	0.647	0.534	1.466	0.528	1.448
23	0.626	0.162	0.633	0.545	1.455	0.539	1.438
24	0.612	0.157	0.619	0.555	1.445	0.549	1.429
25	0.600	0.153	0.606	0.565	1.435	0.559	1.420

8. Calculate the upper and lower control limits (UCL, LCL) for the averages. For subgroup sizes less than 25, use Table 5.19 along with the following formula:

$$\text{LCL}_{\bar{X}} = \bar{\bar{X}} - A_3\bar{s}$$

$$\text{UCL}_{\bar{X}} = \bar{\bar{X}} + A_3\bar{s}$$

Note: Table 5.19 represents approximations of the following (UCL, LCL) calculation. For subgroup sizes larger than 25, use the following formula:

$$\text{LCL}_{\bar{X}} = \bar{\bar{X}} - \frac{3\bar{s}}{\sqrt{n}} = 9.82 - \frac{3(0.3)}{\sqrt{10}} = 9.65$$

$$\text{UCL}_{\bar{X}} = \bar{\bar{X}} + \frac{3\bar{s}}{\sqrt{n}} = 9.82 + \frac{3(0.3)}{\sqrt{10}} = 10.00$$

9. Draft your $\bar{X}$ chart. Plot your data. Draw the central tendency (grand average) as a solid line and the control limits as dashed lines.

Construction with QI Macros

1. Plot your text and data in a spreadsheet.
2. Highlight the text and data.
3. Select **QI Macros > Control Charts > XbarS Chart**.
4. Label the standard deviation chart.
5. Label the $\bar{X}$ chart.

Note: The average of each subgroup represents a data point. Each subgroup is categorized by some unit. In this example, each subgroup is categorized by day. This is your text. Be sure to highlight the data (numbers) and text (day 1...day 32). Doing so will enable the software package to distinguish between the size of the sample (subgroup) and how many samples (subgroups) there are. In this example, there are 32 samples (subgroups), but the sample size (subgroup size) is also 32.

p Chart: Proportion of Defectives Chart

The proportion of defectives chart is used as a metric to measure and graphically display operational performance for discrete data. As the name implies, the p chart is used to track the fraction or *percentage* of defective work products in a given subgroup. The Six Sigma professional often will use the p chart to measure the quality of an operation's work products. A sample p chart is shown in Figure 5.14.

Manual Construction

1. Collect your data. Decide what you want to know and then determine your subgrouping strategy (by shift, by day, weekly, etc.). Draw samples

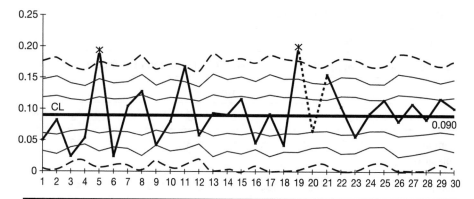

FIGURE 5.14. p Chart: Proportion of Defectives Chart

that are produced under the same conditions. In this example, a local telecommunications company is tracking the percentage of defective calls processed by customer service representatives. The p chart is used to track the percent of calls not resolved to the customer's satisfaction. Plot your data in a data sheet as shown in Table 5.20.

Subgroup Size: Sample sizes for p charts are larger than those of the average and range chart. A statistically valid sample size should be calculated based on the volume of work to be produced during the measurement period.

Number of Subgroups: For reliable and ongoing control limits, the recommended number of subgroups is 25.

2. Determine the percent defective for each subgroup:

$$p = \frac{\text{Number of defectives in the subgroup}}{\text{Subgroup size}}$$

$$p_1 = \frac{5}{100} = 5.0\%$$

$$p_2 = \frac{7}{85} = 8.2\%$$

Plot your data in a data sheet as shown in Table 5.20.

3. Determine the centerline value by calculating the average fraction defective:

TABLE 5.20. p Chart Data Sheet

Operation: Call Center

Service: Customer Support	Measurement: Customer Support Error Rate

	Day									
	1	2	3	4	5	6	7	8	9	10
Number defective	5	7	3	8	19	3	12	10	6	8
Subgroup size	100	85	125	150	98	125	115	78	143	100
Percent defective	5.0	8.2	2.4	5.3	19.4	2.4	10.4	12.8	4.2	8.0

	Day									
	11	12	13	14	15	16	17	18	19	20
Number defective	19	9	7	9	10	5	7	4	19	8
Subgroup size	113	156	75	99	86	110	76	96	95	121
Percent defective	16.8	5.8	9.3	9.1	11.6	4.5	9.2	4.2	20.0	6.6

	Day									
	21	22	23	24	25	26	27	28	29	30
Number defective	20	9	5	12	15	6	9	8	14	10
Subgroup size	129	87	90	129	131	75	83	96	120	99
Percent defective	15.5	10.3	5.6	9.3	11.5	8.0	10.8	8.3	11.7	10.1

$$\bar{p} = \frac{\text{Total number of defectives found}}{\text{Sum of subgroups}} = \frac{286}{3185} = 0.09$$

4. Compute and record the UCL and LCL for *each* subgroup:

$$\text{UCL}_{p_1} = \bar{p} + 3\sqrt{\bar{p}(1 - \bar{p}) / n_1} = 0.09 + 3\sqrt{0.09(1 - 0.09) / 100} = 0.176$$

$$\text{LCL}_{p_1} = \bar{p} - 3\sqrt{\bar{p}(1 - \bar{p}) / n_1} = 0.09 - 3\sqrt{0.09(1 - 0.09) / 100} = 0.04$$

Note: Since the subgroup size varies, the control limits also will vary with each subgroup. In addition, the larger the subgroup size, the tighter the control limits will rest toward the centerline.

5. Draft your p chart. Plot your observations. Draw the central tendency (average percent defective) as a solid line and the control limits as dashed lines.

Construction with QI Macros

1. Plot your text and data in a spreadsheet.
2. Highlight the text and data (three rows: date, number defective, and subgroup size).
3. Select **QI Macros > Control Charts > p Chart**.
4. Label the p chart.

Note: The number of defectives and the subgroup size per subgroup represent one data point. Each subgroup is categorized by some unit. In this example, each subgroup is categorized by day. This is your text. Be sure to highlight the text (day 1…day 30) and data (number defective and sample size) in all three rows. Doing so will enable the software package to perform this construction properly.

np Chart: Number of Defectives Chart

The number of defectives chart is used as a metric to measure and graphically display operational performance for discrete data. As the name implies, the np chart is used to track the *number* of defective work products produced by an operation. The Six Sigma professional often will use the np chart to measure the quality of an operation's work products. When the np chart is used, subgroup sizes are kept constant deliberately. When constancy is not feasible, samples drawn from the operation should not vary more than ±25% from the average subgroup size. This variation is illustrated in Table 5.21 and Figure 5.15.

Manual Construction

1. Collect your data. Decide what you want to know and then determine your subgrouping strategy (by shift, by day, weekly, etc.). Draw samples that are produced under the same conditions. In this example, a local telecommunications company is tracking the number of incorrect invoices. Plot your data in a data sheet as shown in Table 5.21.

   Subgroup Size: Sample sizes for the np chart are larger than those for the average and range chart. A statistically valid sample size should be calculated based on the volume of work to be produced during the measurement period. As mentioned above, when the np chart is used, it is important that the sample size remains constant from subgroup to subgroup. This can be done by deliberately drawing constant sample sizes from the population. If it is not feasible to draw a constant sample size, observations from the process should not vary by more than ±25% from the average subgroup size. This variation is illustrated in Table 5.21.

   Number of Subgroups: For reliable and ongoing control limits, the recommended number of subgroups is 25.

2. Determine the average number of defective observations for each subgroup:

$$\overline{np} = \frac{\text{Total number of defectives}}{\text{Number of subgroups}} = \frac{51 + 72 + 45 + \ldots + 111}{30} = 91.03$$

3. Determine the UCL and LCL for the np chart. *Note*: If the subgroup size varies (within ±25%), then calculate the average subgroup size before determining the control limits.

TABLE 5.21. np Chart Data Sheet

Operation: Billing Process

Service: Invoice and Billing					Measurement: Number of Incorrect Invoices				

					Day					
	1	**2**	**3**	**4**	**5**	**6**	**7**	**8**	**9**	**10**
Number defective	51	72	45	80	91	95	120	105	61	80
Sample size	1000	1214	1125	1150	980	1125	1115	978	1143	1000

					Day					
	11	**12**	**13**	**14**	**15**	**16**	**17**	**18**	**19**	**20**
Number defective	119	119	70	93	102	103	70	114	91	82
Sample size	1113	1156	975	999	986	1110	976	1096	950	1121

					Day					
	21	**22**	**23**	**24**	**25**	**26**	**27**	**28**	**29**	**30**
Number defective	120	99	50	112	115	60	98	89	114	111
Sample size	1129	1187	900	1129	1131	1175	1183	960	1120	990

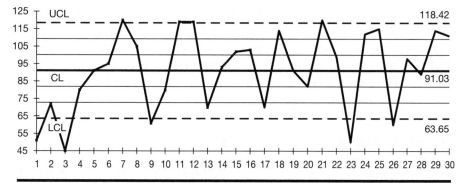

FIGURE 5.15. np Chart: Number of Defectives Chart

$$\bar{n} = \frac{n_1 + n_2 + n_3 + \dots + n_k}{k}$$

$$= \frac{1000 + 1214 + 1125 + \dots + 990}{30} = 1074$$

$$\text{UCL}_{n\bar{p}} = n\bar{p} + 3\sqrt{n\bar{p}(1 - n\bar{p}/\bar{n})}$$

$$= 91.03 + 3\sqrt{91.03(1 - 91.03/1074)} = 118.42$$

$$\text{LCL}_{n\bar{p}} = n\bar{p} - 3\sqrt{n\bar{p}(1 - n\bar{p}/\bar{n})}$$

$$= 91.03 - 3\sqrt{91.03(1 - 91.03/1074)} = 63.65$$

4. Draft your np chart. Plot your observations. Draw the central tendency (average number defectives) as a solid line and the control limits as dashed lines.

Construction with QI Macros

1. Plot your text and data in a spreadsheet.
2. Highlight the text and data (three rows: date, number defective, and subgroup size).
3. Select **QI Macros > Control Charts > np Chart**.
4. Label the np chart.

Note: The number of defectives and the subgroup size per subgroup represent one data point. Each subgroup is categorized by some unit. In this example, each subgroup is categorized by day. This is your text. Be sure to highlight the text (day 1…day 30) and data (number defective and sample size) in all three rows. Doing so will enable the software package to perform the chart construction properly.

c Chart: Number of Defects Chart

The number of defects chart, illustrated in Figure 5.16, is used as a metric to measure and graphically display process performance for discrete or at-

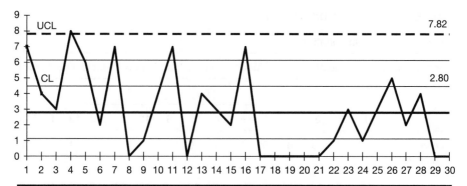

FIGURE 5.16. c Chart: Number of Defects Chart

tribute data. The Six Sigma professional often will use the c chart to measure the quality of an operation's work products. As its name implies, the c chart is used to examine the number of errors or defects per work product produced by an operation. The number of errors/defects in each subgroup is counted, recorded, and plotted on the control chart. The c chart is used when subgroup sizes are deliberately kept constant.

Manual Construction

1. Collect your data. Decide what you want to know and then determine your subgrouping strategy (by shift, by day, weekly, etc.). It is important to draw samples that are produced under the same conditions while keeping subgroup size constant. In this example, a local telecommunications company is tracking the number of installation defects that occur when establishing a business customer's telephone (T1) circuit. See the data sheet shown in Table 5.22.

   Subgroup Size: Sample size is a function of what is being measured and is made up of consecutive measurements from the process. A statistically valid sample size should be calculated based on the volume of work to be produced during the measurement period. In this example, $n = 10$.

   Number of Subgroups: For reliable and ongoing control limits, the recommended number of subgroups is 25.

2. Determine the average number of defects:

TABLE 5.22. c Chart Data Sheet

Operation: Order Installations

Service: Network Installations								Measurement: Installation Defects and Errors						

Day														
1	**2**	**3**	**4**	**5**	**6**	**7**	**8**	**9**	**10**	**11**	**12**	**13**	**14**	**15**
7	4	3	8	6	2	7	0	1	4	7	0	4	3	2
10	10	10	10	10	10	10	10	10	10	10	10	10	10	10

Number of defects (row 1); Sample size (row 2)

Day														
16	**17**	**18**	**19**	**20**	**21**	**22**	**23**	**24**	**25**	**26**	**27**	**28**	**29**	**30**
7	0	0	0	0	0	1	3	1	3	5	2	4	0	0
10	10	10	10	10	10	10	10	10	10	10	10	10	10	10

Number of defects (row 1); Sample size (row 2)

$$\bar{c} = \frac{\text{Total number of defects}}{\text{Number of subgroups}} = \frac{7 + 4 + 3 + \ldots + 0}{30} = 2.80$$

3. Determine the UCL and LCL for the c chart:

$$\text{UCL}_c = \bar{c} + 3\sqrt{\bar{c}} = 2.8 + 3\sqrt{2.8} = 7.82$$

$$\text{LCL}_c = \bar{c} - 3\sqrt{\bar{c}} = 2.8 - 3\sqrt{2.8} < 0$$

4. Draft your c chart. Plot your observations. Draw the central tendency (average number defectives) as a solid line and the control limits as dashed lines.

Construction with QI Macros

1. Plot your text and data in a spreadsheet.
2. Highlight the text and data (two rows: date and number of defects).

3. Select **QI Macros > Control Charts > c Chart**.
4. Label the c chart.

Note: The number of defects per subgroup represents one data point. Each subgroup is categorized by some unit. In this example, each subgroup is categorized by day. This is your text. Be sure to highlight the text (day 1...day 30) and data (number of defects) in both rows. Doing so will enable the software package to perform the chart construction properly.

u Chart: Average Number of Defects per Unit Chart

The average number of defects per unit chart, illustrated in Figure 5.17, is used as a metric to measure and graphically display process performance for discrete or attribute data. The Six Sigma professional often will use the u chart to measure the quality of an operation's work products. As its name implies, the u chart is used to examine the error rate or rate of defects produced by an operation. The number of errors/defects per unit is counted, recorded, and plotted on the control chart. The u chart is used when subgroup size varies.

Manual Construction

1. Collect your data. Decide what you want to know and then determine your subgrouping strategy (by shift, by day, weekly, etc.). It is important to draw samples that are produced under the same conditions. In this example, a local telecommunications company is tracking the rate of

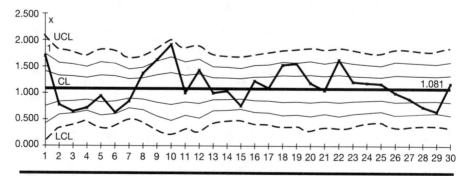

FIGURE 5.17. u Chart: Average Number of Defects per Unit Chart

service order errors that occur when processing new service for business customers. See the data sheet in Table 5.23.

Subgroup Size: Sample size is a function of what is being measured and is made up of consecutive measurements from the process. A statistically valid sample size should be calculated based on the volume of

TABLE 5.23. u Chart Data Sheet

Operation: Service Delivery

Service: New Order Management				Measurement: Customer Order Error Rate					
Day									
1	2	3	4	5	6	7	8	9	10
Number of defects 17	14	13	18	16	12	27	37	26	23
Sample size 10	18	20	25	17	19	32	27	16	12
Defect rate 1.70	0.78	0.65	0.72	0.94	0.63	0.84	1.37	1.63	1.92
Day									
11	12	13	14	15	16	17	18	19	20
Number of defects 17	20	25	27	22	27	23	26	28	19
Sample size 17	14	25	26	29	22	21	17	18	16
Defect rate 1.00	1.43	1.00	1.04	0.76	1.23	1.10	1.53	1.56	1.19
Day									
21	22	23	24	25	26	27	28	29	30
Number of defects 20	26	23	25	27	17	16	14	13	20
Sample size 119	16	19	21	23	17	18	19	20	17
Defect rate 1.05	1.63	1.21	1.19	1.17	1.00	0.89	0.74	0.65	1.18

work to be produced during the measurement period. In this example, $n = 10$. For u charts, subgroup sizes vary.

Number of Subgroups: For reliable and ongoing control limits, the recommended number of subgroups (k) is 25.

2. Determine the error rate for each subgroup:

$$u = \frac{\text{Number of errors for the subgroup}}{\text{Subgroup size}} = \frac{17}{10} = 1.70$$

3. Determine the overall error rate:

$$\bar{u} = \frac{\text{Total number of errors observed}}{\text{Sum of subgroup sizes}}$$

$$= \frac{17 + 14 + 13 + 25 + \ldots + 20}{10 + 18 + 20 + 25 + \ldots + 17} = 1.08$$

4. Determine the UCL and LCL for each plot:

$$\text{UCL}_1 = \bar{u} + 3\sqrt{\bar{u}/n_1} = 1.08 + 3\sqrt{1.08/10} = 2.068$$

$$\text{LCL}_1 = \bar{u} - 3\sqrt{\bar{u}/n_1} = 1.08 - 3\sqrt{1.08/10} = 0.095$$

5. Draft your u chart. Plot your observations. Draw the central tendency (average number defectives) as a solid line and the control limits as dashed lines.

Construction with QI Macros

1. Plot your text and data in a spreadsheet.
2. Highlight the text and data (three rows: date, number of defects, and subgroup size).
3. Select **QI Macros > Control Charts > u Chart**.
4. Label the u chart.

Note: The number of defects and the subgroup size per subgroup represent one data point. Each subgroup is categorized by some unit. In this example, each subgroup is categorized by day. This is your text. Be sure to highlight the text (day 1…day 30) and data (number of defects and sample size) in all three rows. Doing so will enable the software package to perform the chart construction properly.

Performance Variation: A Review

In Chapter 4, two types of variation in operational performance were discussed: common cause variation and special cause variation. Common cause variation is a natural consequence of production factors coming together in the performance of an operation. What factors? The factors of production that management and employees engineer into workflows to influence work activities. These factors of service production are depicted in Figure 5.18.

In a productive workplace, management seeks to engineer an optimum mix of technology, skilled workers, materials, methods, and procedures to create a productive and efficient operation. As a natural consequence of employing these factors of production, operational results will vary. This natural variation is called common cause variation. When only common cause variation exists in an operation, processes are understood to be stable and manageable.

Control charts, as part of a process management regime, provide managers a means to detect instability in operational performance. When data points are observed to fall outside of control limits, an operation is consid-

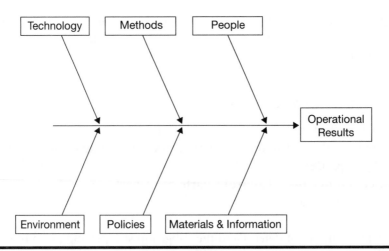

FIGURE 5.18. Factors of Service Production

ered to be *out of statistical control.* At this point, management can be assured that the factors of production are out of sync and are having a disturbing influence over operational performance. Something is causing the process to function abnormally and it is having an unintended consequence on operating results. That something is what was described in Chapter 4 as a *special cause,* and it produces special cause variation in operational performance.

Special cause variation is also referred to as *assignable cause* variation because the variation in operating results can be *assigned* to a specific reason or a unique set of circumstances. To the Six Sigma professional, special cause variation can be like a cancer and must be removed from its source or the results can become very costly.

Control Chart Analysis

Control charts can be likened to an EKG that monitors the heartbeat of a company's core operating processes. If operating performance becomes unstable or out of control, the instability easily can be detected by a control chart. Control chart analysis is governed by the laws of probability. For instance, if an operation's performance only has common cause variation acting on it, there is only a 3 out of 1000 chance that a data point will naturally fall outside of a control limit—generally speaking. If an observation does fall beyond an upper or lower control limit, you can be confident that some unexpected event or influence has caused it. The Six Sigma professional should react to the special cause and identify its source.

To simplify and extend that thought further, Figure 5.19 shows a normal control chart with control limits based on estimates of the mean ±3 standard deviations (±3 sigma). The analysis criterion for the control chart was de-

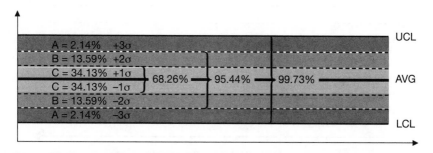

FIGURE 5.19. Control Charting and Normal Probability Rules: The EKG of Performance Management

veloped by Walter Shewhart during the 1930s and has stood the test of time. What Figure 5.19 illustrates is that if only common cause variation is present in operational performance, over the long term 68.26% of the control chart observations will naturally fall within zone *C*, ±1 standard deviation (±1 sigma); 95.44% of the observations will fall within zones *C and B*, ±2 sigma; and 99.73% will fall within zones *A, B, and C*, ±3 sigma. Therefore, the chance that an observation will fall beyond the control limits (UCL, LCL) is 1 − 0.9973 or 0.0027. Thus, if an operation's performance is in statistical control, over the long term its performance is predictable within certain limits—control limits.

The following pages provide an outline of accepted rules used to analyze control charts. They are known as special cause rules and are used to detect when an operation's performance becomes unstable. Violation of the rules indicates the presence of special cause variation.

Special Cause Rules

Shift: A shift serves notice of a *change* in the process average. Violations of the shift rule occur when eight or more consecutive points fall above or below the centerline. An example of a shift rule violation is illustrated in Figure 5.20.

The shift rule is based on the laws of probability. The chance of eight consecutive points falling either above or below the centerline is the same as a coin toss resulting in tails eight times in a row—which is 0.5^8. The chance of eight or more consecutive observations falling above or below the

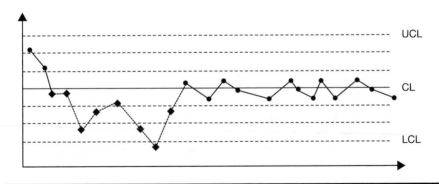

FIGURE 5.20. Shift Rule Violation

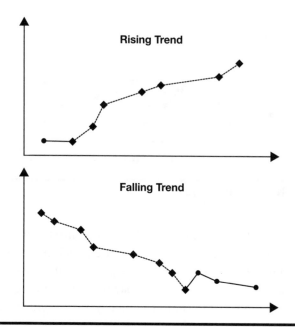

FIGURE 5.21. Trend Rule Violation

process average when only common cause variation is present is 0.004—more than highly unlikely.

Trend: A second special cause violation is a trend. The trend rule is violated when seven consecutive data points flow in the same direction. As depicted in Figure 5.21, a trend can flow in an upward or a downward direction.

A trend usually will present itself after some change has been adopted. It can tell you if any policy adjustments made have had a positive or negative impact on performance. A trend can also illustrate a learning curve associated with some form of training.

Non-Random Cycles: A cycle rule violation is an indication that performance variation is not random. An operation in statistical control will show only random variation. A control chart exhibiting non-random cycles that occur eight or more consecutive times indicates the presence of special cause variation. The pattern in Figure 5.22 illustrates two points above the centerline followed by two points below.

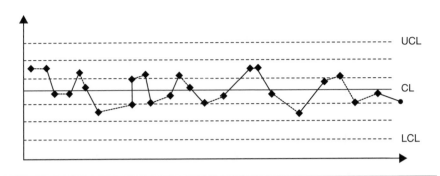

FIGURE 5.22. Non-Random Cycle Rule Violation

Central Tendency (Continuous Data Control Chart): When data points violate the central tendency rule, they indicate a lack of variability among observations. When 15 or more consecutive points that fall within one sigma of the centerline, special cause variation may be present in the operation. An example of a violation of the central tendency rule is illustrated in Figure 5.23.

One-Sigma Variation: A one-sigma rule violation occurs when four out of five points in a row fall more than one sigma away from the performance average. An example of a one-sigma violation is illustrated in Figure 5.24.

Two-Sigma Variation: When two out of three points in a row fall more than two sigma away from the centerline, special cause variation may be present in the process. An example of a two-sigma rule violation is presented in Figure 5.25.

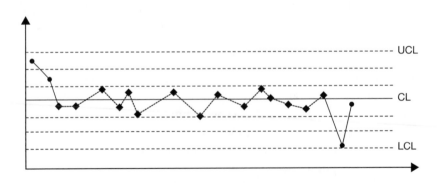

FIGURE 5.23. Central Tendency Rule Violation

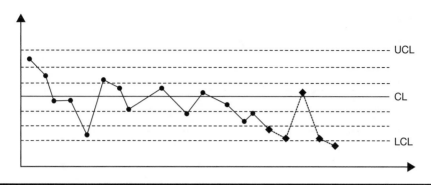

FIGURE 5.24. One-Sigma Rule Violation

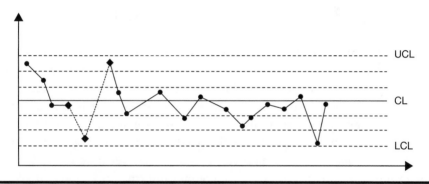

FIGURE 5.25. Two-Sigma Rule Violation

Observation Beyond the Control Limits: This rule is violated when one or more points fall beyond either the upper or lower control limit(s). When this occurs, it may an indication that special cause variation is present in the operation. It does not necessarily mean that corrective action needs to be taken; however, it is important that the reason for the violation is understood. An example of an observation beyond the control limits rule violation is presented in Figure 5.26.

Special Cause Decision Rules

If special cause variation is present in operating results, management should examine its impact. If the impact on performance is favorable, management should find a way to standardize the special cause and make it a standard part of the operation. If the impact on performance is unfavorable, manage-

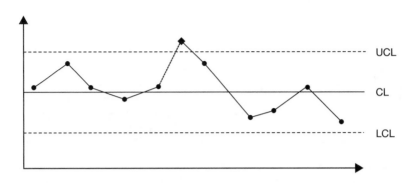

FIGURE 5.26. Observation Beyond the Control Limits Rule Violation

ment should conduct root cause analysis and remove the special cause at its source.

If only common cause variation is present in operating results, no action should be taken. Management should not try to explain the difference between high and low data points; doing so may result in taking unnecessary action. By responding to common cause variation as if it is special cause variation, management may unwittingly introduce special cause variation into the operation. If not satisfied with operating results, management should work to *continuously improve* process performance over time via PDCA by, for example, improving training, upgrading information systems, making process improvements, and enhancing business rules and policies.

Control Chart Analysis Exercise: Restoring Customer Outages

The director of the national network operations center at North Brook Telecommunications is interested in tracking and improving her team's response times to network outages. Table 5.24 shows a month's performance data for the team's time to restore customer outages.

1. Given these data, what is the appropriate control chart to select?
2. Construct the control chart.
3. Analyze the operating results. Is special cause variation present in the process?
4. What action would you take?

Analyses and conclusions are presented in Appendix B.

TABLE 5.24. North Brook Telecommunications Mean Time to Restore (in Minutes) Data Sheet

							Day							
1	2	3	4	5	6	7	8	9	10	11	12	13	14	15
77	99	89	86	80	89	111	98	78	67	80	89	111	98	78
78	87	77	87	88	99	89	90	109	87	88	99	89	90	109
79	85	80	86	91	105	87	87	110	97	91	105	87	87	110
85	88	93	93	93	97	56	89	120	85	93	97	56	89	120
87	85	83	89	90	67	45	76	65	79	90	67	45	76	65

							Day							
16	17	18	19	20	21	22	23	24	25	26	27	28	29	30
67	99	89	86	80	89	111	98	110	97	91	105	87	87	109
87	87	77	87	88	99	89	90	120	85	93	97	56	89	110
97	85	80	86	91	105	87	87	65	79	90	67	45	76	120
85	88	93	93	93	97	56	89	87	88	99	89	90	109	89
79	85	83	89	90	67	45	76	86	91	105	87	87	110	76

Process Capability Analysis

Once processes are defined and measured, Six Sigma teams can proceed with process capability analysis to evaluate operational performance. An operation can be in statistical control but may contain so much natural variation that operating results may stray outside of predetermined performance goals and tolerances. Process capability analysis is a statistical technique used, with continuous data, to compare operating results to specified goals. To obtain a complete assessment of operating performance, process capability analysis is used in conjunction with control charting. Using this technique, a Six Sigma team can determine the potential of a process to deliver unfavorable outcomes.

Performance Evaluation: Process Capability Analysis

Once an operation's performance is recorded, it can be examined to see if the results meet expected standards and requirements. The ability of an operation to meet its expected requirements is referred to as its *process capability*. The measurement of process capability is referred to as the *process capability index* (Cpk). For continuous (variable) data, Cpk is expressed as the ratio of the maximum variation defined by the specification or process standard (customer tolerance) to the level of variation an operation is currently producing. Customer tolerance is expressed as a process requirement that is critical to quality (CTQ) as perceived by the customer.

The process capability analysis procedure is as follows. First, determine customer tolerances:

Upper customer requirement − Lower customer requirement

Then calculate the Cpk. Cpk is calculated as follows. With respect to the upper process requirement:

$$\text{Cpk}_u = \frac{\text{Upper process requirement} - \overline{X}}{3\sigma}$$

With respect to the lower process requirement:

$$\text{Cpk}_l = \frac{\overline{X} - \text{Lower process requirement}}{3\sigma}$$

For the range chart:

$$\sigma = \frac{\overline{R}}{d_2}$$

For the sigma chart:

$$\sigma = \frac{\overline{s}}{c_4}$$

The constants d_2 and c_4 can be found in Table 5.25.

Process Capability Analysis: Business Rules

An operation in statistical control with a Cpk of 1 will yield operating results capable of meeting customer expectations. However, the practice of Six Sigma assumes that the process mean is capable of naturally drifting by 1.5 sigma in either direction. Given that assumption, Six Sigma deems operating re-

TABLE 5.25. Constants for Process Capability Index Calculations

Subgroup/ Sample Size* (n)	Range (d_2)*	Sigma (c_4)
2	1.128	0.7979
3	1.693	0.8862
4	2.059	0.9213
5	2.326	0.9400
6	2.534	0.9515
7	2.704	0.9594
8	2.847	0.9650
9	2.970	0.9693
10	3.078	0.9727
11	3.173	0.9754
12	3.258	0.9776
13	3.336	0.9794
14	3.407	0.9810
15	3.472	0.9823
16	3.532	0.9835
17	3.588	0.9845
18	3.640	0.9854
19	3.689	0.9862
20	3.735	0.9869
21	3.778	0.9876
22	3.819	0.9882
23	3.858	0.9887
24	3.895	0.9892
25	3.931	0.9896

* If the $\overline{R}$ is obtained from an XmR chart, use $d_2 = 1.128$ (subgroup size = 2).

sults with a Cpk of 1.33 as a capable process. For process performance that produces 3.4 errors per million opportunities—Six Sigma performance, a Cpk of 2 is considered process perfect. Review Table 5.26 for an overview of process capability business rules.

Process Capability Analysis and Evaluation: An Example

This example uses the average number of days it takes to deliver and install telecommunications circuits for business customers. The data set is shown in Table 5.27.

TABLE 5.26. Process Capability Rules

If	Then	Explanation
Cpk <1	Process not capable	A considerable share of the process output is not meeting customer requirements
1.00 ≤ Cpk	Process just capable	Process performance meets customer requirements, but it cannot account for the assumed drift of 1.5 sigma
1.33 ≤ Cpk < 2.00	Process capable	Process performance exceeds customer requirements and can account for the assumed 1.5-sigma drift of the process mean
Cpk = 2	Process perfect	Process performance meets customer requirements 99.9997% of the time and can fully account for the assumed 1.5-sigma drift of the process mean

Suppose the CTQ is determined to be 25 to 33 business days for service delivery and acceptance. The process capability analysis would proceed as follows. First, determine customer tolerances:

$$33 \text{ business days} - 25 \text{ business days} = 8 \text{ business days}$$

Then determine process capability (Cpk). With respect to the lower process requirement:

$$\text{Cpk}_l = \frac{\overline{X} - \text{Lower process requirement}}{3\sigma}$$

$$\text{Cpk} = \frac{28.4 - 25}{3\left(\dfrac{7.3}{1.693}\right)} = 0.26284$$

Evaluation and Conclusion

Based on a Cpk of 0.26284, we can conclude that process performance is not adequate. Process performance is not capable of delivering service in the

TABLE 5.27. Control Chart Data Sheet for Cpk Analysis

Operation: New Order Process

| Service: T1 Service Delivery | | | | Measurement: Order Origination to Acceptance | | | | | |

	Day									
	1	**2**	**3**	**4**	**5**	**6**	**7**	**8**	**9**	**10**
S	25	26	30	25	28	27	30	18	27	29
A S	38	16	32	35	27	26	29	19	28	27
M I	26	15	28	27	27	26	19	28	29	20
P Z										
L E										
E										
Average	30	19	30	29	27	26	26	22	28	25
Range	13	11	4	10	1	1	11	10	2	9

	Day									
	11	**12**	**13**	**14**	**15**	**16**	**17**	**18**	**19**	**20**
S	18	22	32	28	17	28	29	27	31	24
A S	42	32	28	30	31	29	30	34	26	27
M I	33	30	31	31	26	35	27	31	27	27
P Z										
L E										
E										
Average	31	28	30	30	25	31	29	31	28	26
Range	24	10	4	3	14	7	3	7	5	3

	Day									
	21	**22**	**23**	**24**	**25**	**26**	**27**	**28**	**29**	**30**
S	35	28	26	27	27	26	25	32	30	27
A S	34	37	37	29	32	36	28	31	30	34
M I	28	25	29	30	33	32	29	28	27	31
P Z										
L E										
E										
Average	32	30	31	29	31	31	27	30	29	31
Range	7	12	11	3	6	10	4	4	3	7

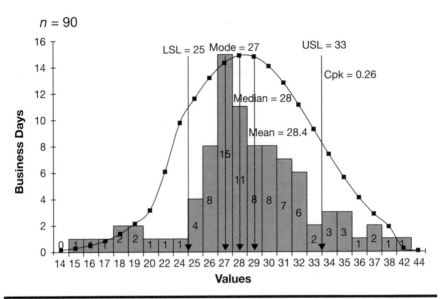

FIGURE 5.27. Process Capability Chart for Circuit Delivery and Install Times

determined standard that is critical to customer quality. An illustration of Cpk analysis is shown in Figure 5.27.

Process Capability Analysis with QI Macros

1. Enter your data in a spreadsheet.
2. Highlight the data set in the spreadsheet.
3. Select **QI Macros > Frequency or Histogram**.
4. Input the upper specification/tolerance limit and click **OK**.
5. Input the lower specification/tolerance limit and click **OK**.

If you have no tolerance or specification limit (i.e., goal), then press cancel.

6. Title the chart and click **OK**.
7. Label the vertical and horizontal axes and click **OK**.
8. Label the histogram according to your preference.
9. Perform the appropriate analysis.

CONCLUSION

In this chapter, we discussed how Six Sigma tools provide decision makers a means to study process performance objectively. We examined how these tools enable decision makers to make decisions and manage by fact instead of basing decisions on opinion and intuition alone. We also discussed how the use of these tools and techniques is essential for achieving operational excellence because they promote the use of facts and data as the basis for decision making.

As you read through this chapter, I hope that you gained an understanding of and an appreciation for the basic Six Sigma analytical took kit. I trust this chapter will serve as a user-friendly reference to the basic analytical tool kit employed by Six Sigma green belts and black belts around the world.

6

PERFORMANCE METRICS AND DASHBOARDS: BUILDING YOUR PERFORMANCE MEASUREMENT SYSTEM

If winning isn't everything, why do they keep score?
—Vince Lombardi, Head Coach
Seven-Time World-Champion
Green Bay Packers

In Chapter 1, we discussed the value that productivity and quality improvement can bring to a company. It was argued that mastering quality and productivity can create a distinctive competence for a company that will empower it to develop a competitive advantage in the marketplace. We went on to examine the fundamentals of process design, the voice of the customer, the impact of performance variation, and the basic analytical tool set of Six Sigma professionals. These are all vital principles and applications for the method, but at the heart of a world-class Six Sigma company is the measurement system of its core operating processes.

This chapter covers the important topic of measuring performance. The major categories of performance measurement for a service organization will be defined and discussed. We will examine how a Six Sigma professional can define and structure a performance measurement system and demonstrate how to use the tools described in earlier chapters to develop an effective dashboard of metrics.

A proper set of metrics will enable those in management to ascertain the relative levels of effectiveness resulting from their efforts and decisions. A strong measurement system will enable management to compare performance among similar functions within a company and also compare the performance of functions relative to the competition. For service organizations and transactional processes, an effective measurement system should be organized into the following categories:

1. **Quality**: Conformance or non-conformance to what customers require
2. **Efficiency**: Measurements of how an organization makes use of its assets
3. **Productivity**: The output of a work group, department, or company
4. **Effectiveness**: The degree to which the process delivers the right service to the right customer at the right time
5. **Cost**: The direct labor and material cost under the control of operations managers and the comparison of budgeted or expected cost to actual cost

THE VALUE STREAM

A factor that separates manufacturing organizations from service environments is the degree to which cross-functional relationships are vital to meeting customer expectations. For the service company, the closer its cross-functional relationships, the more productive and more effective it will be in acquiring, delivering, and keeping a customer's business. In a service company's productive process, everyone has a customer.

A cursory overview of a telecommunications company's service delivery workflow is illustrated in Figure 6.1. In this workflow, the sales organization, which consists of sales representatives and sales engineers, is responsible for assessing client network requirements and translating those requirements into two work products: a network design and a service agreement. The two work products flow to the sales operations department, which executes the

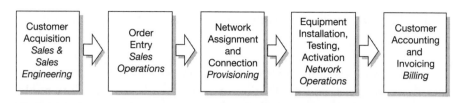

FIGURE 6.1. The Telecommunications Service Delivery Process

service agreement and produces a work order. The sales operations function passes its work product to the provisioning organization. The provisioning organization receives the work order and procures network assignments and connections based on the network design and work order requirements created by the sales engineering and sales operations departments. Then the work order is handed to the network operations group. Network operations procures, installs, tests, and activates the network equipment and circuitry. Once the activation function is complete, the work order is passed from the network operations group to the billing organization. The billing organization establishes a customer account and creates a customer bill for product cost, usage fees, and incidental charges for the service provided.

The workflow described above is a simplified overview of what really takes place in delivering telecommunications services to business customers. The important point to take away from this example is the concept of the value stream. The value stream concept dictates that work products created upstream become marching orders for downstream functions. Products of upstream work groups must conform to the requirements of downstream functions to satisfy customer requirements. As work products flow fluidly, so do profits. That is the basis of how performance is measured.

THE HIDDEN FACTORY

When a work product is created by a work group and passed downstream, at least three outcomes can occur:

1. The work product is deemed useful and acceptable.
2. The work product is accepted and modified by the downstream work group.

3. The work product is rejected and returned to the supplier to *get it right.*

Service processes easily can become encumbered with errors, wasted time, rework, bottlenecks, and duplication of effort. Recall the black box model from Chapter 2. Like any real process, if garbage goes in, then garbage and waste come out. Every service process, in practice, can become what is illustrated in Figure 6.2—the hidden factory.

The hidden factory is an expression used to describe non-value-added work produced by an operation. The hidden factory produces more and more errors and is characterized by the organizational cancer of *re*'s:

- *Re*work
- *Re*check
- *Re*ject
- *Re*send
- *Re*provision
- *Re*install
- *Re*bill

When employees and managers become too tolerant of mistakes, errors, delays, and duplication of effort, they create a drag on productivity and profits. Service companies with large hidden factories in effect pay employees to produce problems and then pay them to correct problems. The lesson

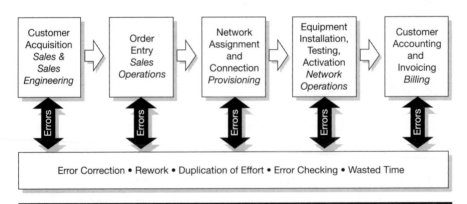

FIGURE 6.2. The Hidden Factory

every manager and executive should learn is that if you pay employees to make mistakes and correct them, the employees will not let you down. The hidden factory will only become progressively worse and more costly until management takes the initiative to measure and manage process performance more effectively.

Measuring performance is a simple five-step process of defining the performance factor, determining the metric, establishing the performance standard, determining the measurement tool, and then implementing the measurement system.

MEASURING SERVICE QUALITY

Step 1. Define quality: In this scenario, quality must be defined as work products that meet downstream workflow requirements with 100% accuracy, complete, and on time. Any deviation from this definition should be considered a non-conformance or defective.

Step 2. Define the quality metric: The quality metric should be defined as an acceptance ratio, where the number of work products accepted by a downstream work group on first submission is divided by the total number of work products delivered to that group during the measurement period.

Step 3. Set the standard: The work standard set should adhere to the SMART principle; it should be:

- Specific
- Measurable
- Attainable
- Realistic
- Time bound

Some may consider a realistic quality standard of 95% to be acceptable. Adherence to a 95% first-pass standard in our telecommunications example would mean that 77% of all service orders initiated will pass through the five-step process without error and on time. A Six Sigma quality standard of 99.9997%, however, dictates that almost 100% (0.999985) of service orders initiated will pass through without error and on time.

A very important concept for service delivery processes reveals itself here. This concept is called *potential maximum performance*. The concept simply states that the productivity of a value stream is determined by the quality of its cross-functional relationships. In our example, if the first-pass acceptance rate of work products from customer acquisition to sales operations is 80%, from sales operations to provisioning is 95%, from provisioning to network operations is 92%, from network operations to billing is 90%, and from billing to the customer is 99%, the potential maximum performance of the process would be:

$$0.80 \times 0.95 \times 0.92 \times 0.90 \times 0.99 = 0.62$$

This means that, at best, this service delivery process can deliver 62% of its services to its customers effectively on the first attempt. This also means that 38% of the customer base will have a poor encounter with this company due to a lack of cross-functional teamwork. Measuring and accounting for performance in this fashion highlights the vital need for Six Sigma performance, especially for a service company.

Step 4. Determine the quality measurement tool: In this scenario, a good quality measurement tool would be the p chart. Figure 6.3 is an example of

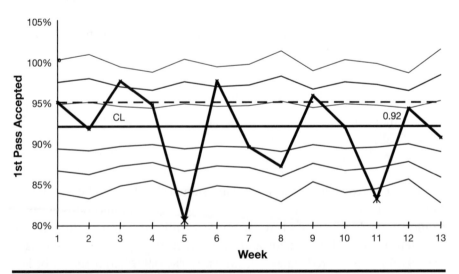

FIGURE 6.3. Quality Measurement Tool: p Chart for First-Pass Acceptance Rate

a p chart that accounts for the quality flow of the sales operations work group. Inserted in the chart is the work standard of 95% first-pass acceptance. With the p chart, management can monitor conformance to standard, average performance, as well as variation in performance.

MEASURING SERVICE EFFICIENCY

A measure of efficiency is how well a work group uses its assets. For service organizations, it is much easier to use time as the basis for an effective efficiency equation.

Step 1. Define efficiency: In our telecommunications service delivery scenario, efficiency would be defined as the time it takes to produce work products that meet downstream workflow requirements. The sales operations unit is responsible for producing new service orders on behalf of the sales team and the customer.

Step 2. Define the efficiency metric: In our scenario, the efficiency metric is defined as the average time to process a new order, where the total time required to process and execute each new order is divided by the total number of new orders executed by the sales operations group.

Step 3. Set the standard: The work standard established should strike the most economical balance between the capability of the work group and the expectations of the customer. Work group efficiency should be a function of procedures, technology, and worker expertise engineered to optimum levels. In our scenario, the manager of the sales operations work group believes it is realistic to expect the group to produce an average order processing time of 30 minutes per order.

Step 4. Determine the efficiency measurement tool: In our scenario, the work group processes fewer than 50 service orders per hour. The stratification strategy involves taking a subgroup of 4 on 5 occasions per day—a total sample size of 20 per day. The measurement tool selected is the average and standard deviation chart or $\overline{X}$,S chart. Figure 6.4 provides an example of an $\overline{X}$,S chart that accounts for the average processing time of the sales operations work group. Inserted in the chart is the work standard of 30

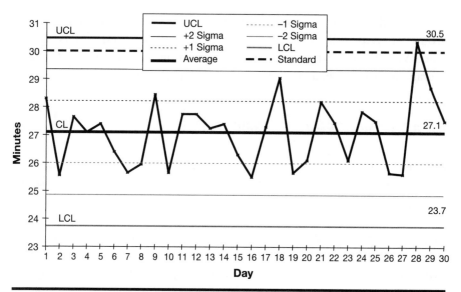

FIGURE 6.4. Efficiency Measurement Tool: X̄,S Chart for Average Processing Time

minutes per order. With the X̄,S chart, management can monitor the average cycle time and the variation in cycle time performance.

It is essential that efficiency be examined in conjunction with quality, cost, and productivity to garner a complete picture of the effectiveness of an operation.

MEASURING SERVICE PRODUCTION

Service production is also a measurement of how a work group makes the most of its assets. It is a measure of the productive output of an operation. For service organizations, it is much easier to measure the total number of work products produced by a work group during a measurement period.

Step 1. Define productivity: In our telecommunications service delivery scenario, production is defined as the total number of work products produced for downstream organizations. The sales operations unit is responsible for producing new service orders on behalf of the sales team and the customer. A definition of productivity for this work group is the total number of service orders produced during the measurement period. It should be noted here that a service order produced is defined as an order that is accepted based on the standard of the downstream organization. An order that does not meet the downstream standard is a defect and is not considered a productive output of the sales operations group.

Step 2. Define the productivity metric: In our scenario, the productivity metric is simply an output metric—the number of accepted service orders processed.

Step 3. Set the standard: The work standard established should strike the most economical balance between the capability of the work group and the expectations of the customer. Work group productivity should be a function of procedures, technology, and worker expertise engineered to optimum levels.

For the purpose of this metric, we will alter the telecommunications scenario slightly. The manager for the sales operations work group believes it is realistic to expect an employee to process 2 service orders each hour. With 10 employees, the work group should produce, on average, 160 acceptable service orders per day.

Step 4. Determine the productivity measurement tool: In our scenario, the appropriate productivity measurement tool is the XmR chart. Figure 6.5 is an example of an XmR chart that accounts for the daily output of the sales operations work group. Inserted in the chart is the work standard of 160 orders per day. With the XmR chart, management can monitor daily output in conjunction with how daily output varies (moving range chart).

MEASURING OPERATIONAL EFFECTIVENESS

Operational effectiveness is the degree to which an operation's service delivery operation furnishes the right service to the right customer at the right time. It is a measure of overall operational excellence. For service organizations, on-time delivery and defects are two important metrics of operational effectiveness.

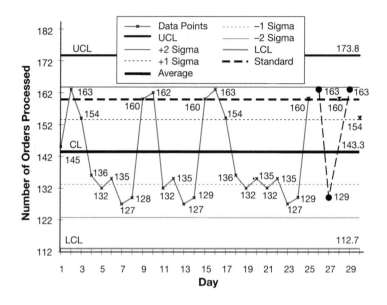

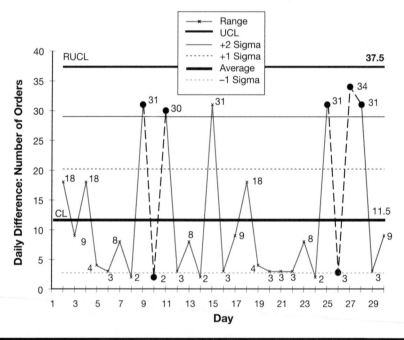

FIGURE 6.5. Productivity Measurement Tool: XmR Chart

Step 1. Define operational effectiveness: In our telecommunications service delivery scenario, operational effectiveness is defined as the cycle time to deliver and install business network services that are free of any circuit, equipment, or technical defects. It is an aggregate quality and efficiency measure of how effectively the cross-functional groups work together to serve the end customer.

Step 2. Define the operational effectiveness metrics: In our scenario, two effectiveness metrics are used: (1) service delivery cycle time and (2) the percentage of error-free installations.

Step 3. Set the standard: This metric will closely match the acceptance rate defined in the quality standard. In our example, the management team believes the operation can accomplish circuit delivery and installation in a cycle time of 15 but no more than 22 business days with a defect-free installation rate of 80%.

Step 4. Determine the operational effectiveness measurement tool: A good cycle time measurement tool is a histogram with tolerances that reflect cycle time requirements. In addition, the fraction defective chart (p chart) will serve to assess the percent of time the quality standard is not met. Figure 6.6 provides an example of both measurement tools to illustrate operational effectiveness for the telecommunications company's service delivery process.

MEASURING COST EFFECTIVENESS

There are many ways to measure cost effectiveness. What is of interest to the Six Sigma professional is measurement of costs which are under the control of operations managers and the comparison of expected costs with actual costs.

Step 1. Define cost: This scenario reflects a different service environment—the *call center*. In a call center, management should measure costs that are under its direct control. The main cost drivers of a call center are labor and those costs related to staffing and managing call center representatives.

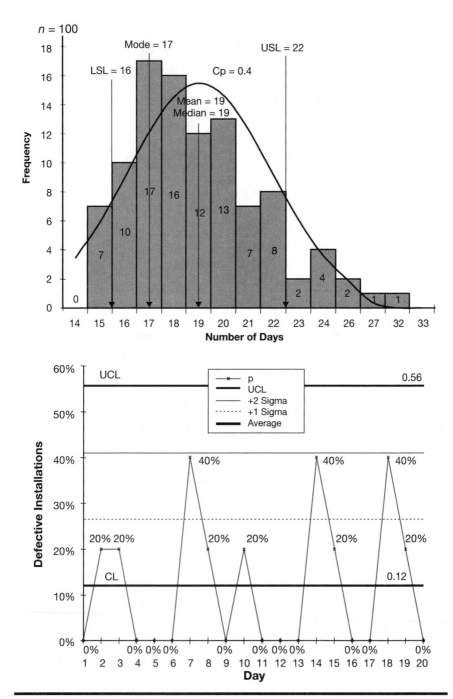

FIGURE 6.6. Operational Effectiveness Measurement Tool: p Chart (Bottom) and Histogram (Top)

Step 2. Define the cost metric: In this scenario, the cost metric is defined as the *loaded cost per second*. Loaded cost per second is the total direct labor cost of the call center representatives divided by the total number of seconds spent processing customer-related calls. Some call centers use the metric *fully loaded cost per second,* which includes indirect labor and overhead costs in the numerator of the equation.

Step 3. Set the standard: The work standard set should adhere to the SMART principle. In this scenario, management has set a loaded cost per second standard of $0.0037.

Step 4. Determine the cost measurement tool: The individual measurement, loaded cost per second, is tracked on a daily basis. An effective tool to monitor cost effectiveness while tracking variation is the XmR chart or the run chart. Figure 6.7 provides an example of both charts to account for the daily cost performance of the call center operation.

CONCLUSION

A proper set of metrics will enable management to ascertain the relative levels of effectiveness and efficiency produced as a result of its efforts and decisions. A proper set of metrics also will empower management to evaluate performance among similar functions within the company and benchmark similar functions relative to the competition.

This chapter covered the important topic of measuring performance. The major categories of performance measurement for a service organization were defined and discussed. We examined how a Six Sigma professional can define and structure a performance measurement system and how to use the tools described in earlier chapters to develop an effective performance measurement system.

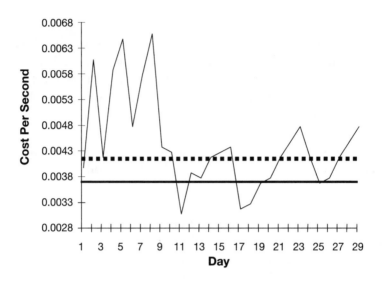

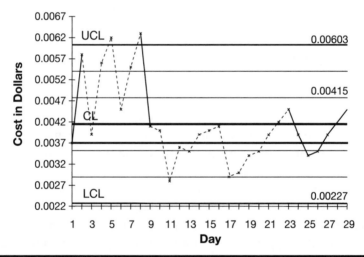

FIGURE 6.7. Cost-Effectiveness Measurement Tool: XmR or Run Chart for Loaded Cost per Second

THE SIX SIGMA PROJECT TEAM

Together
Everyone
Achieves
More

This chapter is devoted to the vital antecedent of a successful Six Sigma program—the Six Sigma project team. Chartered by management to solve specific problems or implement improvements in company operations, Six Sigma project teams serve as the basic building blocks of a Six Sigma effort. The Six Sigma project team is the essential ingredient for an organization to eliminate those barriers to optimum productivity. A project team is comprised of a team leader, team facilitator, and team members. Ideally, a project team should consist of five to seven members. Ordinarily teams are staffed in odd numbers to prevent decision-making impasses.

TEAM ROLES AND RESPONSIBILITIES

Project Team Leader: Black Belt/Green Belt

A project team leader is a member of an organization's management team or a closely connected technical expert who has accountability for leading a Six Sigma improvement effort. Due to his or her special expertise in statistical analysis and his or her level of certification, the project team leader also is known as the black belt. An effective team leader involves all team members and encourages everyone's active participation. The team leader's responsibilities include:

- Leading the team through the defined Six Sigma process (DMAIC)
- Planning, preparing, and executing effective team meetings
- Maintaining the project schedule and effective use of resources
- Utilizing Six Sigma tools and methodologies
- Maintaining and cultivating organizational and political relationships while communicating team progress
- Executing and ensuring the timely completion of all project duties and action plans

Successful project team leaders tend to be experienced natural leaders skilled in several areas. Some of those areas are people skills, some are technical, and others political. In terms of people skills, a successful team leader will be a good listener, a good coach, an effective negotiator, and a good evaluator of performance. A successful leader will listen and comprehend issues with objectivity and empathy. He or she will possess the keen ability to assess, describe, and evaluate behaviors and their influence on a situation. The leader will constructively provide the team with feedback in order to produce an effective level of performance. He or she also will demonstrate an innate ability to produce win-win outcomes while successfully balancing the needs of the project team with the needs of the business.

In terms of technical skills, a successful team leader will possess strong investigative skills and good project management skills and will demonstrate competence in applying Six Sigma tools. The successful leader will use methods such as interviews, surveys, focus groups, and data collection effectively to obtain an objective account of a given situation. An effective team leader will demonstrate the skill to scope and plan a project, define and sequence project activities, resource a project, and bring a project to a successful conclusion. He or she also will be expertly trained and certified in the selection and use of statistical analysis and performance improvement tools.

In terms of political skills, a successful team leader will show an ability to develop and manage relationships and use group dynamics to his or her advantage. Like a politician, a successful team leader will be a social chameleon, modifying his or her attitudes and behaviors in order to maintain trust and confidence across a broad range of groups. He or she will be open-minded in the pursuit of ideas and practices and demonstrate the ability to use creativity and logic without holding onto professional precedent or personal prejudgments. He or she will understand the four stages of team development (forming, storming, norming, and performing) and influence people to take care of the task at hand while successfully managing the personalities of the team.

One of the most important decisions a management team can make in a Six Sigma project is the selection of a project team leader. All of the skills and abilities mentioned above should be taken into account when selecting a leader for a Six Sigma project team.

Project Team Facilitator: Master Black Belt/Black Belt

A project team facilitator is a technical expert dedicated to the project team from the company's organizational development department. The facilitator serves as a partner to the team leader and a consultant to the team. He or she works with the project team as a Six Sigma expert to support team meetings and data collection efforts and provides feedback on the accurate use of Six Sigma methods to ensure the implementation of measurable improvements. Responsibilities of the team facilitator include:

- **Facilitation**: Instructing project teams in the proper use of Six Sigma methods and statistical tools
- **Support**: Aiding team leaders in meeting preparation and follow-up
- **Coaching**: Promoting team improvement by critiquing team effectiveness and providing feedback, and inspiring and motivating the team to succeed with Six Sigma methods
- **Consulting**: Influencing team leaders and team members to accurately and effectively deploy the Six Sigma DMAIC process

Successful project facilitators tend to be natural helpers and teachers skilled in several areas. Similar to the team leader, those areas include people skills, technical abilities, and political savvy. An effective facilitator will display his or her knowledge and talent in training and developing professionals in new principles and practices. He or she will understand how adult learners obtain new knowledge and will be able to use different techniques to encourage learning. The successful facilitator will demonstrate his or her ability to comprehend the structural and political landscape of organizations and use this understanding to facilitate change. Trained and certified in the selection and use of statistical analysis and Six Sigma methods, the facilitator is the designated on-site expert

Project Team Member: Green Belt or Yellow Belt

If the Six Sigma project team is the building block of performance improvement in an organization, then the Six Sigma project team member is the building block of the project team. A project team member is a Six Sigma–trained employee working on a project team to solve a specific performance problem and implement improvements in company operations. Each team member is responsible for using Six Sigma methods and is accountable for the overall success of the team. A team member's responsibilities include:

- Developing metrics and tracking performance
- Attending all team meetings prepared and on time
- Collecting, organizing, and analyzing data
- Conducting root cause analysis of performance problems
- Generating solutions for improvement
- Recommending and implementing solutions

When seeking to staff a project team, one should look for individual contributors with a strong need to get a job done, get a job done right, and get along with others. Effective team members contribute to the orderly conduct of meetings. They listen to the ideas of others without prejudgments. They judge the merit of ideas and solutions based on objective facts and data. They effectively use the tools and methods of Six Sigma to guide their decisions and actions. Most importantly, they follow through on assignments and action items.

Table 7.1 provides a suggested structure for Six Sigma team roles and responsibilities.

TABLE 7.1. Six Sigma Team Roles and Responsibilities

Role and Expertise	Responsibility
Project team leader: black belt/green belt	Primary project accountability; successfully oversee and guide project to its conclusion
Project team facilitator: master black belt/black belt	Coach and facilitate project completion and support team leader
Team members: green belt/yellow belt	Measure, analyze, and implement performance improvements

HOW TO ESTABLISH A SIX SIGMA PROJECT TEAM

During an organization's ordinary business and operations review, a performance gap or reason for improvement may be identified. Management charters a project team to close the performance gap or achieve a strategic goal for improvement. The management charter:

- Defines the team's mission
- Selects the team's leader, members, and facilitator
- Establishes the team's tentative schedule and resource requirements
- Defines the team's scope and cross-functional relationships

The author of the charter must ensure that team members have completed all required Six Sigma training before the team has its first meeting. The author of the charter becomes the team leader and conducts a kickoff meeting to outline the team's goals, mission, performance indicators, timeline, roles and responsibilities, and expected reporting. The chartering process is discussed in greater detail in Chapter 9.

HOW TO SUPPORT SIX SIGMA PROJECT TEAMS

Six Sigma project teams are best supported through the structure, communication, and commitment of a company. In order for Six Sigma teams to become successful, executive management needs to champion, sponsor, and support project teams through their performance improvement projects. Success with Six Sigma starts with the leadership—an executive in charge. The executive in charge is accountable for making Six Sigma the method of management for the company, division, or department. He or she gives constant direction and management support for implementing Six Sigma so there is no distinction between the Six Sigma method and the way employees ordinarily meet the needs of the business. He or she is responsible for reviewing team progress and actual improvements made by the division(s). He or she also periodically participates in process improvement efforts and publicly recognizes and rewards the efforts and results of project teams.

The commitment to Six Sigma project teams is established through designation of a Six Sigma leader in the organization. A director of Six Sigma drives the deployment of Six Sigma throughout the defined scope of the company. He or she is accountable for organizing project teams, scheduling progress and results sessions, periodically assessing departmental indicators, assigning facilitators for each project team, and providing ongoing consultation to each department. The director's staff is responsible for providing support for team development, training, and coaching in the use of Six Sigma tools. In addition, the director and staff will provide ongoing Six Sigma course development and program evaluation.

STAGES OF TEAM EVOLUTION

A project team, like any other relationship, develops over time. In a team's early stages, people do not really know each other and the experience can be quite surreal. Over time, however, a team and its relationships mature through four predictable stages of development: forming, storming, norming, and performing. Each stage has its own emotional state, which is important for each member to recognize in order to overcome the pitfalls that can throw a team off track. The stages and their related emotional states are outlined in Figure 7.1.

Forming

Forming, the first stage of team development, can be characterized as both exciting and anxious. The excitement comes from the novelty of the task at

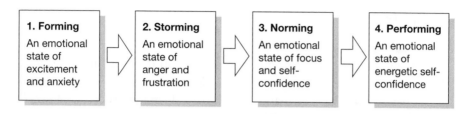

FIGURE 7.1. The Stages of Team Development

hand and the special feeling each team member has about being selected. The anxiety is derived from the challenge of a project's objectives, the expectations of the team, and the team members' unfamiliarity with each other. At this stage, people are not completely themselves. It is this stage where you don't really meet the individuals—you meet their *representatives*. At this stage, team members usually are diplomatic and conciliatory. Consequently, there is little open conflict and everyone typically is on their best behavior.

Storming

In the second stage, storming, team members struggle to balance satisfying personalities with the need to get the job done. In the storming stage, team members experience anger, frustration, issue wrangling, and open hostilities. At this stage, teams work through personality conflicts and open disagreements. In the storming stage, successful teams find ways to deal with the new personalities while succeeding at the job at hand.

Norming

In the norming stage, team members adjust to each other's working style and find ways to successfully resolve their personality differences. Reaching the norming stage indicates that team members have consciously and subconsciously negotiated the terms and conditions upon which their relationships will function. Strong evidence of norming is that teams focus less on personality and more on the task at hand. The residue of the prior stage may still exist as some team members may harbor a reluctance to deal with delicate situations or offer ideas. Overall, reaching norming indicates the team has found a way to function and make progress.

Performing

In the final stage of team development, performing, team members succeed in maintaining good relations and getting the job done at the same time. They deal with conflicts as they arise, challenge ideas without getting personal, operate at peak performance, and take pride in their success. At times, the team hardly seems to need a leader.

Every team will progress through the four cycles mentioned above. It is not uncommon for teams to return to earlier phases. For example, the dynamic of introducing a new team member can cause a return to the storming stage. It is vital for a team leader and facilitator to have the competence to recognize and understand these stages in order to shape, mold, and facilitate the progression of the team.

REMEDIES FOR THE PROBLEMS OF TEAM EVOLUTION

Forming

Since team anxiety is primarily derived from uncertainty, a team leader's success can be marked by how well he or she structures the team's goals and expectations. This can be accomplished by developing and communicating a strong business case and charter for the project's existence. The business case should explain the current undesirable situation, cite a strong business reason for improvement, and establish the expected outcomes for the project. The leader and facilitator also should structure a set of ground rules to which team members can reconcile their behavior. Helpful ground rules include:

- Be on time to all meetings.
- Ask questions.
- Be a devil's advocate.
- Listen to the ideas of others.
- Complete assignments on time.
- Follow the facts.
- Follow the meeting agenda closely.

Storming

Since the second stage is marked by a team's struggle to balance personalities with the need to get the job done, a team leader can best serve this stage by recognizing and accepting that conflict is a natural part of the process. His or her task is to function as a mediator and referee to create focus on what is right vs. who is right. The actions of the leader and facilitator should shape and mold the team to produce disagreements and agreements without people being disagreeable.

Norming

As team members find ways to successfully use their relations to get the job done, the best thing a leader can do is to promote smooth relations and increase responsibilities. At this stage, a team leader best serves the team through the art of delegation.

Performing

At this stage, a team leader is more of a communicator and an administrator. The team leader best serves the project by maintaining its schedule, promoting the team's work amongst the management team, and communicating to the company through the team's executive champion.

CONCLUSION

This chapter was devoted to the vital antecedent of a successful Six Sigma program—the Six Sigma project team. Team roles and responsibilities, how to establish and support a Six Sigma project team, and the stages of team evolution were discussed. When combined with the next chapter, the concepts and subject matter become a powerful tool to implement Six Sigma within an organization.

SIX SIGMA SOFT SKILLS: WORKING WITH AND THROUGH OTHERS

No matter what you do or how sophisticated things get,
it still all comes down to people!

—*Tim Auen*

A Six Sigma project team is somewhat of an enigma in any organization within which it operates. The life of a team is limited, it has no legitimate authority to compel others to act in its interest, and although it has an executive sponsor, it has no formal superior. Its only true power is its standing with the executive sponsor and the influence it derives from the organization to solve its problems, the latter of which is under direct control of the Six Sigma team.

The purpose of this chapter is to help you learn and understand the necessary skills required to effectively work with and through others. The focus is on how to work within a team to produce effective decisions and solve problems. The basic elements of change and how to create and nurture change for successful project completion also are discussed.

The following team dynamics skills are covered:

- Successful team attributes
- Consensus building
- Groupthink
- Understanding and managing change

SUCCESSFUL TEAM ATTRIBUTES

Success for teams does not just happen; it must be planned for, structured, and coached. Whether a temporary Six Sigma project team or an ongoing work unit, some key ingredients are required in order for a team to be successful:

- **Structure**: A team requires defined roles, responsibilities, ground rules, and procedures by which it will operate.
- **Acceptable norms**: Team members require an expected manner of conduct not only within the team but also within the organizations it supports.
- **Purpose**: A team needs to know what it is to accomplish, how the accomplishments will be measured, and the significance of the accomplishments to the organization it serves.

These key ingredients set the stage for a productive and effective effort. Successful teams also have one additional element that is worth mentioning—self-interest. A personal stake or professional advantage in being part of a Six Sigma project team can encourage a high degree of personal commitment.

Acceptable Norms: Ground Rules

As the last chapter addressed the structure and responsibilities of a Six Sigma team, the key ingredient this chapter will start with is how to establish acceptable norms and ground rules. In order to work together productively, employees have basic needs and expectations that must be met:

- **Respect**: Those participating in an effort require basic regard for and acknowledgment of their talent, background, and work experience.

- **Shared responsibility**: Team members expect that everyone will be accountable for carrying out their duties and upholding their obligations.
- **Physical safety**: Team members expect to work in an environment that is safe and secure.
- **Psychological security**: Everyone has a degree of self-esteem they bring to the workplace. No one expects to be ridiculed or harangued.
- **Opportunity for professional growth**: Everyone expects a chance to exercise initiative.

One way to establish acceptable norms is for everyone to come together and agree on a set of ground rules that will be observed as the team goes about its business. The team leader's first responsibility is to make sure his or her team builds a strong consensus around an acceptable code of conduct. Figure 8.1 provides a sample code of conduct a team can adopt or modify to suit its organizational climate. Ground rules established by a team can govern member conduct during meetings, consensus-building sessions, ad hoc discussions, and other situations.

**Team Taylor's
Guide to Corporate Citizenship**

- We will criticize ideas, not people.
- We will listen without any prejudgments.
- We will listen constructively.
- We will attend all meetings on time and will come prepared.
- We will question and participate.
- We will work together and share responsibility.
- We will respect each person.
- We will understand what is required and follow through.

FIGURE 8.1. Team Code of Conduct

Purpose

Funk and Wagnalls Standard Dictionary defines purpose as "an idea or ideal kept before the mind as an end of an effort or action; a design or aim." In order for a team to be successful, it needs to know what it is supposed to accomplish. What is its design or aim? This is especially true for a Six Sigma project team. Without a shared understanding of the team's purpose, a team's membership cannot have shared responsibility. A mission statement can make clear a team's role in an organization and its significance in achieving overarching objectives. A strong mission statement can serve a very useful purpose for a temporary project team and an established work group.

Developing a Mission Statement

For a temporary project team, a strong mission statement will:

- Define the team's shared responsibility
- Define a project team's end product
- Serve as a point of reference in resolving conflicts of understanding
- Serve as the guide that keeps the team's effort on track

A strong mission statement for a temporary project team is more precise than that of an established work group. A temporary project team's mission statement should have the following elements:

- **Project statement**: The clear and compelling business reason to initiate a project
- **Goal statement**: A specific statement of purpose toward which the team's objectives, work activities, and tasks will point
- **Scope statement**: The physical or departmental limits of the project

Figure 8.2 is an example of a mission statement for a Six Sigma project team. Creating a mission statement for a Six Sigma project team is covered in greater detail in Chapter 9.

For an established work group, a strong mission statement can:

SIX SIGMA CUSTOMER SERVICE TEAM

Project Statement

Our call center's average speed of answer is consistently one to two minutes beyond what is planned and staffed for. Over 78% of customer calls are not being answered within customer requirements and call center actual staffing levels and overtime are 52% beyond what is budgeted for. The current situation is hurting our company image of five-star service, and if continued staffing levels persist, they will have a significant adverse impact on operating margins.

Goal Statement

Improve average speed of answer coverage to 95% by end of third quarter 2008 and cut overtime in half by the same time period.

Project Scope

The scope of this project is limited to direct root causes of the problem stated above and where they reside.

FIGURE 8.2. Sample Project Team Mission Statement

- Clarify the work group's part in achieving corporate objectives
- Communicate a department's role in the corporation
- Answer the "what we will do" question for the organization
- Define a department's shared responsibility

A mission statement for an established work group should be a statement of commitment for those who (co)operate and manage under the mission. A strong mission statement should have the following elements:

1. **"Who we are" statement**: An expression of the team's identity
2. **"What we do" statement**: A definition of the team's function
3. **"We will" statements**: A collection of statements that clarify what the team's role is in achieving organizational and corporate objectives

---

The Order-to-Cash Process Mission Statement

We are Company X's order-to-cash process team that consists of the sales, sales operations, inventory control, distribution, shipping, and billing departments. Our purpose is to ensure our customers receive the right product at the right place at the right time. To achieve that end, we will:

1. Produce internal work products that meet our downstream process requirements as measured by our quality standards and metrics.

2. Forecast, plan, and staff to levels that are appropriate for us to meet our customer requirements.

3. Use the proper mix of people, technology, methods, and procedures to achieve and maintain high productivity and cost effectiveness as measured by our production standards.

4. Provide our customers with key access mechanisms to facilitate their ability to conduct business and seek assistance.

FIGURE 8.3. Sample Departmental Mission Statement

A departmental mission statement can create focus and commitment and can generate enthusiasm for what a team is organized to accomplish. Figure 8.3 is an example of a solid departmental mission statement for a service company.

A strong mission statement will enable a team to focus on what it is supposed to accomplish, how its accomplishments will be measured, and the significance of those accomplishments to the organization. The following steps can be used to create a strong departmental or interdepartmental mission statement:

1. Determine the scope and define which work groups will operate under the mission.
2. Identify key personnel to participate in the development of the mission statement, including those who are accountable for departmental objectives along with those who have a great deal of experience working in or with the departments.
3. Prepare the materials and meeting room. Materials should include a large sheet of butcher-block paper, felt-tip markers, and masking tape or a large white board and erasable markers.

What Is Your Vision?

Name:	Company:

Take this time to create an image of what your company/operation would look like 6 to 12 months from now if you had things completely your way! What is your vision?

1. What is your vision for the working environment?
   (processes, procedures, productivity, performance, technology)

2. How are people working differently from the way they work today?
   (meetings, goal setting, planning, departmental communication)

3. How different will your business results be from what they are today?
   (financial, internal operations, customer/market, employee/workforce)

4. What will your customers (internal and external) be saying about you?

FIGURE 8.4. Vision Worksheet

4. Use the visioning document in Figure 8.4 as a tool to facilitate discussion.
5. Develop the mission statement's *who we are, what we do,* and *we will* statements.

CONSENSUS BUILDING

Consensus is defined as the general acceptance of a decision by a group of people, along with their commitment to support a course of action. Consensus does not mean that unanimity among everyone has been achieved; it means team members commit, in varying degrees, to a decision and course of action. For some members, a decision may not have been their first or second choice, but they can live with the results and support the outcome.

Generally speaking, consensus is the most effective kind of decision making when working with and through others. Table 8.1 compares consensus with other types of group decision making.

Consensus building is an essential skill for working with and through others. It is a method of decision making in which everyone actively dis-

TABLE 8.1. Consensus Compared with Other Types of Decision Making

Type of Decision Making	Advantage	Disadvantage
Minority or individual	■ Fastest	■ Low commitment from group ■ Animosity
Majority rules	■ Fast ■ Useful with large number of decision makers	■ Majority "wins," others "lose" ■ In the long run, no one wants to work with a loser
Unanimous	■ High commitment and everybody wins	■ Time consuming ■ Can overlook options ■ Groupthink can occur
Consensus	■ High creativity, high commitment, no losers ■ Useful when both quality and acceptance of decisions are important	■ Takes time and requires good facilitation skills ■ Can be frustrating

cusses issues, weighs the pros and cons, and ultimately arrives at a common decision. The goals of a consensus builder are simple. A consensus builder works to create a situation where everyone wins; he or she works to engender team ownership of a course of action and works to eliminate an *us* vs. *them* feeling among the team members.

A team knows consensus has been reached when each team member can walk away from a consensus-building session saying:

- "I have listened to everyone else's opinion regarding the subject."
- "I have been able to fully communicate my position to everyone."
- "I believe the decision is a good one."
- "I can support the course of action."

How to Reach Consensus

The following list outlines the steps in consensus building:

1. State the issue at hand and explain the desire to use consensus to make the decision.

2. Each team member gathers related facts and prepares his or her own position.
3. The team meets and each member explains his or her position and provides his or her rationale for the decision.
4. Everyone listens to each other's position and, if logic dictates, team members modify their positions.
5. Create a number of appropriate options and evaluate them based on logic and priorities.
6. Select one course of action to which everyone can, in varying degrees, commit.
7. Develop an action plan to implement the course of action.

With consensus, more comprehensive decisions are produced through open discussion. With consensus, ideas are fully vetted and problems are resolved with the pooled knowledge and creativity of a team. As a result, better quality decisions are formed, along with a relatively high level of commitment from team members.

GROUPTHINK

To this point, this chapter has described and encouraged ways for people to "work together" in order to achieve objectives. In Chapter 7, the four stages of team development were described to provide information on how to recognize when a project team has achieved the benefits that come from leading a cohesive work group. In a cohesive work group, members see themselves as *we* as opposed to *I*. A *performing* group has learned to maintain good relations while getting the job done well. A cohesive work group is a true team.

This section is somewhat of a caveat for teamwork and group cohesion. Performing teams sometimes enter into a phenomenon called *groupthink*. Groupthink, a negative by-product of group cohesiveness, is defined by psychologist Dr. Irving L. Janis as "a mode of thinking that people engage in when they are deeply involved in a cohesive in-group. Groupthink happens when members' striving for unanimity overrides their motivation to realistically appraise alternative courses of action."[*]

---

[*] Janis, I. (1982). *Groupthink*, Boston: Houghton Mifflin.

After studying the accounts of several successful and unsuccessful U.S. government foreign policy decisions, Dr. Janis was able to explain how experienced, intelligent policy makers can sometimes make incredible errors. In the findings of his study, Dr. Janis described eight symptoms that, if present, can be an indication that groupthink exists. Other researchers agree with his conclusion that the more of these symptoms that are present, the more likely it is that a team can and will develop groupthink.

The eight symptoms of groupthink are as follows:

1. **The illusion of invulnerability**: The feeling of power and authority that causes a team to think that any decision it reaches will be the right one. This feeling of invulnerability causes a team to take undue risks.
2. **An unquestioned belief in the inherent morality of the group**: A team's extreme belief in the rightness of its actions. This inflated sense of "it is the right thing to do" can cause a team's membership to ignore the ethical and moral consequences of its actions.
3. **Irrational exuberance**: A collective effort to rationalize and downplay legitimate objections to courses of action.
4. **Stereotyping of out-groups**: An attitude of *us* vs. *them* that can cause an opposing viewpoint or legitimate criticism to be caricaturized.
5. **Self-censorship**: The overwhelming idea that the reaction of going against the team is of greater negative personal impact than keeping quiet. This sort of censorship typically occurs under the guise of group loyalty, team spirit, or adherence to company policy.
6. **Direct pressure**: Pressure and intimidation brought to bear on team members to the extent they not only are conditioned to keep counter viewpoints to themselves but also are convinced that to believe differently is contrary to what is expected of all *loyal* team members.
7. **Mind guards**: The desires and actions of team members that surface to protect the group from disconcerting thoughts and ideas. Data, facts, and information may be manipulated or deliberately kept out of the purview of the team.
8. **Illusion of unanimity**: Also known as false consensus, this happens when the team coalesces around a course of action. Those who may have had legitimate criticisms have even put their doubts to rest.

Avoiding the Effects of Groupthink*

Six Sigma teams can experience groupthink if they come through a particularly tough and extended storming phase. A team's desire to avoid the wrangling, resistance, and hostility experienced while storming may override the desire to logically and objectively arrive at conclusions. To avoid the effects of groupthink, a team leader can do a variety of things, including:

1. **Be a coach**: Know the symptoms of groupthink. Consistently evaluate behaviors, based on ground rules, and provide feedback that will shape and mold acceptable conduct.
2. **Maintain an open climate**: Avoid stating preferences and expectations at the outset. Encourage free discussion, non-judgmental attitudes, and acceptance of divergent thinking.
3. **Avoid the isolation of the group**: Bring in outsiders to provide critical reactions to the team's assumptions and decisions.
4. **Appoint a devil's advocate**: Appoint a team member to be a critical evaluator. By giving someone the power to question sacred cows and uncontested team assumptions, the team will be encouraged to re-examine its own logic and rationalizations.
5. **Avoid being too directive**: The team leader should not exert undue influence upon the team. A team leader should encourage consensus building and perhaps even remove himself or herself from some deliberations to allow other members to facilitate a meeting in his or her absence.

This author encourages the reader to continuously evaluate team interaction based on the eight symptoms of groupthink described by Dr. Janis. When the symptoms consistently reveal themselves, prescribe and implement the solutions based upon the prescriptions outlined above.

UNDERSTANDING AND MANAGING CHANGE

What is change? To effect change is to make different or make something become different. Organizational change comes in all shapes and sizes. A company may implement a new IT system, re-engineer a process, execute

---

* Derived from CRM Learning, "Groupthink."

a merger, introduce a new performance appraisal program, or announce a layoff. Whatever the change, it can be likened to a rock being tossed into still waters. Change can cause ripple effects throughout an organization, often with unintended consequences.

A common reaction to organizational change is resistance from those whose jobs may be directly affected. Employees can resist change for many reasons. The most common reasons are:

- **Insecurity**: Change introduced with almost no warning can create a sense of discomfort among employees.
- **Stubbornness**: "This is the way we do it!" is the battle cry of employees who wish to maintain the predictable company status quo.
- **Lack of trust**: When employees do not trust management, it is unlikely that management's comments and actions will be well received.
- **Poor employee relations**: An unpopular and disliked management team can be a very poor agent of change.
- **Job status**: Employees can feel a loss of esteem or status due to a pending change.

There are many more reasons why employees resist change; however, for the purpose of our efforts, we will focus on the main reason that affects the business context: introducing Six Sigma as a quality improvement initiative.

Change and the Six Sigma Experience

As mentioned above, organizational change, in and of itself, can be an emotionally and occupationally disruptive experience. Working with and through others in an effort to achieve Six Sigma performance is no different. General Electric identified three specific forms of resistance usually encountered when trying to introduce a quality improvement effort into an organization:

1. **Technical system resistance***: Employees enjoy and are comfortable with certain ways and means for getting things done. They

---

* General Electric Corporate Management Development—Corporate Entry-Level Programs (1993). GE Problem Solving and Project Management Tool Kit, Fairfield, CT: General Electric Company.

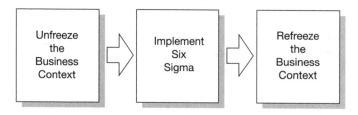

FIGURE 8.5. Change Theory

like their system and are likely to resist unfamiliar methods, suggestions, or mandates.

2. **Political system resistance***: Office politics exist for a reason. Employees create and foster coalitions to control power and influence. A method of managing by fact can threaten these power bases.

3. **Cultural system resistance***: Every organization operates off of a basic set of assumptions, values, and experiences that has set a precedent for the present and future. A corporate culture can become so ingrained that often it creates an inherent barrier to change.

To make Six Sigma performance a reality, a company must overcome these three forms of resistance. The Performance Management Group recommends a change management method first made popular by the social scientist Kurt Lewin. As depicted in Figure 8.5, Kurt Lewin sees an organization as a social system which can be unfrozen, changed, and then refrozen.

The business context can be defined as the organizational structures, systems, circumstances, and expectations of a business enterprise and its employees. To achieve Six Sigma performance, a company may impact one or more of the elements of a business context in a significant way.

Unfreezing the Business Context

To unfreeze the business context, a company uses a method to create a shared belief that there is a need and rationale for a change in order for the

---

* General Electric Corporate Management Development—Corporate Entry-Level Programs (1993). GE Problem Solving and Project Management Tool Kit, Fairfield, CT: General Electric Company.

company to succeed or survive. A case is made that the need for change is greater than the desire to stay the same.

A business case can be made in many ways; The Performance Management Group recommends the following:

- Use a quality-readiness survey to cultivate the prevailing thought among the employee base affected about the company's actual performance. A majority of the time, the quality-readiness survey will uncover a strong need for improvement.
- Generate internal or external data to induce change. Performance audits that compare company results to standards, objectives, and competitive benchmarks also can make the case.
- It is typical for an employee base to have a vision of what employees want their work environment to become. More often than not, employees see the potential to do more and to do better. Work with them, using the visioning document introduced earlier, to create a strong consensus on what their organization can become.

Any combination of the above three can have a substantial impact on unfreezing the business context and overcoming the initial resistance to change.

Implement Six Sigma

Form a coalition of key players to be advocates, sponsors, and change agents. Train and certify technical experts, champions, and individual contributors in the Six Sigma methodology. Use the following steps to introduce Six Sigma to the organization:

1. **Identify executive sponsors**: Achieving Six Sigma performance derives its power from the legitimate hierarchy in a company.
2. **Identify Six Sigma practitioners**: Whether serving in a full-time capacity or implementing Six Sigma as a secondary accountability, trained black belts, green belts, and individual contributors can derive significant influence from executing their improvement projects competently and successfully.
3. **Assign responsibility for making Six Sigma successful**: At General Electric, it is said that managers must demonstrate their ex-

pertise using the Six Sigma methodology in order to be considered for promotion.

4. **Get results**: Look for *low-hanging fruit* as an effective and feasible first project. Drive favorable financial and operational results through the use of Six Sigma tools and methods.

Refreeze the Business Context

Support and reinforce the Six Sigma culture. Follow up and correct unintended project consequences. Track and share the success stories. Develop metrics and track company performance in terms of quality, productivity, and cost. Share results widely and provide feedback. Hold people accountable for results. Share credit and recognition with others. Reward Six Sigma performance excellence! These steps will ensure that the change to a high-performance organization takes hold.

CONCLUSION

The purpose of this chapter was to provide you with an understanding of the skills required to effectively work with and through others on a Six Sigma team. The chapter covered the relevant people skill tools to successfully work within a team to produce effective decisions and solve problems. Also discussed were the basic elements of change and how to create and nurture change for successful project completion. Through understanding successful team attributes, how to use consensus building, how to recognize and protect against groupthink, and how to manage the change a Six Sigma team produces, you will be empowered to effectively lead and function within a Six Sigma team.

This book has free materials available for download from the
Web Added Value™ Resource Center at www.jrosspub.com.

9

MANAGEMENT BY FACT: THE DMAIC APPROACH TO PERFORMANCE IMPROVEMENT

To this point, we have discussed the purpose, methods, and tools used in the practice of Six Sigma. This chapter is devoted to further defining what Six Sigma is in the context of a concept called management by fact.

FIRE FIGHTING

When managers problem solve, often they have a gut feeling or intuition regarding the nature of the issue with which they are dealing. They frequently formulate and implement solutions with little or no supporting information regarding the problem. Their educated guess may be based on past experience or a familiar anecdote. More often than not, the solution they implement resolves the problem for a short time or establishes a workaround to serve a short-term business need. Effectively, they put the fire out, but they do not resolve the underlying issue that caused the fire. As a consequence, the issue soon revisits them. Does this sound familiar?

The practice of Six Sigma uses the vast experience of managers coupled with supporting information to analyze problems at their root causes in order to formulate and implement permanent solutions. This concept of decision making and problem solving with data and information is known as management by fact.

WHAT IS MANAGEMENT BY FACT?

As opposed to management by opinion or management by intuition, management by fact is a business practice of decision making and problem solving with numerical facts and information along with the experience and expertise of managers. Decision makers who manage by fact depend on the continual measurement and analysis of operating performance. They collect performance data and analyze the data for the purpose of evaluation, planning, change management, and benchmarking. Decision makers are empowered to manage by fact only when they know what their work processes involve. They must know their process:

- **Requirements**: Inputs, information, and materials
- **Activities**: Methods, procedures, and techniques
- **Work products**: Work product descriptions and standards

Decision makers who manage by fact solve problems with data. When faced with an issue, they collect numerical facts and information, organize them, analyze them, and draw fact-based conclusions. Six Sigma is a powerful method that gives managers and employees the knowledge and skills to manage by fact in order to produce higher levels of productivity, efficiency, and quality.

The remainder of this chapter is devoted to defining the practice of Six Sigma. We will discuss what Six Sigma is and it will be described in terms of what it is not. Six Sigma will be contrasted with other quality methods, key Six Sigma concepts will be explored, and an overview of how to manage a Six Sigma project will be provided.

WHAT IS SIX SIGMA?

Six Sigma has been described in many different ways. It is known as a measure of performance that approaches perfection. It is described as a fact-based, data-driven management approach used primarily to eliminate defects and errors from manufacturing processes and non-manufacturing workflows. It is called a statistical measure that represents how a process is performing. A process can be described as achieving Six Sigma performance when it produces no more than 3.4 defects per million opportunities. The Performance Management Group likes to think of Six Sigma in very simple terms and defines Six Sigma as:

1. A *quality improvement* business practice that strives to produce perfection in the delivery of products and services
2. A *method of management* that uses facts, information, and data to make decisions and manage business performance
3. A *problem-solving method* that identifies root causes of problems and determines permanent solutions

The practice of Six Sigma is applied through two main methods: DMAIC and DFSS. DMAIC is an acronym which stands for define, measure, analyze, improve, and control. The DMAIC method is a systematic problem-solving methodology that resolves issues at the root cause. DFSS (Design for Six Sigma) is also known as DMADV, which stands for define, measure, analyze, design, and verify. DFSS is used primarily to design and develop new products and processes.

Both Six Sigma methods are deployed by Six Sigma green belts and black belts, and Six Sigma projects are supervised master black belts. The belt designations are borrowed from the martial arts to establish the level of expertise an individual has achieved in the selection and use of statistical applications and performance improvement tools. Those with advanced backgrounds are certified as black belts, and those with intermediate competencies are certified as green belts. The highest level of expertise is the master black belt. The master black belt not only possesses a superior level of competency using statistical applications but also is a designated master with respect to Six Sigma strategy, coaching, and training.

WHAT SIX SIGMA IS NOT

Six Sigma has been defined in terms of what it is and will now be further defined in terms of what it is not. Six Sigma is *not*:

- **A flavor-of-the-month program**: Whereas many programs are fly-by-night, packed with slogans and signs, Six Sigma is a new way of doing business. The goal of Six Sigma is to ensure that everyone efficiently produces something of value.
- **A cost-cutting strategy**: Six Sigma is a management practice designed to obtain the highest levels of customer loyalty and produce the highest levels of productivity in order to avoid cost-cutting strategies that can be destructive.
- **Solely a focus on people**: Focusing on people alone only accounts for 25% of work activity. Six Sigma strives to improve the system of work. Evaluating procedures, technology, material, information flows, as well as people is essential to make the system work better.
- **Fire fighting**: The purpose of Six Sigma is not to find defects and fix them; Six Sigma means prevention. The goal of the method is to eliminate problems at the root cause to prevent defects and errors.
- **Just the voice of the metric**: Six Sigma involves listening to the voice of the customer. The practice wants you to know and understand your customer. The method encourages you to understand and satisfy your customer requirements with perfection.

We have defined Six Sigma in terms of what it is and what it is not. Table 9.1 provides an overview of how Six Sigma compares and contrasts with other well-known quality improvement methods.

KEY SIX SIGMA CONCEPTS

General Electric presents a notion that describes the key aspects of Six Sigma: "Customers don't judge us on averages, they feel the variance in each transaction, in each product we ship."* Six Sigma focuses on reducing process variation and then improving process capability. Other defining concepts of the practice are as follows:

---

* www.ge.com/sixsigma/sixsigstrategy.html.

TABLE 9.1. Six Sigma vs. Other Quality Methods

Element	ISO	Kaizen	Lean	Six Sigma
Organization type	Designed for manufacturing	Manufacturing or services	Primarily designed for manufacturing	Manufacturing, services, product development
Strategic intent	Concerned with standardization of rules	Concerned primarily with small incremental improvements	Concerned with overproduction, inventory or work in process, plant formation, time and motion, and defective parts	Concerned with improving return on investments, prevention of wasteful problems, and satisfying the customer
Application	Establishment of a bureaucracy, audit procedures, and conformance to accepted quality standards	Informal use of continuous improvement tools to produce incremental improvements	Training of entire employee body, establishment of an executive oversight organization, and structured project approvals and implementations	Limited project teams with time constraints focused on delivering significant return on investments and improved customer loyalty
Outcomes	Not focused on delivering business results; the goal is to maintain ISO quality standard certification	Delivers small incremental improvements	Returns are delivered after overhauling approaches and methods of manufacturing	Achievement of 3.4 defects per million opportunities and process-perfect outcomes; Six Sigma projects return on average $230,000 per project*

* www.isixsigma.com/sixsigma/six_sigma.as.

1. **Voice of the customer:** The idea of comprehending and reacting to the market's needs, attitudes, and perceptions for the purpose of moving beyond customer satisfaction to engender true customer loyalty.
2. **Critical to quality (CTQ):** The idea of translating the voice of the customer into specific tangible product or service requirements for the purpose of meeting and exceeding a customer's needs and expectations.
3. **Defect/error:** A failure of the production or service delivery process to meet those established product or service requirements derived from customer CTQs.
4. **Process capability:** Refers to the ability of a process to meet customer requirements or the ability of a process to produce a defect-free product or error-free service.
5. **Management by fact:** As opposed to "cause jumping" or "management by anecdote," management by fact is a dictate which states that decisions and solutions to problems will be determined by the best available data and information.

FROM ROOT CAUSE TO PERFORMANCE IMPROVEMENT: PDCA

Six Sigma provides a structured approach to solving problems and improving the value of what a company produces. Approaches may vary by company and by consulting firm, but an effectively structured approach will closely follow W. Edwards Deming's PDCA (plan, do, check, act) approach illustrated in Figure 9.1.

The PDCA cycle is a flow diagram for learning and for improving a product or service. PDCA is the quality circle established by the Japanese as taught by Deming during the 1950s. As its name implies, after every action, there will be evaluations of what has happened, followed by further action. As the quality circle turns, it models the concept of continuous improvement. The four-step PDCA cycle is outlined as follows:

1. **Plan:** Someone might have an idea to improve a product or a process. The first step is to study the process to decide what change

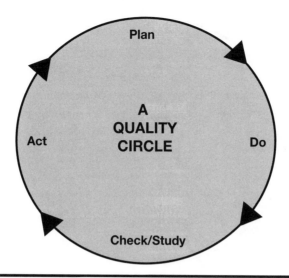

FIGURE 9.1. PDCA Cycle

might improve it. An appropriate team is organized to test the improvement idea. A plan with expected outcomes is created.

2. **Do**: The improvement is piloted and tested on a small scale.
3. **Check**: The outcomes are studied and evaluated. A determination is made regarding whether the expectations as a result of the change are realized.
4. **Act**: The improvement is adopted, the idea is abandoned, or the cycle is run again under different conditions.

The objective of the PDCA cycle is to achieve process-perfect performance. As mentioned earlier, the PDCA cycle is a quality circle, and as it rolls, it produces more and more knowledge about how operating performance can be improved.

THE DMAIC PROCESS: A STRUCTURED APPROACH TO IMPROVEMENT

The DMAIC (define, measure, analyze, improve, and control) improvement model, illustrated in Figure 9.2, is the generally accepted approach to process

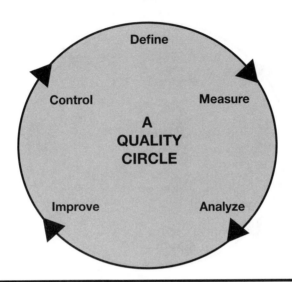

FIGURE 9.2. DMAIC Improvement Model

improvement for Six Sigma efforts. It is systematic, scientific, and fact based. This closed-loop process eliminates unproductive steps and improves a company's ability to remain number one in the eyes of its customer.

As mentioned earlier, structured approaches to improving products and processes differ from company to company and from consulting firm to consulting firm. The Performance Management Group models its method after the generally accepted Six Sigma approach—DMAIC.

Define Phase   D▶

The purpose of the define stage of the DMAIC process is to discover a *clear and compelling business reason* for improving a product or a process. The work product of this step consists of a preliminary business case with an identified issue and its defined impact on the customer, the process, and the business, along with a preliminary financial impact analysis (optional). The business case should include relevant information uncovered during due diligence. A framework for a proper business case diagnosis is outlined in Table 9.2.

Oftentimes, a compelling issue may be obvious because of its impact on the business. As a result, a Six Sigma project may be chartered. A Six Sigma project also may be chartered due to an executive's desire to achieve a spe-

TABLE 9.2. A Business Case Diagnosis

What	What is the issue? What is the process affected?
Who	Who is the customer? Who is the supplier?
Where	Where is the issue occurring? ■ Department ■ Region ■ Company-wide
Impact analysis	How often is the issue arising? What is the impact on the customer? What is the impact on process capability? What is the financial impact on the business?
Project objective	Outline the target of the project and write a goal statement that meets the SMART criteria
Project team	Qualified members to whom the issue is relevant and important
Project scope	Defined boundaries relating to the direct issue Defined time limits (estimated)

cific strategic objective. In either case, a Six Sigma team can get started by conducting an assessment. This activity will include:

- Conducting voice of the customer assessments (internal and external)
- Examining departmental methods, procedures, and indicators
- Identifying what a work group and its managers know
- Reviewing departmental audits and reports
- Identifying gaps between actual performance and performance standards
- Displaying and communicating performance gaps in financial terms

Through this assessment, customer requirements not being consistently met, inefficiencies, rework, and waste can be uncovered. These issues can be documented to produce a problem statement. The following are examples of typical problems:

- Twenty-five percent of the entries in our department are in error.
- Sales of our product were down 30% in each of the past three months.
- Seventeen of 25 service delivery dates were missed last month.
- Overall customer satisfaction ratings have been falling 10% every month for the last two quarters.

Once an issue has been uncovered, its impact can be quantified and a financial impact analysis can be produced.

The work product of this step is a preliminary business case. The formal business case is a living document. It is a diary of the Six Sigma project which documents the major milestones and business implications of the project. At the define stage, the business case is an immature situational analysis that states a *clear and compelling* business reason to proceed with an improvement project. Elements of a preliminary business case are as follows:

1. **Problem statement**: The problem statement describes what the facts of the assessment reveal. It is an *as is* statement that defines the present undesirable situation and avoids jumping to causes or solutions. The criteria for a good problem statement include:
   - A good problem statement is specific. In measurable terms, it tells you the extent of the problem. For example: "Our mean time to resolve south region outages is more than 15 hours compared to our standard of 4 hours."
   - A good problem statement states the results. It states what is wrong and identifies no causes. It avoids *cause* or *solution* statements like: "Our mean time to resolve south region outages is more than 15 hours *because we have a lack of technicians.*"
   - A good problem statement has a measurable financial impact.
   - A good problem statement proposes no solutions and jumps to no conclusions.
2. **Goal statement**: While the problem statement describes the pain, a goal statement defines the relief.* Goal statements can be standardized into three elements:
   - A statement of outcome or what will be achieved

---

* Pande, Peter S., Neuman, Robert P., and Cavanagh, Roland R. (2000). *The Six Sigma Way*, New York: McGraw-Hill, p. 241.

- A specific target with respect to productivity, quality, and/or cost
- A general deadline for delivering the results

For clarity, you may want to include two deadlines in a goal statement—one date for implementing solutions and the second for when you expect to show measurable results.

3. **Team roles and responsibilities**: Team members are listed along with their designated accountabilities and qualifications (black belt, green belt, etc.).

4. **Project scope**: The physical, departmental, or cause boundaries of the project. A cause boundary is a border for wherever a root cause of an effect resides.

5. **Constraints**: Any resource limitations.

6. **Assumptions**: Any relevant issues, concerns, or business implications.

7. **Team guidelines**: Any special considerations for teams that relate to how they function.

8. **Communication plan**: How progress reports will be made, to whom, and in what form.

9. **Preliminary project plan**: A suggested start date, estimated completion date, and suggested project milestones.

Once approved, the business case will become the draft project charter for the Six Sigma improvement team. As stated before, this document is a living document and a diary of the project as it develops. An example of a preliminary business case is illustrated in Figure 9.3. As time progresses and milestones are achieved, major decisions, adjustments, and results will be documented and enclosed.

Measure Phase

The purpose of the measure phase is to fully account for the frequency and severity of the problem. In addition, this step provides the groundwork for the analyze phase of the project by narrowing the problem to its major factors. As a result of this phase, the Six Sigma project team will have:

- Validated the problem defined in the prior step
- Refined the goal of the project team

**SIX SIGMA CUSTOMER SERVICE TEAM
BUSINESS CASE**

Problem Statement

Our call center's average speed of answer is consistently one to two minutes beyond what is planned and staffed for. Over 78% of customer calls are not being answered within customer requirements, and call center actual staffing levels and overtime are 52% beyond what is budgeted for. The current situation is hurting our company image of five-star service, and if continued staffing levels persist, they will have a significant adverse impact on operating margins.

Goal Statement

Improve average speed of answer coverage to 95% by end of third quarter 2008 and cut overtime in half by the same time period.

Project Scope

The scope of this project is limited to direct root causes of the problem stated above and where they reside.

Constraints

This will be a special project. Team members will be expected to be 100% dedicated to this project until completion. Accommodations for additional resources will be made as needed.

Assumptions

No reasonable solutions will be considered "out of bounds," but the focus of the team will be on improving the operating results discussed in the problem statement and not on designing or redesigning new processes.

Team Guidelines

The team will meet continually as determined by the team leader. Decisions will be made by consensus and guided by data, facts, and logic. If consensus cannot be reached, the team leader will make the final call.

FIGURE 9.3. Sample Preliminary Business Case

Team Members

John Sartan, Customer Service Manager (Team Leader)
Jeff Martin, Network Technician (Team Member)
Rick Mayer, Customer Service Supervisor (Team Member)
Jerry Ricke, Lead Customer Service Representative (Team Member)
Johnson Liberty, Six Sigma Coach (Team Facilitator)

Communication Plan

Monthly business case review (toll gate) presentation to executive sponsor and direct reports. Weekly written project updates to executive sponsor.

Preliminary Project Plan

The following are milestones for completing each phase of the DMAIC process:

Define	2 weeks
Measure	2.5 weeks
Analyze	3 weeks
Improve	3 weeks
Control	5 weeks

Total estimated project time: 15.5 weeks to be initiated this coming Monday.

FIGURE 9.3. Sample Preliminary Business Case (continued)

- Measured key process inputs and outcomes
- Improved on the preliminary financial impact analysis

Major activities of this step support fact-based decision making by gathering data and obtaining a full intellectual grasp of the situation. Major activities of the measure phase include:

- Identifying key measures and process errors
- Planning and executing data collection efforts
- Charting and communicating process variation
- Calculating sigma performance baseline

The work products of this phase amend the business case with sound business analyses and conclusions. The types of analysis typically completed in the measure phase include:

- **Process analysis:** An *as is* flowchart is mapped and charted.
- **Data collection planned and completed:** Solid data collection plans are created and executed. These plans may include Pareto analysis, correlation analysis, and process capability analysis.
- **Performance baseline analysis:** Operational performance of quality, productivity, and efficiency is trended over time, and sigma-related levels are calculated.
- **Cost analysis:** The cost of poor quality is compiled and evaluated. Any significant budget variances are evaluated and reported.

Analyze Phase

The purpose of the analyze phase is to identify and verify the *root cause* of a problem. In Six Sigma language, we want to know "what special cause is disrupting our business."

The Performance Management Group takes special care in understanding what a root cause is, as it is easy to jump to conclusions when trying to conduct root cause analysis. As depicted in Figure 9.4, problems are seen in three dimensions: the pain, the symptom, and the root cause.

The first dimension is the pain. At the pain level, problems are recognized due to some discomfort or annoyance experienced by employees or customers. Employees may devote great effort to satisfying a seemingly simple task or completing an activity for which they otherwise may not be responsible.

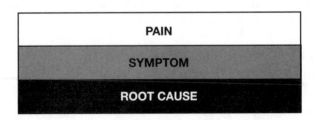

FIGURE 9.4. Dimensions of a Problem

At this level, customers often experience great inconvenience or a loss of value for their time, effort, or money.

The second dimension is the symptom. Often confused with the cause, the symptom lies closer to the problem. A symptom is a sign or indication that a problem exists; it is an observable characteristic produced by a process and indicates that there is some sort of disorder.

The third dimension is the root cause. The root cause is the primary agent or force producing the error, defect, or effect. Once the root cause is removed or corrected, the undesirable condition ceases to exist and the process functions as designed.

Note: People often have "gut" feelings, intuitions, or opinions about the cause of a problem and try to solve the problem with little or no information. Educated guesses often are based on past experience, but these ideas are only the first step in analyzing a problem. The purpose of the analysis step is to rely on information and data for decision making and to prevent jumping to causes and poor solutions.

Root Cause Analysis

In the analyze phase, relevant data are collected and analyzed to identify causes and confirm their impact. The service quality root cause analysis model illustrated in Figure 9.5 calls for first performing cause and effect analysis in order to generate a list of *possible* root causes. The next step is to stratify the list of possible causes and continue the analysis to the level of actionable special causes. The special cause(s) with the probable greatest impact must be selected and prioritized. Finally, the team investigates and verifies the selected root causes before targeting them for removal.

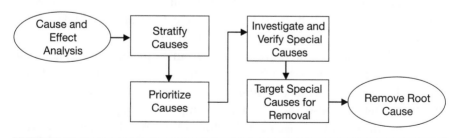

FIGURE 9.5. Service Quality Root Cause Analysis Process

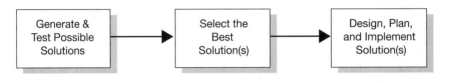

FIGURE 9.6. Improve Phase

Improve Phase

Once the analysis phase is complete, the process moves from analysis to action. Figure 9.6 outlines the three-step process of the improve phase. The purpose of the improve phase is to generate and implement viable solutions that will root out special causes. These solutions must be effective in performing corrective action on root causes and must be financially feasible to implement. Once the one best solution is found, an effective implementation plan to install the solution must be designed.

There are several activities through which a project team can generate and test possible solutions, some of which are as follows:

- Brainstorming
- Benchmarking
- Plan, do, check, act (PDCA)

Once a Six Sigma team identifies a solution, the solution is optimized based on testing and analysis. The team should confirm that the problem and its root causes have been removed before proceeding to implementation. The team can contrast the problem before and after the test using the same indicators, reports, or customer feedback. Results also can be compared to targeted performance. When testing is complete, the team should design the new process and its new inputs and requirements.

This phase calls for the development of an implementation plan. The plan should answer the basic who, what, when, where, and how questions. It should include a schedule, resource requirements, and a work breakdown structure. The plan also should have the appropriate approvals from the executive sponsor and management structure. Once completed and approved, the plan should be fully implemented.

Control Phase   D > M > A > I > C

The purpose of this phase is to control future operational performance. At this stage, the intent is to *burn in* the solution to the operation and ensure it delivers the expected and long-term performance promised.

The team must show success by validating real-time process capability. In order to do so, the team develops and deploys new standard operating procedures and also establishes a measurement and control system. Along with departmental management, the team selects the appropriate control chart and implements a statistical process control regime. The outcome of the team's efforts should yield favorable performance trends and cost savings through the control phase. Once the control phase is complete, the team leader brings the DMAIC project to an administrative close.

SIX SIGMA PROJECT MANAGEMENT OVERVIEW

The purpose of this section is to provide a concise overview of the key aspects of what should be accomplished in managing a Six Sigma project. This section is not intended to be a complete lesson in project management, but if used in conjunction with the information in the preceding chapters, it will provide a good basis to help you plan, prepare, and execute an effective Six Sigma project.

The primary reason to initiate a Six Sigma project is to make a favorable impact on the needs of the business. The effectiveness of a project can be defined in terms of improving cycle times, reducing rework and waste, cutting cost, or improving customer loyalty. Management may charter a project team to target a specific issue in the operation or to ensure the achievement of a strategic objective. A project team should, by virtue of its purpose, improve the productivity, cost effectiveness, or customer goodwill of an operation.

Six Sigma projects have many characteristics, a few of which are:

- They are performed by people.
- They are constrained by limited resources.
- They are planned, executed, and controlled.
- They are goal oriented.

Six Sigma projects are temporary and unique. They are temporary in that a project has a definite beginning and a definite end; once the objectives of a project have been achieved, or when it becomes clear that they cannot be met, the project is terminated. Unique means that the specific intent and purpose of a project carry special influence, authority, and purview. When properly defined, the scope of a project should remain constant.

One of the basic building blocks of a Six Sigma project is the Six Sigma Master Project Plan, shown in Figure 9.7. Used in conjunction with the Six Sigma Personal Action Plan, shown in Figure 9.8, it becomes a means by which a project team can maintain project discipline.

Six Sigma Master Project Plan

The Six Sigma Master Project Plan (SSMPP) is a template to be used as a guide for a Six Sigma project. It defines which DMAIC phase a project is in and the input requirements, output/work product, target completion date, and actual completion date of the phase, along with any relevant comments. As an essential element of a project's structure, the SSMPP is a tool a project's black belt can use to maintain project discipline.

The SSMPP often is used as an executive summary for the ongoing business case of a project. It serves as a cover sheet for the project's diary of activities and events. It is a brief documented profile of project accomplishments to date, along with any significant events.

Six Sigma Personal Action Plan

The Six Sigma Personal Action Plan (SSPAP) is a template used by a project team member as his or her personal guide for a project. By articulating directly into the SSMPP, the personal action plan becomes an account of a project team member's action items. It defines the action the project team member should take, the scheduled start and completion dates, and the actual start and completion dates, along with any relevant and important comments. As an essential element of a project's structure, the SSPAP is a tool the project leader can use to maintain project discipline. The SSPAP is used in conjunction with the SSMPP as a documented profile of project issues, accomplishments, and significant events.

Business Reviews and Project Briefings

Business reviews and project briefings are toll gate meetings held to assess project status and progress. In a business review, a Six Sigma team presents to management an update of its progress through the DMAIC improvement process. Its purpose is to communicate the operating results from a business case perspective, give management a means to assess what is going well, and convey any special needs of the project team. The briefing, if executed correctly, will accomplish the following:

- Presentation of key project indicators and results
- Approvals and action plans designed to support project success factors
- Reinforcement of the commitment to the project and to the understanding of the DMAIC process

The following outline is a concise overview of a generic project briefing schedule:

1. Project briefing after Phase 1 (Define)
   a. Business case is presented. A clear and compelling case is made to move forward with the project.
   b. Financial impact and/or strategic intent is defined.
   c. Business case is amended and updated.
2. Project briefing after Phase 4 (Improve)
   a. Root cause analysis is presented. Data analysis and verification of special causes are presented.
   b. Alternative solutions and related cost-benefit analyses are presented, along with the project team's recommendations. A decision is made.
   c. Business case is amended and updated.
   d. Project variances, if any, are reported.
3. Project briefing after Phase 5 (Control)
   a. Solution implementation and verification that the root cause has been eliminated.
   b. Earned value analysis of payback of project is compared to the payback period schedule prescribed in the business case.

Team Name:				Team Number:	
Problem Statement:					
Goal Statement:					

Project Step	Input Requirements	Objective and Work Product	Target Date	Completion Date	Comments
1 **Define**	Business case diagnosis Flowcharting Histogram Data sheets Pareto charts Voice of the customer Control charts	To establish a *clear and compelling reason* for improving a product or a process 1. Business case 2. Financial impact analysis			
2 **Measure**	Pareto analysis Sigma calculation Run chart Data collection plan Process flowchart Process capability analysis Net present value, return on investment, payback period Measurement system analysis	To factually understand the strength and extent of the problem 1. Process flowchart "as is" 2. Data collection planned and completed 3. Amended financial impact analysis completed (if needed) 4. Amended business case to include facts and data collected			

Project Step	Input Requirements	Objective and Work Product	Target Date	Completion Date	Comments
3 Analyze	Pareto charts _____ Ishikawa diagram _____ Scatter diagram _____ Hypothesis testing _____ Design of Experiments _____ Regression analysis _____ Data sheets _____ Run charts _____ Histograms _____	To identify and *verify* the root cause of a problem			
		The work product is the amended business case with data and results from the process analysis, root cause analysis, and quantification of the performance gap			
4 Improve	Brainstorming _____ Cost-benefit _____ Benchmarking _____ Failure Mode and Effects Analysis _____ Simulations _____ Scatter diagrams _____ Design of Experiments _____ Action plans _____	To generate and implement viable solutions that will root out the root causes			
		An amended business case that includes each alternative solution, its related cost-benefit analysis, a "should be" process map, and any related data			
5 Control	Process sigma calculation _____ Control charts _____ Control plans _____ Cost savings calculation _____	To control future process performance			
		An amended business case that includes a documented monitoring plan, standardized process and procedures, and a documented transfer of ownership to process owner and management team			

FIGURE 9.7. Six Sigma Master Project Plan

Team Member Name:		Team Name:		
Problem Statement:		Goal Statement:		
Action Item	Scheduled Start	Scheduled Completion		Comments
	Actual Start	Actual Completion		
Action Item	Scheduled Start	Scheduled Completion		Comments
	Actual Start	Actual Completion		
Action Item	Scheduled Start	Scheduled Completion		Comments
	Actual Start	Actual Completion		
Action Item	Scheduled Start	Scheduled Completion		Comments
	Actual Start	Actual Completion		

FIGURE 9.8. Six Sigma Personal Action Plan

c. Administrative closure means the business case is accepted and signed off on by the executive sponsor. Good performance is recognized and rewarded.

Project briefings should be relatively informal, and all team members should be encouraged to participate. Management should set a tone of curiosity and pleasant anticipation. Project briefings should not be "do-or-die" situations; rather, they should be opportunities for the business to be improved and for professional development.

CONCLUSION

This chapter was devoted to further defining Six Sigma in the context of a concept called management by fact. The practice of Six Sigma was defined in terms of what it is and in terms of what it is not. This chapter also described the DMAIC improvement process and provided an overview of how to manage a Six Sigma project.

10

DEPLOYING YOUR PERFORMANCE EXCELLENCE SYSTEM

Exceed (ik SEED): to surpass or to be superior, to go beyond (a limit).
Excel (ik SEL): to surpass; outstrip; be outstanding.
Excellent (EK sə lənt): being of the best quality; exceptionally good.
—Funk and Wagnalls Standard Dictionary

To achieve Six Sigma performance, the right conditions must be present. Six Sigma requires an assertive employee base, where people are willing to step outside the scope of their primary duties. The method requires a leadership team that trusts its employees and one that expects people at all levels to take full responsibility for their work. In addition, companies need employees with a strong desire to make things better. Finally, executive leadership and employees must work well together toward a common goal to make things happen.

To that end, The Performance Management Group advocates the promotion of three key ingredients within a company: corporate integration, teamwork, and commitment to the basic principles of Six Sigma. Corporate integration is the idea that executive management—through personal accountability—sets the stage by strategically deploying the Six Sigma methodology as a company's *method of operation*. The corporate mantra "if Six

Sigma is successful, then our company is successful" should be the war cry of executive management.

Teamwork, in terms of Six Sigma service excellence, is more than just working well together. Teamwork is the idea of truly becoming a *cross-functional* organization as an essential element of success. Cross-functional organizations encourage working relationships based not on a department's function but based on processes that cut across organizational boundaries. Through becoming more cross-functional, a company can base process requirements on customer expectations so the needs of the customer can be articulated throughout the company. When a company views its efforts in this fashion, its employees begin to improve their *shared* responsibilities, resulting in improved products and services for customers.

Finally, a commitment to the basic principles of Six Sigma means that everyone is behaving in a particular fashion and acting on specific tasks, which include:

- Assessing, evaluating, and satisfying customer requirements
- Looking at issues from a systems perspective and not just as employee-related problems
- Constantly examining work processes
- Eliminating duplication of effort, workarounds, and waste
- Promoting teamwork across functions
- Committing to continuous improvement throughout the company
- Measuring, measuring, and measuring
- Using statistical tools to manage by fact

The purpose of this chapter is to concisely present a step-by-step strategy that can be used to establish a performance excellence system for a service environment. This overview will define the attributes of a strong performance excellence system, explain how to focus performance efforts on an organization's core processes, describe how to integrate a measurement system, and discuss how to eliminate non-value-added tasks.

ATTRIBUTES OF A STRONG PERFORMANCE EXCELLENCE SYSTEM

A strong performance excellence system should have very specific characteristics. A Six Sigma professional should be able to judge how well a performance excellence system is established through examination of three basic dimensions: the system's approach, its deployment, and its results.

The approach of a performance excellence system relates to the management techniques and practices used to establish, monitor, and improve operational performance. A performance excellence system is strong to the degree its techniques and practices are:

- Repeatable, integrated, and consistently applied
- Subject to continuous evaluation and improvement
- Based on reliable information, facts, and data

Deployment of a performance excellence system relates to the extent to which the approach is applied to a company's core operating processes. A performance excellence system is well deployed to the degree that:

- An effective and systematic approach is fully responsive to customer and process requirements
- A very strong fact-based evaluation, improvement, and knowledge-sharing system is evident
- The approach is fully deployed throughout a company's core operating processes without significant weaknesses or gaps in any functions or departments

Results of a performance excellence system relate to the performance outcomes of a company's core operating processes. A performance excellence system is well deployed to the extent that the basis for analyzing operating performance evaluates:

- Current performance measured against a company's key success factors, standards, and goals
- Process performance and trends relative to past performance and benchmarks
- Depth, breadth, and importance of the performance improvements
- The linkage of operating results to key customer requirements, process targets, and strategic objectives

The attributes of a performance excellence system mentioned above can serve as a guideline and as an instrument for reviewing the management system of a company. A performance excellence system worksheet is available as part of the Service Excellence Handbook at the Web Added Value™ Download Resource Center at www.jrosspub.com.

FOCUSING ON CORE OPERATING PROCESSES

The key processes that are essential to the success of most service providers are:

- **Customer acquisition**: Key activities exercised to source, qualify, and establish a business relationship
- **Service delivery**: Key activities exercised to support and fulfill the obligations of the business relationship established through acquisition
- **Customer support**: Key value-added activities provided to supplement the service delivery processes and sustain customer relationships
- **Invoice and collection**: The business and transactional process (es)that facilitates the means of exchange between customer and service provider
- **Supplier and partnering processes**: Support activities which sustain the value creation chain between a company and its customers

Whether a company's processes already exist or are being established, the Six Sigma professional must answer fundamental questions regarding the design and performance of each process. Those questions include:

1. What is the purpose of each process—what services are produced or delivered?
2. Who are the customers (internal and external) of the process and what are their critical-to-quality requirements (CTQs)?
3. How does the day-to-day operation of the process ensure the company is meeting the stated customer/performance requirements?
4. What are the key performance metrics used for the control and improvement of the core processes?
5. What are the performance results and how do they relate to the goals of the processes?

Those responsible for conducting process analysis are encouraged to first analyze the extent to which their current management system promotes performance excellence and second analyze each core service operating process to determine the current corporate strengths and weaknesses. A work product of this evaluation is the performance management book. Whether this book is kept on-line or in a binder, it should serve as a source document for an organization's performance excellence program. It is an invaluable tool for management reviews. Managers will find that this tool not only will help keep track of what is important but also will serve as a historical document of operating performance. This book should be available for everyone's review. The topics in the book also should include:

- Survey information on customer needs and expectations
- Lists of process key success factors and requirements
- Process maps and performance matrices of core operating processes
- Current and historical measures of performance results (graphs, control charts, etc.)
- Current business cases relating to an ongoing DMAIC effort

Once created, the book will serve as a valuable source document and a sound basis for performance improvement within a company.

As a second work product, a process storyboard, another aid, should be produced. The purpose of the storyboard is to provide a public picture of a process and how it is performing. It can serve as a useful way to solicit suggestions for improving a process across work groups. An example of a process storyboard is shown in Figure 10.1.

A process storyboard can be created on a dry erase board and designed to convey current process performance or designed to depict the stages of a process improvement project. It can be updated to reflect quarterly, monthly, and daily performance results.

INTEGRATING MEASUREMENTS

Proper measurements are the heart and soul of an effective performance excellence system. The expression "what gets measured gets better!" is true. The objective of integrating measurements is to implement measures that

Process: Telecommunications Service Delivery	Metric	Results	Process Improvement
Customer	Quality	Cpk = 1	
Sales Engineering	Productivity	Cpk = 1.21	
Provisioning	Productivity and quality	Cpk = 1.34	
Provider/ Carrier	Timeliness	Cpk = 0.94	Integrate master service schedule with vendor
Network Operations	Timeliness and quality	Cpk = 0.85	The preceding step is a constraint; the fix will improve the capability of this step

FIGURE 10.1. Process Storyboard

govern the productivity, quality, cost, and overall effectiveness of a process and its outcomes. By measuring, an organization can:

- Accurately assess process performance and customer satisfaction
- Illustrate cause and effect relationships
- Communicate with a common vernacular among business partners and customers

The specific steps required to define process measurements were outlined in preceding chapters. Refer to the discussion of Requirements Based Process Design™ in Chapter 2 and to Chapter 6 for effective techniques to develop key success factors and performance indicators.

Control charts are very effective tools to measure operational performance. Control charts traditionally are utilized in manufacturing environments. However, service providers also have benefited greatly from the application of control charts. CTQs have been "control charted" to track cost, on-time delivery, cycle time, and safety. Control charts also are used to identify the frequency of errors and other quality characteristics. Quality characteristics should at the least be tracked whether or not they are detected by customers.

A company's performance excellence system should work to exceed customer requirements. Thus, performance targets should be realistic expectations derived from CTQs and voice of the customer assessments. The targets also should reflect the balance between what the customer is willing to pay for and what a company can realistically provide. Good performance targets will reconcile to the SMART criteria.

As mentioned earlier, Six Sigma performance is an expression of process-perfect performance. When an organization achieves Six Sigma performance, it in effect produces 3.4 defects per million opportunities. The following equation can be used as a guide to calculate the effectiveness of an operation's efforts to achieve Six Sigma process performance:

$$\frac{\text{Number of defects (errors)}}{\text{Number of opportunities} \times \text{Number of units}} \times 1,000,000$$

ELIMINATING NON-VALUE-ADDED TASKS

In everything a business does—every job, every task, and every duty, the work should directly contribute to the economic value created by the company. Moreover, these tasks should contribute directly to meeting or exceeding customer requirements. Those activities which do not contribute to value creation or customer loyalty are considered non-value-added tasks. All work that happens in a company should be derived from this way of looking at value. By understanding work in this manner, a company can create what is known as a value chain. A *value chain* is defined as a system of work and processes that directly creates value for the customer and economic profit for the company. Table 10.1 compares and contrasts value-added tasks vs. non-value-added tasks.

In building a performance excellence system, one must understand that every task creates cost. An effective performance excellence system creates a program of measurement and continuous improvement to ensure that

TABLE 10.1. Value-Added Tasks vs. Non-Value-Added Tasks

Value-Added Tasks	Non-Value-Added Tasks
▪ Preventing errors and defects	▪ Getting numerous approvals
▪ Assessing changing customer requirements	▪ Duplicating work and effort
▪ Resolving customer issues	▪ Waiting for information and producing workarounds
▪ Delivering services	▪ Creating reports that are not used
▪ Processing customer orders	▪ Attending non-productive meetings
▪ Moving, adding, or changing customer services	▪ Reworking the work products of upstream functions and work groups
▪ Developing new products	▪ Retrieving information and collecting data that are not relevant to the needs of the business
▪ Assessing customer satisfaction	
▪ Providing feedback to partners and suppliers	

economic value created by a job always exceeds its cost. To that end, a work group should critically question "why" each step in a process is performed. Interestingly enough, by scrutinizing work activities in this manner, managers often find many non-value-added tasks that exist only because of tradition. They also find other tasks that exist only because formal bureaucratic procedure ordains it. The practicality of each step should be questioned by asking "why" five times and removing those steps that common sense says you can do without. A caveat, however, is to question process steps in the presence of downstream (internal) customers. Doing so will empower you to prevent unintended consequences which potentially can occur downstream.

Once you have focused on your core processes, integrated your measurements, and eliminated non-value-added tasks, the next step is to deploy the DMAIC approach as your primary method to continuously improve your business. The DMAIC improvement model, depicted in Figure 10.2, is the generally accepted approach to process improvement for Six Sigma efforts. It is systematic, scientific, and fact based. This closed-loop process eliminates unproductive steps and improves a company's ability to remain number one in its customers' eyes. This model is the recognized quality circle. As you continually turn it, you continuously improve your company's efforts to achieve Six Sigma performance excellence.

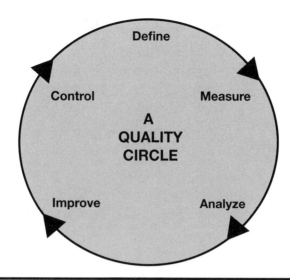

FIGURE 10.2. DMAIC Improvement Model

CONCLUSION

Hopefully, you will find value in the principles, applications, and exercises in this book. Every manager who aims to improve the productivity, efficiency, and cost effectiveness in his or her area of accountability can benefit from what this book promotes. Although the practice of Six Sigma can be a very powerful weapon for a company to use, it is not a panacea. Companies, especially service providers, should feel very confident in the applicability of these methods to their core operating processes.

You may ask: "Why is the use of statistics so important? Can't we improve things just by common sense?" The answer to this question is simple. It is true that you can improve performance by simply using common sense, but common sense can take your performance only so far. At some point in time in your effort to improve performance, you will run into the laws of probability—the "mother" of all natural laws. Statistical analysis empowers you with the knowledge to understand the laws of probability so you can make educated and informed decisions about how to improve the short- and long-term cost effectiveness of your company's operation. The practice of Six Sigma gives managers a simple and easy context for examining common cause and special cause variation and conducting root cause analysis and a method to manage and control the performance of their accountabilities. Therefore, the knowledge of statistics is vital to performance improvement. Besides, we all know that we can't fight Mother Nature, we can't fight city hall, and as managers we now know that we can't fight the laws of probability.

11

THE FUNDAMENTALS OF LEAN THINKING FOR SERVICE EXCELLENCE: DOING MORE WITH LESS!

LEAN THINKING

Thus far, we have discussed how the applications of Six Sigma are used to improve the quality, productivity, and cost effectiveness of a service operation. This book not only is dedicated to using Six Sigma as a means to achieve service excellence but is also devoted to employing Lean thinking to improve an organization's operating efficiencies. Earlier chapters alluded to the application of Lean tools without specific reference to the practice of Lean. The purpose of this chapter is to, in more explicit ways, define what Lean thinking is and how its principles are applied in a service environment.

WHAT IS LEAN?

Lean production and total quality management have a shared history. When the ideas of Deming, Juran, and Shewhart gained wide acceptance and broad implementation in post-World War II Japan, the concepts of Lean production, through the championing of Taiichi Ohno, also came to fruition. Lean manufacturing was initiated at Toyota during the 1920s by Sakichi Toyoda. In the late 1940s, Taiichi Ohno, a Toyota executive, achieved a great deal of success implementing the ideas originally conceived by Toyoda. During that time, Japanese manufacturers were plagued with a variety of problems related to quality and cost. Chief among them was the challenge of serving a Japanese market that demanded product variety, as opposed to U.S. markets and American manufacturers that followed the mantra of Henry Ford: "You can paint it [the car] any color, so long as it's black."

The traditional American system of mass production, propagated by the success of Henry Ford, lent itself to large production runs and huge inventories. The objective was to manufacture as many units of a standard part at a given time in order to take advantage of economies of scale. This method of production encouraged employees to work faster and not to worry about quality; it also encouraged companies to hold massive amounts of work-in-process and finished goods inventories. As a consequence, companies produced massive amounts of waste. There was waste in terms of scrap, defects, warranty returns, wasted time, unnecessary movement of goods, and unnecessary processing, along with the huge cost of working capital tied up in inventories. In addition, these companies were ill-equipped to deal with the product variety demanded by a marketplace growing more sophisticated. One solution to the problem was the concept and application of total quality management; another solution was the implementation of Lean manufacturing principles.

What is Lean thinking? The Lean approach refers to a company's style of inventory management and operational effectiveness. Made popular by the Toyota method of production, also known as Total Productive Maintenance, Lean thinking was given life in North America as a result of the work of MIT researchers led by James Womack, Daniel Jones, and Daniel Roos. The team of Womack, Jones, and Roos introduced the term Lean production to North America and the West in their 1990 publication *The Machine That Changed the World.** In 1996, Womack and Jones wrote another work that described the principles and applications of converting a mass production operation to a Lean operation. That book, *Lean Thinking:*

---

* Womack, J., Jones, D., and Roos, D. (1990). *The Machine That Changed the World*, New York: Harper Perennial.

*Banish Waste and Create Wealth in Your Corporation,** offers five guiding principles for practitioners:

- Determine value by product/service offering.
- Identify value streams by each product and service offering.
- Make value flow.
- Let the customer pull value from the producer.
- Pursue perfection.

So, what is Lean? In an attempt to keep things simple, Lean can be described as:

- A method of management employed to minimize operational waste
- A system of operation employed to deliver value-added products and services to customers
- A practice of producing goods just in time for customer orders to keep the inventory holding cost down
- A company's journey to eliminate the cost of operational waste from selling prices

Lean production is fundamentally a manufacturing philosophy. It has been a popular manufacturing approach because it has empowered companies to produce more with less. Successful Lean manufacturers have been able to produce more in less time, with less capital and fewer resources. Like Six Sigma, the principles of Lean can be translated into a service context. The remainder of this chapter will do just that. It is devoted to providing an introduction to certain concepts of Lean production and their applicability in a non-manufacturing setting. This chapter focuses on the concepts of value, waste, value stream mapping, and the 5S of Lean thinking.

VALUE: VALUE CREATION AND VALUE ADDED

Many books discuss value and many business professors, economists, and consultants talk extensively about value. It is this author's experience, how-

---

* Womack, J. and Jones, D. (1996). *Lean Thinking: Banish Waste and Create Wealth in Your Corporation,* New York: Simon and Schuster.

ever, that very little time is actually dedicated to defining value. Few books, lectures, economic analyses, and consultant recommendations define value in concrete terms. In the following paragraphs, this author hopes to accomplish that task.

What is value? Value is the reason a company is empowered to pursue the profit motive. It is the difference between the benefits enjoyed by a firm's customers and its cost of production.* Value is a financial concept, value is an economic concept, and value is a marketing concept. The first thing to understand about value is that it begins with the customer.

In discussing the voice of the customer in Chapter 3, it was stated that forces drive people to accomplish important tasks. It also was noted that forces drive strong and sometimes overwhelming needs for people to solve significant problems. More often than not, it is uneconomical for people to solve all of their problems or accomplish all of their goals within their own intellectual and practical means, so people go to the marketplace for solutions and assistance. When you or I go to the marketplace to achieve an objective, we become constituents of the economy. The economy answers us by providing solutions to our problems and support for our tasks. For example, suppose a college professor needs a tune-up on his BMW. He recognizes that it is an unproductive pursuit for him to seek the latest knowledge and skills of automobile maintenance just to perform a tune-up on his BMW. The economy acknowledges this fact by providing BMW automotive specialists. Economically speaking, society's utilization of both the automotive specialist and the professor is optimized when both solely dedicate themselves to their career pursuits. Society benefits from this relationship and value is created in the economy.

When the tune-up is performed, value is transferred from the automotive specialist to the professor. Market forces determine the economic and financial significance of this exchange by way of the prevailing price for service. The professor's need for maintenance on his BMW is resolved in the marketplace by the automotive specialist, and the benefit of having that problem solved is transferred from the professor to the automotive specialist by way of payment.

The automotive specialist is not the only one responsible for creating value in this exchange. She is merely the point of transaction where value

---

* Dranove, D. and Marciano, S. (2005). *Kellogg on Strategy*, Hoboken, NJ: John Wiley & Sons, p. 30.

is recognized, provided, and transacted. She needs automotive parts to produce value for the professor. Her effort and the auto parts used create value for the professor. Behind her is an entire chain of activities, transactions, and production to support the economic opportunity that resolves the professor's maintenance issue.

In the auto parts value chain, raw materials are sourced to make the auto parts. Once sourced, the materials are processed. They are then manufactured, transported to an auto parts distributor, and sold by the distributor to the BMW automotive service center. At each stage, resources are brought to bear to make the parts usable to both the professor and the automotive specialist. At each stage, resources add value to the parts so they can resolve the professor's maintenance issue. At each stage, an exchange of currency is transacted to account for the cost of the resources applied. At each stage, land, labor, and capital are compensated for the role they play in this economic value chain. This chain is illustrated in Figure 11.1.

As mentioned earlier, the economic reward for both the professor and the automotive specialist is conveyed through the market price for service. While searching for a solution to his car maintenance problem, the professor's goal is to obtain the best automotive service available at the lowest possible price. If he accomplishes his goal, he finds value and wins. The automotive specialist hopes the service she provides is respected and the wage she is provided is tendered at a premium. If she accomplishes her task, she receives value and wins. If they both accomplish their tasks, the economy has rewarded them efficiently for the value they provide.

From this example, we can safely conclude that value is an economic concept in that every person, every organization, every task, and every resource has its most efficient place in the economy. We also can conclude that value is a financial concept in that the production of products and provision of service are made meaningful through the transfer of currency from the

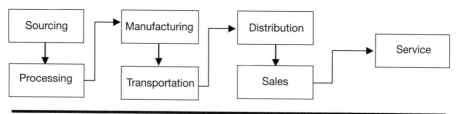

FIGURE 11.1. The Parts Value Chain

receiver of value to the provider of value. We can further conclude that value is a marketing concept in that market forces determine the price and significance that every person, every organization, every task, and every resource has in the marketplace. Let us not forget, however, that the value in our example was recognized only when the professor was driven (no pun intended) to the automotive service center out of his need to maintain his vehicle. Value starts with the customer.

A successful company wins market share when its value proposition is greater than that of its rivals. This can be accomplished in a variety of ways, many of which were discussed in Chapter 3. With respect to Lean thinking, the objective for a company is to respond to customer requirements while establishing an optimum market price for its products and services. Lean practices become a strategic competence for a company when the elimination of its waste produces a circumstance where the difference between the company's average cost to produce a product and the product's market price is significantly greater than that of its rivals. This difference provides a company with pricing power that can drive either excess profit margins for shareholders or greater market share for the company. It is in this context that we will discuss the value of Lean thinking to a services operation.

MUDA: WASTE, WASTE, WASTE

Muda (無駄) is a traditional Japanese term for activity that is wasteful, does not add value, or is unproductive. Lean's first major champion, Taiichi Ohno, described seven sources of manufacturing muda:

- **Defects and defectives**: It is very costly and wasteful to manufacture products only to rework them or throw them away. It is a waste of working capital, material, and people's time. Moreover, the cost of reworked or rejected items is almost double the cost of units produced correctly the first time.
- **Huge inventories**: Inventories tie up a company's working capital in non-productive activities. If customers change their requirements, inventories could be made obsolete and thus wasted.
- **Wasted motion**: Physical waste of movement over time has the effect of compounding interest. In an environment where speed of product to market is important, wasted time is wasted money.

- **Overproduction:** Producing more than is consumed causes a crunch of cash flow.
- **Processing:** While modifying a work product for the next phase can be a value-added activity, it does not preclude the fact that processing can involve removing some unneeded feature or attribute.
- **Waiting:** Idle operator time and large amounts of inventory waiting for the next production stage are indications of potentially large non-value-added cost.
- **Transportation of materials:** Collocating production cells can eliminate the unnecessary handling of materials and the risk and cost associated with it.

Six Sources of Service Muda

Given that this book is dedicated to service providers, The Performance Management Group has identified six typical sources of service muda that rob non-manufacturers of productivity and profits. These sources of service muda are confined to typical non-value-added activities and the cost associated with them. Non-value-added activities are those tasks which do not contribute to a company's wealth creation or customer loyalty. In a service context, non-value activities can be eliminated with no deterioration of service quality, operational performance, or perceived value to the customer. These sources of service muda are as follows:

1. **Rework:** Reworking of inaccuracies created in service orders and billing statements is the equivalent of manufacturing defects in a production operation. Reworked inaccuracies produce wasted employee time and delays and can lead to service bottlenecks.
2. **Recheck:** Some service organizations attempt to inspect quality and accuracy into their processes. Insurance claims operations, loan documentation processing, and telecommunications work orders often require job functions dedicated solely to inspecting the accuracy and completeness of documents. Accuracy and completeness of work cannot be inspected into a service process any more than quality can be inspected into a manufacturing process. Garbage, in garbage out.
3. **Reject:** Rejected service orders, loan documents, and claims cause major time delays, arguments, and customer dissatisfaction.

4. **Reprovision**: As a consequence of rejects, errors, and mistakes, service companies often are adversely impacted by reprovisioning services.

5. **Reinstall**: For many utilities, cable companies, and satellite service providers, missed service calls and improperly and erroneously provided services often require second or third attempts. Additional truck rolls can be an expensive misuse of manpower, fuel, and time. This misuse often results in greater head count requirements and/or significant use of overtime.

6. **Rebill**: Misaccounting of customer service usage contributes to customer frustration and dissatisfaction. Something done so often (billing for service) should be so easy. Rebilling customers robs a company of time, customer satisfaction, and productive use of employees.

These six sources of service muda often go unrecognized and are viewed as unimportant sources of waste by most service companies. In an attempt to control the negative consequences associated with the six sources of service muda, many service company executives merely toss more people and money at lower level managers. As a consequence, service companies operate 25 to 30% more expensively than they should.

VALUE STREAM MAPPING: ELIMINATING THE SIX SOURCES OF SERVICE MUDA

Value stream mapping is a Lean tool used to identify and eliminate non-value-added activities and the costs associated with them. The purpose of value stream mapping is to identify and document the significant activities in a corporation's core operating processes. Once the activities are identified, they are investigated and analyzed for their purpose. The conclusions of this type of analysis reveal:

■ **If the activities are necessary**: Are there manual steps that can be automated?

■ **If the activities are efficiently performed**: Is there is a significant amount of rework or an excessive number of handoffs? Is there a

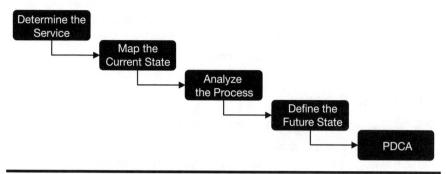

FIGURE 11.2. Value Stream Mapping

mismatch between the skill level of those performing the work and the skill level required to perform the work?

■ **If the activities serve a useful purpose**: Are there levels of approvals that are unnecessary?

Value stream mapping is an active exercise for the Six Sigma professional. The steps are shown in Figure 11.2.

Determine the Service Process

In determining the set of service activities a Six Sigma professional will map, it is best to begin with the end in mind. First understand the end work product that will be consumed by the customer. For example, a utility company may want to examine the work order process for service activation.

Map the Current State

Beginning with the end in mind, the Six Sigma professional can use the following guidelines:

1. Start with the physical activation.
2. Personally follow the flow of the work order.
3. Map what actually occurs in a backward flow.
4. Document the data personally. Document the physical information flow requirements and functional work products. Document the actual start and completion times and calculate the cycle times.
5. Map the entire workflow.

The map itself should highlight the muda in the process. An example of a value stream map is available from the Web Added Value™ Download Resource Center at www.jrosspub.com.

Analyze the Process

Value stream process analysis should include cycle time measurements, slack time at each stage of the value stream, the number of resources required to produce a work product, and the actual work time involved. Additional analysis should include any steps with significant amounts of rework, steps with large bottlenecks, steps with an excessive number of accuracy checks, or data entry steps used merely to change software applications in routing.

Once wasteful activities are identified, four techniques can be used to reduce the resulting costs:*

- **Activity reduction**: Scale back the activity by reducing the time or other resources devoted to it.
- **Activity elimination**: If the activity does not contribute to the activation of the customer's service or the invoicing of service usage, stop performing the activity.
- **Automation**: If there is an excessive amount of data entry along the value stream, opportunities for automation may exist. For example, a company may use technology and programming to dispatch service orders.
- **Activity sharing**: Combine functions in a more efficient manner. Combine the jobs of taking commercial and residential service orders. Take advantage of economies of scale.

Define the Future State

The future state value stream map is a modified workflow used to "lean" out the process and streamline activities in order to improve service efficiencies. The Six Sigma professional will work with his or her team to design individual Lean improvements. The team will recommend and document pro-

---

* Turney, Peter B.B. (1991). "How Activity-Based Costing Helps Reduce Cost," *Journal of Cost Management*, Winter, pp. 29–35.

posed activity changes, technology adoptions, or structural modifications. The map will serve as a communications tool that offers proposed solutions along with related benefits. Remember that Lean thinking is a systems improvement method; not all individual Lean improvements will result in meaningful or measurable performance improvements. Individual improvements will, over time, make the system work better and more productively.

PDCA: Plan, Do, Check, Act

The PDCA cycle is as follows:

- **Plan:** The future process state is designed and documented. An appropriate team is organized to test the improvement ideas. A plan with expected outcomes is created.
- **Do:** The improvement is piloted and tested on a small scale.
- **Check:** The outcomes are studied and evaluated. A determination is made regarding whether the expected value from the change is realized.
- **Act:** The improvement is adopted or the cycle is run again under different conditions.

The objective of the PDCA cycle is to achieve process-perfect performance. As mentioned in Chapter 9, the PDCA cycle is a quality circle, and as it rolls forward, it produces more and more knowledge about how service excellence can be achieved.

5S: GETTING YOUR SERVICE HOUSE IN ORDER

"There is a place for everything and everything in its place" is the 5S motto. 5S is the starting place for Lean thinking in a service organization. 5S stands for sort, set in order, shine, standardize, and sustain. It is the foundation of a service excellence environment in that it provides for a clean, organized, and orderly environment in which people can conduct business. The objective of 5S is to set the standards for total service efficiency, cycle time reduction, and a clean and orderly work environment. In effect, 5S is a service organization makeover.

Sort

First, determine what you want to accomplish by getting your house in order. Establish an objective of creating an environment that is free from the causes of waste. For example, a team may want to:

- Shorten the time to find the right loan documents for the appropriate loan product
- Shorten the time to find and install the right replacement part for the right vehicle
- Shorten the time to process the right claim for the right claim profile

Outside of the special causes discussed in prior chapters, waste can be caused by the work environment when people search for supplies and cannot find them. Time is wasted when people unsuccessfully sift through piles of documents and files. Wasted time is compounded when the unsuccessful searcher enlists the help of others in his or her effort. Whatever your circumstance, establish your objectives before initiating the 5S program.

Next, assess the current working conditions of the value chain from end to end. Inspect and take pictures of the workplace in order to baseline the current state of affairs. Look at your service operation for improvement. Assess your:

- Order-taking call center
- Dispatch area
- Expediting operation
- Warehouse
- Service yard
- Service vehicles

The service operation is where value is created; it must be maintained in the highest order. Search everyplace where clutter, supplies, documents, or stock might be. Look for excessive supply inventory, clutter, or documents that are out of place. Look at the big picture. Determine if functional groups in the same value chain are located near each other. If your service organization is a financial institution, see if loan documents and files are piled on tables or stacked inside of boxes put in a corner. If your organization is a service center, determine whether supplies are in their correct bin space and if bins are correctly labeled.

Afterward, distinguish which work items are necessary to do the job from those that are not. Remove the unnecessary items from the work area. Sort out all accumulated and unnecessary supplies and documents. Remove any miscellaneous items that are not for customer use. Also, sift out those items that are either outdated or obsolete. Move all unrelated items to a holding place for evaluation. Form an evaluation team and conduct an assessment for disposal of outdated and unusable items. Then put the needed items in their appropriate place to allow for easy access and use.

Set in Order

Once clutter has been removed from the value chain, the team should think about how to redesign it for the most efficient way to conduct business. First, if possible, configure the work area so the links in the value chain are located physically close to each other. Place the order takers close to the dispatch operators, align the sales operations clerks close to the provisioning department, and put the credit department close to sales operations. The closer you configure work groups that are part of the same value chain, the greater the communication and the better the production of quality work products. The process can be improved through a reduction of time and space between work groups.

Shine

The new workplace should be clutter free. A clutter-free work environment is conducive to a more orderly and productive work product flow. Set a new level of orderliness for the workplace. Afterward, carryout routine inspections. Make the results of the audits visible.

Standardize

Standardized work should include work instructions for each activity in the value chain. The work instructions should always be displayed in the workplace. Expectations of quality, quantity, and effort should be embedded in the work instructions. The instructions and performance expectations should reconcile to the workflow requirements demanded by the customer and planned for by the business. For additional tools used in the standardized value chain, refer to the process storyboard in Chapter 10.

Sustain

The Japanese word for sustain is *shitsucke,* which means self-discipline. The purpose of the sustain portion of 5S is to maintain the high standards established in the first four phases. The intent of shitsucke is for each individual to maintain a high level of personal and professional commitment to the continuous improvement of the 5S standards. 5S is the foundation for Lean principles in a service organization.

CONCLUSION

The purpose of this chapter was to define what Lean thinking is and how its principles are applied in a service environment. I write this chapter with one caveat: you should read it with the understanding that Lean principles are primarily manufacturing tools for the Six Sigma professional. My intent was to provide an overview of the fundamentals of Lean methodology that are applicable in a non-manufacturing context.

12

LEAN SIX SIGMA SERVICE EXCELLENCE: A ROAD MAP TO GREEN BELT CERTIFICATION

The Six Sigma green belt is a Six Sigma–certified individual working on a project team to solve a specific performance problem and implement improvements in company operations. Each green belt is responsible for using Six Sigma methods and is accountable for the overall success of the team. A green belt's responsibility includes:

- Developing metrics and tracking performance
- Attending all team meetings prepared and on time
- Collecting, organizing, and analyzing data
- Conducting root cause analysis of performance problems
- Generating solutions for improvement
- Successfully implementing solutions

To become green belt certified, a candidate must demonstrate:

1. The successful application of Lean Six Sigma tools and techniques
2. The aptitude to work successfully with and through others to achieve results
3. The ability to successfully complete the DMAIC process

LEAN SIX SIGMA SERVICE EXCELLENCE GREEN BELT CERTIFICATION PROGRAM

By virtue of reading this book, you have embarked on an inexpensive path to becoming green belt certified. Through The Performance Management Group (TPMG) on-line classroom, you can participate in an intensive 40-hour on-line training and certification program. The program consists of:

1. The Roots of Six Sigma
2. Process Design and Management
3. The Voice of the Customer
4. The Six Sigma Analytical Tool Set
5. Statistical Process Control for Service Excellence
6. Measurement Systems Analysis—Gage R&R
7. Failure Mode and Effects Analysis
8. Team Dynamics and People Skills
9. Financial Impact Analysis
10. DMAIC Project Management

TPMG's on-line training offers two environments—interactive and self-paced:

- **Interactive on-line:** A real-time training environment driven by a TPMG master black belt (MBB). The real-time environment provides for a real classroom setting with student participants from around the globe. On-line MBB instruction is conducted in a most dynamic on-line environment.
- **Self-paced on-line:** Similar to the interactive classroom in every respect with the exception that the MBB coaching is on an as-needed basis and you can drive the time and place for your on-line sessions.

TOOLS

By now, you should have purchased your Six Sigma software application (QI Macros) either from TPMG directly or from http://www.qimacros.com/products.php?PARTNER=tpmgllc. If you have not, you are encouraged to do so before registering for your green belt on-line training. In addition, visit the Web Added Value™ Download Resource Center at www.jrosspub.com. The Lean Six Sigma for Service Excellence download is a required resource, in addition to this book, to proceed through the training experience.

At the end of your training, you will be provided with a comprehensive green belt examination. Upon successful completion of the examination, you will be certified as a Lean Six Sigma Green Belt.

We at TPMG have worked with a variety of service-oriented companies and are humbled by the creativity of people and their new perspectives on this topic. We are very excited about the fact that Lean Six Sigma is becoming very popular with retailers, utility companies, government agencies, financial and insurance companies, health care organizations, call center operations, and other service providers around the globe. As you embark on your performance excellence journey, we would like to hear from you about how this book has helped you. Feel free to e-mail us at info@helpingmakeithappen.com.

GLOSSARY

Baldrige Criteria for Performance Excellence: The criteria used as the basis for organizational self-assessment and for making awards in the Malcolm Baldrige National Quality Award program. The criteria include assessment of organizational leadership; strategic planning; customer and market focus; measurement, analysis, and knowledge management; workforce focus; process management; and business results.

Bell curve: Also known as the Gaussian distribution, the bell curve is a cumulative distribution function where the average is in the middle and the curve has a perfectly symmetrical shape.

Black belt: Technical expert, trained and certified in statistical analysis and the DMAIC method, who has accountability for leading a Six Sigma improvement effort.

Business context: The organizational structures, systems, circumstances, and expectations of a business enterprise.

Cause and effect diagram: Also known as the fishbone or Ishikawa diagram, the cause and effect diagram is a tool used during brainstorming sessions to study the factors that may have some bearing on a given situation.

c chart (number of defects chart): Used as a metric to measure and graphically display process performance for discrete or attribute data. As its name implies, the c chart is used to examine the number of errors or defects per work product produced by an operation. The c chart is used when the subgroup size is constant.

Central tendency rule: A special cause analysis rule, used in analyzing control charts, that indicates the presence of special cause variation in operating performance if 15 or more consecutive points fall within one sigma of the centerline.

Common cause variation: A natural consequence of production factors coming together in the performance of a process. Common cause variation is performance variation that is free from special cause variation.

Consensus: The general acceptance of a decision by a group along with the commitment of group members to support a course of action.

Continuous data: The type of data that yields a measurement or number for each unit measured. Continuous data most often are used to measure an operation's productivity, efficiency, or cost effectiveness.

Continuous process improvement: A quality improvement method and business practice aimed at increasing productivity of and eliminating waste in manufacturing and service delivery operations.

Cost of poor quality: The price, in terms of excess cost, a company pays for not being process perfect. It includes those costs associated with failing to produce quality work products or deliver a quality service.

Critical-to-quality requirement (CTQ): The voice of the customer expressed as quantitative measures and qualitative expectations.

Cross-functional organization: An organizational design and management style that promotes structuring process accountabilities across departments and functions.

Customer(s): The receiver of an output(s). Customers may be either internal or external to a company. The ultimate customer is the end user or the recipient of the final product.

Customer attitude: A customer's tendency to evaluate a company's product or service in a favorable or unfavorable way.

Customer loyalty: A customer's commitment to a company's product or service. A loyal customer operates with extreme prejudice toward a company's products and services.

Customer need: The force that directs customers toward the achievement of certain goals.

Cycle rule: A special cause analysis rule, used in analyzing control charts, that indicates the presence of special cause variation if any non-random pattern recurs eight or more consecutive times.

Customer perception: The way customers organize and interpret information about a company and its products and services.

Data sheet: A spreadsheet used to collect, record, and inventory data for evaluation.

Defect: The lack of conformance to a specification for a single portion of a work product.

Defective: A non-conforming/non-performing product or service that in some way fails to conform to one or more requirements.

Design for Six Sigma (DFSS): Also known as DMADV, which stands for define, measure, analyze, design, and verify. It is used primarily to design and develop new products and processes.

Design of Experiments: A structured, organized method, used in Six Sigma, for determining cause and effect relationships. Design of Experiments methods are used for conducting and analyzing controlled tests to evaluate factors that control a parameter or group of parameters.

Discrete data: The type of data that is categorical or where the attributes measured relate to defects or defective units. Discrete data most often are used to measure the quality of an operation's work product.

DMAIC: Acronym that stands for define, measure, analyze, improve, and control. The DMAIC method is a systematic problem-solving methodology that resolves issues at the root cause.

External failure cost: The cost of poor quality that occurs after the delivery of a product or service to a customer. Examples of external failure cost for services include the cost of patient returns, complaint investigations, warranty claims, fines and penalties, lawsuits, returned food, customer credits, lost customers, and reprovision and redelivery of services.

5S: The starting place for Lean thinking in a service organization. 5S is an acronym for a series of Lean activities that stands for sort, set in order, shine, standardize, and sustain.

Flowchart: A process design and analysis method that structures a process as a series of steps an operation performs to produce a work product or deliver a service.

Focus group: Informal loosely structured customer interview with a group of roughly 8 to 12 participants.

Green belt: A Six Sigma–trained individual working on a project team to solve a specific performance problem and implement improvements in company operations.

Groupthink: Occurs when team members striving for unanimity overrides their motivation to realistically appraise alternative courses of action.*

Hidden factory: The resources engaged in error correction and rework activities.

Histogram: A type of bar chart that enables a decision maker to display operational performance in a graphical representation.

Input(s): Work product of the supplier that meets the requirements of the customer.

Internal failure cost: The cost of poor quality that occurs before or during the delivery of a product or service to a customer. It is typically a negative by-product of the lack of quality in a service delivery operation. Examples of internal failure cost for services include the cost of process rework, redesigning networks, post-operation infections, longer hospital stays, incorrect billing, and on-the-job accidents.

ISO 9000:2000: The standard that provides a set of standardized guidelines for quality management systems in the private and public sectors.

Kaizen: Applied to management, kaizen is a Japanese philosophy and business practice that focuses on continuous improvement throughout all aspects of the workplace. Kaizen activities continually improve all functions of a business from manufacturing to service management and from the assembly line workers to a company's chief executive.

Key performance indicator: Indicator that directly measures the productivity, efficiency, or quality of an organization's core operating processes.

---

* Janis, Irving I. (1982). *Groupthink*, Boston: Houghton Mifflin.

Lean production: A method of management employed to minimize operational waste. A system of operation employed to deliver value-added products and services to customers. A practice of producing goods just in time for customer orders to keep the inventory holding cost down. A company's journey to eliminate the cost of operational waste from the selling price.

Malcolm Baldrige National Quality Award: A national award created in 1987 to promote the principles, values, and practices of quality improvement. Principal support for the program comes from the Foundation for the Malcolm Baldrige National Quality Award. The program is managed by the National Institute of Standards and Technology, an agency of the U.S. Department of Commerce.

Management by fact: A business practice of decision making and problem solving with numerical facts and information along with the experience and expertise of managers.

Mean: The simple average of a set of values.

Median: The halfway point in a set of data.

Metric: The measurement tool and operational definition of a key performance indicator.

Mode: The most frequently occurring value in an array or range of data.

Muda (無駄): A traditional Japanese term for activity that is wasteful, does not add value, or is unproductive.

np chart (number of defectives chart): Used as a metric to measure and graphically display operational performance for discrete data. As the name implies, the np chart is used to track the number of defective work products produced by an operation. The np chart is used when the subgroup size is constant.

Observation beyond the control limits: A special cause analysis rule, used in analyzing control charts, that indicates the presence of special cause variation if one or more points fall beyond either the upper or lower control limit(s).

One-sigma variation: A special cause analysis rule, used in analyzing control charts, that indicates the presence of special cause variation if four out of five points in a row fall more than one sigma away from the performance average.

Output(s): The product of both the inputs and work process applied. Outputs become inputs to another process. Outputs may be either tangible products or intangible services.

Pareto analysis: A method used to clarify the most significant factors that can have bearing on a given situation.

Pareto diagram: A bar chart that organizes data according to significance.

Pareto principle: Also known as the 80/20 rule, it states that 80% of a problem is caused by 20% of its contributors. This principle seeks to separate the vital few issues from the trivial many.

p chart (proportion of defectives chart): Used as a metric to measure and graphically display operational performance for discrete data. As the name implies, the p chart is used to track the fraction or *percentage* of defective work products in a given subgroup. The p chart is used when the subgroup size varies.

PDCA: Acronym for plan, do, check, act. PDCA is the quality circle established by the Japanese as taught by Deming during the 1950s. As its name implies, after every action, there will be evaluations of what has happened, followed by further action.

Performance: To fulfill an obligation or requirement; to accomplish something as promised or expected.

Process: A series of requirements that must be satisfied in order to produce something of value. A process consists of steps, methods, and techniques applied to inputs that result in work products and outputs.

Process capability: The ability of an operation to meet its expected requirements.

Process capability index (Cpk): For continuous (variable) data, Cpk is expressed as the ratio of the maximum variation defined by a specification or process standard (customer tolerance) to the level of variation an operation is currently producing.

Process manager: The individual who is accountable for process results, who allocates resources, and who resolves or escalates process issues.

Process owner(s): The individual who actually produces an output. The process owner is the "voice of the process" to the organization and also is responsible for validating plans for changes in the work process, gathering performance data and information, and implementing changes.

Process re-engineering: A management approach aimed at improvements by means of optimizing the variables in work processes that exist within and across organizations. It achieves this end through management looking at business processes as a clean slate and then designing or redesigning the system in the best configuration that will produce an optimal level of performance.

Productivity: A measure of the output of an organization divided by its inputs. It is also defined as the output, or increase in the output, of a department(s) for which a manager has accountability and departments with which a manager has a significant working relationship.

Quality: Quality work is producing a product or service that conforms to customer wants, needs, and expectations as defined by "customer requirements." It means creating a product or a service that is "fit" for customer use.

Requirements: Customer wants, needs, and expectations of an output—also known as critical-to-quality requirements. Requirements may be expressed as measures of quantity, timeliness, accuracy, and other characteristics.

Requirements Based Process Design™: A process design and analysis method that structures a process as a series of requirements that must be satisfied to produce a work product or deliver a service.

Root cause analysis: Analyzing a problem until the primary agent or force producing an error is identified.

Run chart: Also known as a line graph and trend chart, a run chart is a graph of performance data captured over time.

Scatter diagram: Also known as a scatter plot, a scatter diagram is a tool used to graphically illustrate the possible relationship between two quantitative variables.

Shift rule: A special cause analysis rule, used in analyzing run charts and control charts, that indicates the presence of special cause variation if eight or more consecutive points fall above or below the process average.

SIPOC diagram: A process scoping and analysis tool that structures a process in terms of its suppliers, inputs, processes, outputs, and customers.

Six Sigma: A *quality improvement business practice* that strives to produce perfection in the delivery of products and services. A *management method* that uses facts, information, and data to make decisions and manage business performance. A *problem-solving method* that identifies root causes of problems and determines permanent solutions.

Special cause variation: Performance variation that can be attributed to an extraordinary factor or set of factors acting on an operation. Also known as assignable cause variation.

Statistical process control: A method of analyzing operational performance by taking samples of operational results, at specified time intervals, and charting the outcomes in a graphical summary. Statistical process control is used for process assessment, process comparison, and process verification.

Subgroup: A sample drawn from an operation under controlled circumstances for the purpose of observation and conducting statistical analysis.

Suppliers: Individuals and organizations, whether internal or external to an organization, whose work products serve as inputs.

Survey: A quantitative form of information gathering and data collection that provides a company a way to express its customers' needs, attitudes, and perceptions numerically.

System: The elements and components of a process leveraged by a management team to produce a product or deliver a service. A system consists of people, methods and procedures, technology, materials, information, and management decision making.

Transaction: The exchange of assets or work products as a means to create a work product or deliver a service.

Trend rule: A special cause analysis rule, used in analyzing run charts and control charts, that indicates the presence of special cause variation if seven consecutive points move in the same direction.

Two-sigma variation: A special cause analysis rule, used in analyzing control charts, that indicates the presence of special cause variation if two out of three points in a row fall more than two sigma away from the centerline.

u chart (average number of defects per unit chart): Used as a metric to measure and graphically display process performance for discrete or attribute data. As its name implies, the u chart is used to examine the error rate or rate of defects produced by an operation. The u chart is used when subgroup size varies.

Value: Economically speaking, value is the benefit an organization brings to the market less the cost to bring the benefit to the market.

Value chain: The chain of activities facilitated in order to bring value to the marketplace.

Voice of the customer: A customer's positive or negative predisposition toward a company's products or services. This predisposition is based on the customer's needs, attitude, and perception of a company's products and services.

$\overline{X}$,R chart (average and range chart): Used as a metric to measure and graphically display operational performance for continuous data. The average chart (the upper chart) is used to evaluate the central tendency of operational performance by measuring process average over time. It also is used to measure and evaluate performance variation between subgroups. The range chart (the lower chart) is used to evaluate the dispersion or process variation within subgroups over time. Average and range charts are used when subgroup sizes are greater than 1 but less than 10.

$\overline{X}$,S chart (average and standard deviation chart): Similar to average and range charts in all but one respect: the subgroup standard deviation is used to measure within-group variation standard deviation rather than the subgroup range. Like $\overline{X}$,R charts, $\overline{X}$,S charts also are used as a metric to measure and graphically display operational performance for continuous data. They should be used in situations where subgroup size is large ($n \geq 10$).

XmR chart (individual measurement with moving range chart): Used as a metric to measure and graphically display operational performance for continuous data. As the name implies, XmR charts track individual measures.

REFERENCES

Assael, H. (1990). *Marketing Principles and Strategy,* Chicago: The Dryden Press, p. 125.

Brewer, R.F. (1996). *Design of Experiments for Process Improvement and Quality Assurance,* Engineering & Management Press.

Costanzo, C. (2002). "Bank Takes on Six Sigma: Service at Morgan, Processing at SunTrust," *American Banker,* June 5.

Dalesio, E. (2003). "Girl in Botched Heart-Lung Transplant Dies," Associated Press, February 23.

Dobbs, L. (2005). "The Global Outlook on Outsourcing," CNN.com, January 31, posted 1927 GMT (0327 HKT).

Dranove, D. and Marciano, S. (2005). *Kellogg on Strategy,* Hoboken, NJ: John Wiley & Sons.

General Electric Corporate Management Development—Corporate Entry-Level Programs (1993). GE Problem Solving and Project Management Tool Kit, Fairfield, CT: General Electric Company.

General Electric Corporate Management Development—Corporate Entry-Level Programs (1993). GE Problem Solving and Project Management Users Guide, Fairfield, CT: General Electric Company.

General Electric Web site: http://www.ge.com/sixsigma/sixsigstrategy.html, http://www.ge.com/sixsigma/keyelements.html.

Hilton, R.W. (1994). *Managerial Accounting,* New York: McGraw-Hill.

isixsigma Web site: isixsigma.com.

Janis, I. (1982). *Groupthink,* Boston: Houghton Mifflin.

The Juran Institute (2002). *The Six Sigma Basic Training Kit,* New York: McGraw-Hill.

Kreitner, R. (1989). *Management,* Boston: Houghton Mifflin.

Pande, P., Neuman, R., and Cavanagh, R. (2000). *The Six Sigma Way: How GE, Motorola, and Other Top Companies Are Honing Their Performance,* New York: McGraw-Hill.

Peter, B. and Turney, B. (1991). "How Activity-Based Costing Helps Reduce Cost," *Journal of Cost Management,* Winter, pp. 29–35.

Pyzdek, T. (2003). *The Six Sigma Handbook: A Guide to Green Belts, Black Belts and Managers at All Levels,* New York: McGraw-Hill.

Rue, L.W. and Byars, L.L. (1999). *Supervision: Key Link to Productivity,* New York: McGraw-Hill.

U.S. Department of Commerce, National Institute of Standards and Technology (2003). Criteria for Performance Excellence, Baldrige National Quality Program.

U.S. Department of Labor, Employment and Training Administration (1998). Voice of the Customer Manual, 2nd edition.

U.S. Department of Labor, Employment and Training Administration (1998). Voice of the Customer Workbook, 2nd edition.

Walton, M. (1986). *The Deming Management Method,* New York: Perigee Books/ Putnam Publishing Group.

Whitehouse, M. and Aeppel, T. (2006). "Pause Stirs Concern That Growth in Productivity May Be Flattening," *Wall Street Journal,* November 3.

Womack, J. and Jones, D. (1996). *Lean Thinking: Banish Waste and Create Wealth in Your Corporation,* New York: Simon and Schuster.

Womack, J., Jones, D., and Roos, D. (1990). *The Machine That Changed the World,* New York: Harper Perennial.

Zenger, J.H., Mussel, E., Hurson, K., and Perrin, C. (1994). *Leading Teams: Mastering the New Role,* New York: McGraw-Hill.

APPENDIX A:
CHAPTER 4
EXERCISE ANSWERS

RUN CHART CONSTRUCTION EXERCISE

Call Center Response Times

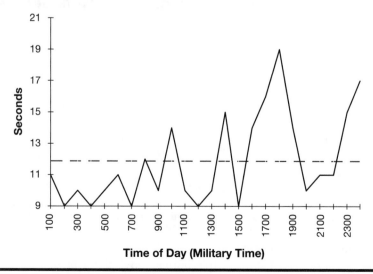

Run Chart for Average Speed of Answer

RUN CHART ANALYSIS EXERCISES

Run Chart Analysis Exercise 1:
Number of Application Errors

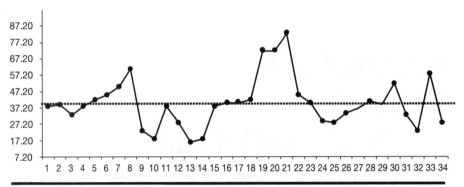

Run Chart for Number of Application Errors

Conclusion: No special cause is present.
Rationale: No rules are violated.

Run Chart Analysis Exercise 2:
Monthly Cost of Telecommunications Network Services

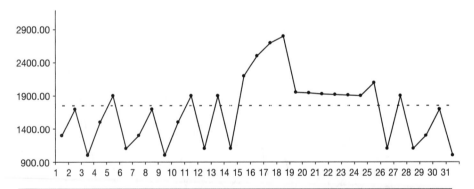

Run Chart for Monthly Cost of Telecommunications Network Services

Conclusion: A shift is present.
Rationale: There are 11 consecutive points above the average.

Run Chart Analysis Exercise 3: Total Defects

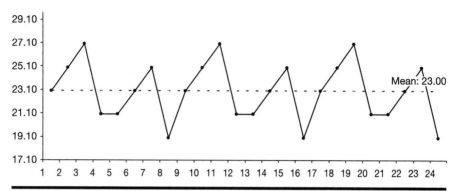

Run Chart for Total Defects Found on Visual Inspection

Conclusion: No special cause is present.
Rationale: No rule is violated.

APPENDIX B: CHAPTER 5 EXERCISE ANSWERS

HISTOGRAM EXERCISE

Understanding Call Center Efficiencies

Number of data points $N = 100$
Range $R = 217 - 192 = 25$
Classes $K = 10$
Class width $H = 25/10 = 2.5$ rounded up to 3

Class Number	Class Limits	Tally	Frequency
1	192–194	///// ///// ////	14
2	195–197	///// ///// ///// ///// ///// //	27
3	198–200	///// ///// ///// ///// ///// /////	30
4	201–203	///// ///// //	12
5	204–206	///	3
6	207–209	//	2
7	210–212	///// ////	9
8	213–215	//	2
9	216–218	/	1
10	219–221		0
		Total	100

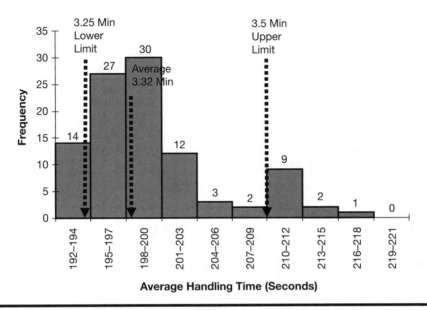

Histogram for Average Handling Time

The call center's ability to meet its efficiency standard varies. The mean time to process calls to the center is 3.3 minutes—well within the center's acceptable efficiency standard. Almost three-fourths of the calls are handled in between 195 and 209 seconds—which is considered to be within the call center's acceptable efficiency standard. However, 12% of the call volume is observed to be beyond the center's acceptable efficiency standard, while 14% of the call volume is processed at a faster rate than expected. A review of the call mix during certain time periods may enable management to better understand the reason for the variation.

CAUSE AND EFFECT DIAGRAM EXERCISE

A Hot Time in the City

It has been almost a year since you changed the oil in your car. Your engine overheated due to a lack of viscosity in the oil. Does this cause appear on your fishbone diagram?

SCATTER DIAGRAM EXERCISE

Field Operations Supervisor

The scatter diagram below conveys a couple of obvious things. First, there seems to be a correlation between experience and productivity. With the exception of three employees, years on the job seems to explain weekly production. At first glance, it seems the only way to improve the production of the installation team is to hire experienced personnel. However, outliers do exist. After further analysis, it seems that certification training may have a favorable impact on inexperienced employees.

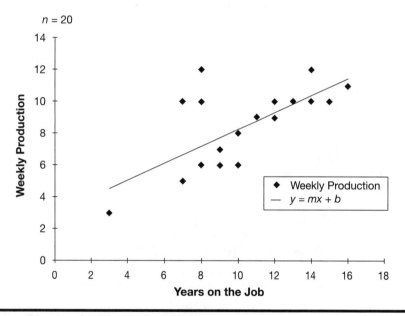

Scatter Diagram for Weekly Installation Production

PARETO ANALYSIS EXERCISE

Cost Due to Poor Health Care Quality

Stratification #1: By Error Type

Error Type	Number of Occurrences	Cumulative Percentages
Invoicing errors	560	51%
Medication errors	210	71%
Instrument in body	140	83%
Wound reopening	120	94%
Blood infection	60	100%

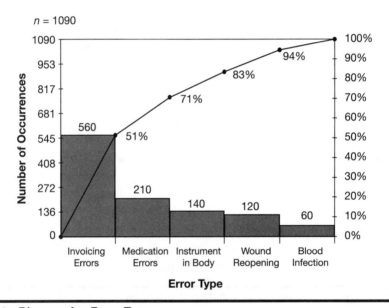

Pareto Diagram for Error Type

Stratification #2: By Month

Month	Number of Errors	Cumulative Percent
February	200	18%
March	200	35%
May	190	52%
January	180	68%
April	180	84%
June	180	100%

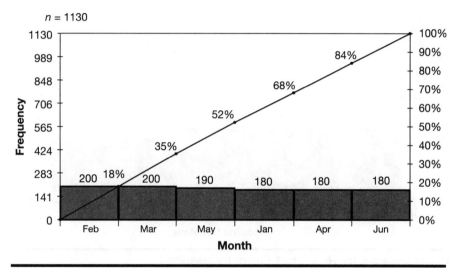

Pareto Diagram for Number of Errors by Month

Stratification #3: By Hospital Facility

Hospital Facility	Number of Errors	Cumulative Percent
West	380	35%
South	380	70%
North	330	100%

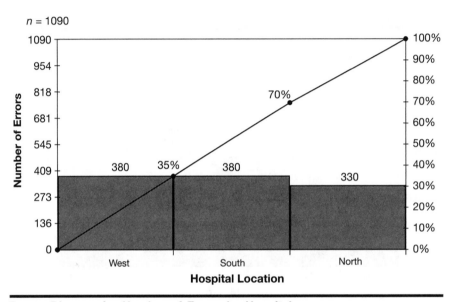

Pareto Diagram for Number of Errors by Hospital

Stratification #4: By Cost of Error Type

Error Type	Cost	Cumulative Percent
Wound reopening	$639,000	47%
Blood infection	$416,100	78%
Instrument in body	$182,000	91%
Medication errors	$105,000	99%
Invoicing errors	$14,280	100%

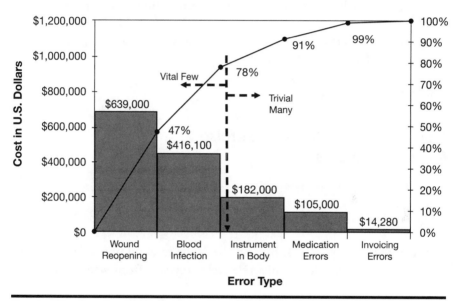

Pareto Diagram for Total Cost by Error Type

Conclusion

The fourth and fifth greatest number of errors account for the first and second highest level of cost due to poor quality. The Pareto diagram for total cost by error type does not reveal the Pareto principle in the strictest sense, but starkly separates the vital few from the trivial many with respect to the cost of wound reopening and blood infections—almost 80% of the excess costs are due to these two issues. The next step should be to move forward in understanding what is at the root of these error types and take corrective action.

CONTROL CHART SELECTION EXERCISES

Control Chart Selection Exercise 1: Filling Job Vacancies

Type of Data: Discrete data.

CTQ Tracked: Count the number of jobs filled by external candidates out of the total number of vacancies. The data are "defectives" data, where the count indicates whether jobs were filled by promotion (conforming) or not.

Subgroup Size Vary?: The number of job vacancies (subgroup size) varies considerably from month to month.

Control Chart: p chart.

Control Chart Selection Exercise 2: Reworked Orders

Type of Data: Discrete data.

CTQ Tracked: Track the total number of reworked orders per week.

Subgroup Size Vary?: The subgroup size is the total number of new service orders per week, and it remains relatively constant from week to week.

Control Chart: np chart.

Control Chart Selection Exercise 3: Call Center Response Times

Type of Data: Continuous data.

CTQ Tracked: Average speed of answer (in seconds) taken every hour.

Subgroup Size Vary?: No. A sample of one is taken once every hour.

Control Chart: XmR chart (individual measurement with moving range chart).

Control Chart Selection Exercise 4: Monthly Revenue

Type of Data: Continuous data.

CTQ Tracked: Total revenue recorded on a monthly basis.

Subgroup Size Vary?: No. Subgroup of one—total revenue at month end.

Control Chart: XmR chart (individual measurement with moving range chart).

CONTROL CHART ANALYSIS EXERCISE

Restoring Customer Outages

1. The appropriate chart to use is the $\overline{X}$,R chart. Subgroup size is 5, it is a continuous data set, and there are 30 subgroups.
2. Constructed as shown on the next page.
3. The $\overline{X}$ chart shows no evidence of special cause variation present in the process outcomes. However, there does appear to be some within-group variation observed in the range chart that may deserve some attention.
   Note: It is common practice to evaluate the range chart for special cause variation first before examining the $\overline{X}$ chart. The accepted understanding is that a range chart must indicate within-group stability in order for the control limits of the average chart to be deemed valid. The value of this consideration is the subject of much debate; the value of range charts has not been demonstrated by academics. Six Sigma professionals, however, can use range charts for closer scrutiny when examining process performance.
4. It is appropriate to monitor process performance and continuously improve how the national network operations center executes its work.

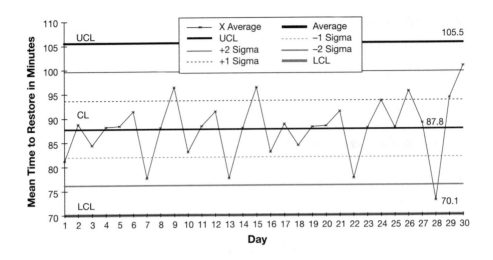

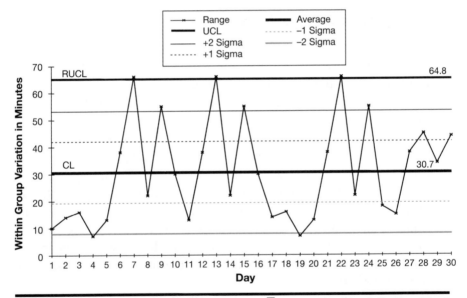

Control Charts for Mean Time to Restore: X̄ Chart (Top) and Range Chart (Bottom)

APPENDIX C: ADDITIONAL LEAN SIX SIGMA TOOLS AND METHODS

CORRELATION AND REGRESSION ANALYSIS

Correlation and regression analysis is used to determine the strength and direction of a linear relationship that exists between two continuous variables. Correlation and regression analysis can be used for three major reasons:

- **Prediction**: To estimate how the number of sales calls made in a month translates into the number of units sold
- **Explanation**: To determine to what extent the amount of money spent on customer service training impacts customer satisfaction
- **Optimization**: To determine the strength of the relationship between the call center service level and staffing levels

Correlation Analysis

The strength and direction of a correlation are defined and measured by its correlation coefficient (r). The value of r will always fall between -1 and 1:

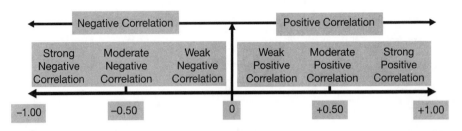

FIGURE 1. **Relative Strength of the Correlation Coefficient**

- 1 indicates a perfect positive correlation.
- 0 indicates no correlation.
- −1 indicates a perfect negative correlation.

The scale for the relative strength of the correlation coefficient (r) is illustrated in Figure 1.

When the formula for the correlation coefficient (r) is used, the sign is determined automatically, without the need to observe or calculate the slope of the regression line. The formula is:

$$r = \frac{\sum (X_i - \overline{X})(Y_i - \overline{Y})}{\sqrt{\sum (X_i - \overline{X})^2 \sum (Y_i - \overline{Y})^2}}$$

Construction with QI Macros

1. Format the data in the same fashion as for scatter plot construction.
2. Highlight the labels and data in two columns (independent and dependent variables).
3. Select **QI Macros > ANOVA and Analysis Tools**.
4. Select **Correlation > OK**.

Example

You are a Six Sigma green belt who works for a regional transportation trucking company. You are interested in the relationship between distance in miles and the number of days to deliver. You take a sample of 15 recent deliveries. The data for the analysis are shown in Table 1.

TABLE 1. Correlation Analysis Data Sheet

Trip	Distance (Miles)	Deliver Time (Days)
1	935	8.5
2	325	6.0
3	1180	9.0
4	660	7.0
5	590	6.0
6	1030	8.0
7	1460	8.5
8	435	6.5
9	780	8.0
10	1325	10.0
11	675	7.0
12	1512	11.0
13	510	5.0
14	1585	11.5
15	1172	9.0

The results of correlation analysis on these data are shown in Table 2. Based on the data, you find a very strong relationship between distance in miles and the number of days to deliver service. Your conclusion justifies your assumptions before you performed the analysis.

Correlation Analysis Exercise

Purpose: To conduct correlation analysis and draw a conclusion.

Action: Use the example and data from the scatter diagram exercise in Chapter 5 to conduct correlation analysis.

Scenario: You are a supervisor for a cable company's field operations. You have observed a somewhat linear relationship between the level of experience

TABLE 2. Results of Correlation Analysis

	Distance (Miles)	Deliver Time (Days)
Distance (miles)	1	
Deliver time (days)	0.922686186	1

TABLE 3. Results for Correlation Analysis Exercise

	Years on the Job	Weekly Production
Years on the job		
Weekly production		

of an installation technician and the total number of installations he or she can perform in a week. Your aim now is to quantify your results and analyze the overall strength and direction of that relationship. Based on the data in Table 5.9, perform correlation analysis and enter your results in Table 3.

Your Conclusion: The correlation matrix confirms a _____ correlation with a calculated correlation coefficient of $r =$ _____.

Simple Linear Regression Analysis

Simple linear regression analysis is used to express, in greater depth, the relationship between a continuous response variable and a continuous explanatory variable. This relationship is expressed in an equation that allows the use of numerical facts to explain, predict, and optimize circumstances in a work situation. It can reveal what percent of the outcomes for a response variable can be explained by its linear relationship with an explanatory variable.

The general equation for a simple linear regression model* is:

$$\hat{y} = a + bx + \varepsilon$$

where $\hat{y}$ = the value of the response variable predicted by the slope and y intercept of the regression equation, a = the y intercept of the estimated regression equation or the point where the regression line crosses the y-axis, b = the average change in y for each unit change in x, and ε = random error.

Simple linear regression can help answer questions like:

■ How is the number of errors made in the application process related to cycle time?

---

* The linear regression equation is just an estimate of the relationship between two variables in a population. The values of a and b, thus, usually are referred to as *estimated regression coefficients*.

- What impact would an additional five employees have on the call center's average speed of answer?
- How much will annual bookstore sales increase given a 10% increase in the student population?

Simple linear regression is used when *y* is continuous and you have a single *x* variable. The following conditions also must be met:

- *x* can be ordinal or continuous.
- The residuals are normally distributed.
- The residuals are independent.
- The residuals have constant variance across all values of *x*.

Some General Terms

Figure 2 shows a scatter diagram for the cable company field operations supervisor exercise in Chapter 5. It is used here to illustrate some general terms associated with linear regression analysis. The first term is the regres-

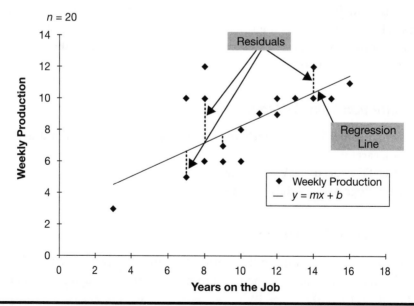

FIGURE 2. Scatter Diagram for Weekly Productivity

sion line. The regression line is the line that illustrates and approximates the linear relationship that exists between the x and y variables.

The least squares regression line (equation) is the best-fitting line that makes the residuals as a group as short as possible. The object of fitting the least squares line is to minimize the sum of the squares of the residuals.

If the general equation for the regression line is

$$\hat{y} = a + bx + \varepsilon$$

then the formulas by which the values of a and b in the regression equation can be established for the equation that satisfies the least squares regression criterion are:

$$b = \frac{\sum XY - n\overline{X}\overline{Y}}{\sum X^2 - n\overline{X}^2}$$

$$a = \overline{Y} - m\overline{X}$$

The regression line can be used as a graphical tool to explain, forecast, and draw conclusions about the relationship that exists between two variables. The second term is the residual. A residual is the difference between an actual observed value of y (response value) and the value predicted by the regression line (equation).

Construction with QI Macros

1. Highlight the data and labels in two columns (independent and dependant variables).
2. Select **QI Macros > ANOVA and Analysis Tools.**
3. Select **Regression Analysis > OK.**

Analysis and Conclusion

The regression was run using the scatter diagram exercise in Chapter 5 and the related data in Table 5.9, and the summary output (the regression model) is shown in Table 4.

TABLE 4. Summary Output

Regression Statistics	
Multiple R	0.683924
R square	0.467753
Adjusted R square	0.438183
Standard error	1.900886
Observation	20

Total variation = Regression variation + Unexplained variation (error or residual)
Observations = 20
Total variation = 3863.80
Residual or error variation = 711.97
Regression variation = 3151.63
Coefficient of determination = 0.46 (the percent of the variation of y explained by its linear relationship with x)
Regression equation = $y = 2.92 + 0.53x$ (For each year of experience added to an employee on the job, average weekly productive output increases by 0.53 units.)

ANOVA

	df	SS	MS	F	Significance F
Regression	1	57.15937	57.15937	15.81886	0.000883
Residual	18	65.04063	3.613369		
Total	19	122.2			

	Coefficients	Standard Error	t Stat	P-value
Intercept	2.924678	1.416767	2.064333	0.053704
Years on the job	0.53221	0.133812	3.977293	0.000883

Testing the Regression Model

The purpose of testing the regression model in the summary output is to ascertain if the regression equation is useful in explaining the behavior in the outcomes of the response variable. Put in the form of a question: Are the outcomes illustrated by the observations of the response variable explained by their linear relationship with the explanatory variable or do the outcomes occur by chance?

To relate this question to our example, we will test whether average weekly productive output is a function of number of years on the job. In order to answer that question, ANOVA is used to compare the present regression model to a restricted model:

Regression model $\quad \hat{y} = a + bx + \varepsilon$

Restricted model $\quad \hat{y} = a + \varepsilon$

where ε = random error.

The restricted model states that changes in the response variable are due solely to random error (ε), or the explanatory variable has zero net regression coefficients. Thus, the hypotheses for ANOVA are:

Null or given hypothesis (H_0) $\quad\quad b = 0$

Alternative hypothesis (H_1) $\quad\quad b \neq 0$

The analysis and conclusion of whether the regression model is acceptable are partially based upon the hypothesis mentioned above. Considering our summary output, the decision rule is simple:

- If the significance F value (also known as the p-value) is less than or equal to 0.05, then the null hypothesis (H_0) is rejected. The impact on the response variable is more than a function of random error or chance.
- If the significance F value (also known as the p-value) is greater than or equal to 0.05, then the null hypothesis (H_0) cannot be rejected. The impact on the response variable is a function of chance or random error.

Interpreting the Regression Equation

The regression equation tells us to what extent weekly productive output is a function of years on the job. Given that

$$\hat{y} = a + bx + \varepsilon$$

then our equation states that

$$y = 2.92 + 0.53x + \varepsilon$$

or for each year of experience added to an employee on the job, average weekly productive output increases by 0.53 units.

Standard Error of the Estimate

Standard error indicates how accurate a predictor the regression equation is. The more accurate the equation is as a predictor of the response variable, the lower the value of the standard error of the estimate.

R^2: Coefficient of Determination

R^2 is the proportion of the total variation in the response variable that is explained by its linear relationship with the explanatory variable. In our example, only 46% of the variation in weekly production can be explained by its linear relationship with number of years on the job. A strong R^2 is 0.71 or higher.

Analysis of the Residuals

The basic assumptions required for regression and correlation analysis were outlined earlier. With respect to the residuals, the following are carried forward:

1. The residuals must be independent and random.
2. The residuals must be normally distributed.
3. The residuals must have a constant variance across all values of X.

The chart output of the normal probability and line fit plots is as follows:

■ **Normal probability plot**: The normal probability plot (Figure 3) of the residuals should roughly follow a straight line. Based on this plot, the residuals appear to be approximately normal.

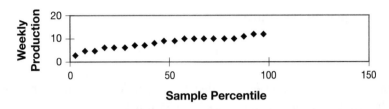

FIGURE 3.   Normal Probability Plot

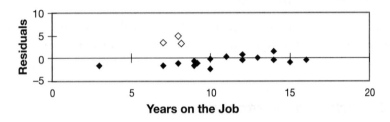

FIGURE 4.   Years on the Job Residual Plot

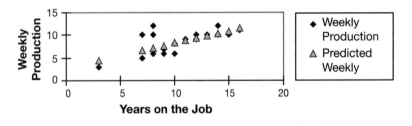

FIGURE 5.   Years on the Job Line Fit Plot

■ **Residual vs. fitted line values plot**: In the residual (Figure 4) vs. fitted values (Figure 5) plot, the residuals should be scattered randomly about zero. Based on these two plots, some residuals appear not randomly scattered about zero. Why?

Regression Analysis Exercise

Using the data in Table 1, conduct a regression analysis and answer the following questions:

1. Is the regression equation an acceptable one?   Yes ☐   No ☐
   Why or why not?

2. If the regression equation is an acceptable one,   Yes ☐   No ☐
   is it an accurate predictor?
   Why or why not?

3. Is the regression equation a strong predictor?   Yes ☐   No ☐
   Why or why not?

4. Does the regression equation satisfy the   Yes ☐   No ☐
   required assumptions?

FINANCIAL IMPACT ANALYSIS: NET PRESENT VALUE, RETURN ON INVESTMENT, AND PAYBACK PERIOD

Net Present Value

A Six Sigma project's net present value (NPV) is its contribution to a company's bottom line through the production of cost savings or revenue enhancements, over time, minus the initial investment of the resources to produce the cost savings or revenue enhancements. It is a project's current worth of future cost savings or revenue enhancements minus its initial investment. As indicated in the preceding sentences, NPV takes into account the *time value of money:*

NPV = Present value of projected cost savings/revenue enhancements

   − Project's initial investment

NPV is calculated by subtracting a project's initial investment from the present value of the project's projected benefits discounted at a rate equal to the company's cost of capital. The formula for NPV is defined as follows:

$$NPV = \sum_{t=1}^{n} \frac{CF_t}{(1 + k)^t} = II$$

where CF = cash flows derived from projected cost savings or revenue enhancements discounted at a firm's cost of capital, k = the firm's cost of capital, and II = the project's initial investment.

The decision rule for accepting or rejecting a Six Sigma project using NPV is as follows: If the NPV of a Six Sigma solution is greater than or equal to zero, then accept the Six Sigma solution; otherwise reject the solution. If the NPV is greater than or equal to zero, the company will earn a return greater than or equal to its cost of capital. Such an action would enhance or maintain the company's profitability.

Manual Calculation

1. Estimate the known cost and potential investments associated with the solution.
2. Quantify and project the estimated benefits secured by the solution for a reasonable period of time (three to five years).
3. Use the present value chart in Table 5 in to determine the present value of cost savings over the next three to five years.
4. Determine the company's cost of capital. Each company estimates its own cost of capital. Traditionally, a safe figure to use has been 8.4%. Another widely accepted standard is an average return of 12% on equities and stocks since 1926. Locate your estimate figure across the top of Table 5.
5. Determine the period (number of years) over which the analysis is to be calculated and locate the figure in the left column of Table 5. The NPV is the point where your required return and the period cross.
6. Multiply the present value interest factor by the cost savings or revenue enhancement for one period.
7. Compare the project's cost to the present value of the cost savings over time and make a decision about whether or not to accept the project solution.

Present Value of an Ordinary Annuity Table

Present value interest factors for a one-dollar annuity discounted at k% for n periods:

$$\text{PVIFA}_{k,n} = \sum_{t=1}^{n} \frac{1}{(1+k)^t}$$

TABLE 5. Present Value Chart

Period	1%	2%	3%	4%	5%	6%	8%	10%	12%
1	0.990	0.980	0.971	0.962	0.952	0.943	0.926	0.909	0.893
2	1.970	1.942	1.913	1.886	1.859	1.833	1.783	1.736	1.690
3	2.941	2.884	2.829	2.775	2.723	2.673	2.577	2.487	2.402
4	3.902	3.808	3.717	3.630	3.546	3.465	3.312	3.170	3.037
5	4.853	4.713	4.580	4.452	4.329	4.212	3.993	3.791	3.605
6	5.795	5.601	5.417	5.242	5.076	4.917	4.623	4.355	4.111
7	6.728	6.472	6.230	6.002	5.786	5.582	5.206	4.868	4.564
8	7.652	7.325	7.020	6.733	6.463	6.210	5.747	5.335	4.968
9	8.566	8.162	7.786	7.435	7.108	6.802	6.247	5.759	5.328
10	9.471	8.983	8.530	8.111	7.722	7.360	6.710	6.145	5.650

Calculation with Excel

1. Estimate the known cost and potential investments associated with the solution.
2. Quantify and project the estimated benefits secured by the solution for a reasonable period of time (three to five years).
3. Organize your data in a spreadsheet, as illustrated in Table 6.*
4. Select **Insert > Function**.
5. Under **Search for a Function**, type **npv** and click **OK**.
6. Place the cursor inside **RATE** and select the cell with the cost of capital.
7. Place the cursor inside **Value1** and select the remaining cells.
8. Click **OK**.

Your answer for the data in Table 6 should be $7740.10.

TABLE 6. Data for Net Present Value Calculation

	A	B
1	12%	Annual discount rate
2	−100,000	Initial cost of investment one year from today
3	30,000	Return from first year
4	42,000	Return from second year
5	68,000	Return from third year

* Derived from Microsoft Excel® Help—NPV.

Net Present Value Exercise

Purpose: To conduct an NPV analysis and draw a conclusion.

Action: Use the example and data below to conduct an NPV analysis and determine the best course of action for the operation.

Scenario: A project team is using NPV analysis to determine whether a recommended Six Sigma solution is financially feasible. Team members have been looking at the increasing volume of calls to the call center. While performing root cause analysis, they discover that a significant share of calls could be handled over the Internet or through integrated voice response (IVR) processing. They identify a number of ways to handle the increased call volume and decide that purchasing and programming an IVR unit (at a cost of $327,000) and augmenting the company's Web site (at a cost of $7000) is the less expensive alternative compared to outsourcing the call center.

The team members analyze all the relevant costs to acquire, install, and utilize the IVR system and the cost to augment the Web site. They examine the value of the capital purchase over its estimated useful life (five years) and assume 12% as the cost of capital. Their analysis is outlined in Table 7.

Conduct an NPV analysis and determine if the team's solution is financially feasible. The answer to this exercise can be found at the end of this appendix.

Return on Investment

Return on investment (ROI) is an estimate and measure of the overall effectiveness of a Six Sigma project team's ability to produce a favorable project

TABLE 7. Net Present Value Exercise Analysis

Investments	Related Expense	Annual Benefit	Savings
IVR and programming	$327,000	Reduced overtime	$112,000
Web site upgrade	7,000	Reduced training expenses	12,499
Lost production	1,000	Reduction in temporary workforce	21,000
Estimated total investment	**($335,000)**	Estimated annual savings	**$145,499**

outcome. ROI, which also can be called a project team's return on resources applied (RORA) or return on project assets (ROPA), estimates and measures a team's overall effectiveness in generating a favorable financial return on a project effort. The higher a project team's ROI, the better.

A project's ROI is calculated as follows:

$$ROI = \frac{\text{Cost savings}}{\text{Asset investment} + \text{Labor cost} + \text{Miscellaneous investment}}$$

The numerator in the equation can represent either the estimated cost savings when initially evaluating a project or the estimated cost savings of a solution as part of a feasibility study. The denominator in the equation represents the total investment derived from the project cost and solution offered.

Using the data from the example in the preceding section, we can calculate the project team's ROI as:

- Project's projected cost savings (before tax) = $729,995
- Project's projected investment = $335,000
- Estimated project team investment (labor and materials) = $60,000

$$ROI = \frac{\$729,995}{\$335,000 + \$60,000} = 1.84$$

This project's solution has a favorable ROI; it provides a return that more than covers the value of the resources applied.

Payback Period

Payback period is an estimate of the amount of time required for a project team's solution to recover the cost incurred from implementing the solution. Payback period can be used in conjunction with NPV and ROI calculations as criteria for evaluating proposed project solutions.

Payback Period Example

Data for project solutions X and Y are outlined in Table 8. The payback period for solution X is two quarters and for solution Y is four quarters. Using the payback period as the only criterion, solution X would be pref-

TABLE 8. Data for Payback Period Analysis

Date: 5/25/08 Total Investment	Solution X $100,000	Solution Y $95,000
Quarter	Cost Savings	Cost Savings
3Q/08	$75,000	$20,000
4Q/08	60,000	20,000
1Q/09	20,000	40,000
2Q/09	30,000	90,000
3Q/09	10,000	60,000
Payback period	2 quarters	4 quarters
Net present value	$189,674.27	$216,021.73
Return on investment	190%	227%

erable to solution Y—especially if management's goal is to recover cost savings within the fiscal year. However, using the payback period in conjunction with NPV and ROI assessments shows solution Y to be a more favorable alternative and may cause management to re-evaluate its decision rule to recover cost savings within the fiscal year.

By measuring how quickly a project can recover its initial investment, payback period as a criterion only implicitly considers the timing of cost savings. By using payback period analysis in conjunction with the NPV calculation, decision makers can explicitly consider the time value of project cost savings as part of their final determination.

Financial Impact Analysis Exercise

Members of a Six Sigma project team are looking at the problem of rework in their area. While analyzing the problem for root cause, they discover that the largest piece of the problem is rejects. They identify various ways to improve the existing technology and processes. They also consider implementing a more intensive inspection process. Finally, they decide that a new IT system is needed.

The team members survey several companies and identify five IT systems that meet the requirements of their operation. After considering all the costs related to installing the new system and getting it up and running, as well

TABLE 9. Data for Financial Impact Analysis Exercise

Initial Investment	System A $26,000	System B $500,000	System C $170,000	System D $950,000	System E $80,000
Year			Cost Savings ($)		
1	4,000	100,000	20,000	230,000	0
2	4,000	120,000	19,000	230,000	0
3	4,000	140,000	18,000	230,000	0
4	4,000	160,000	17,000	230,000	20,000
5	4,000	180,000	16,000	230,000	30,000
6	4,000	200,000	15,000	230,000	0
7	4,000		14,000	230,000	50,000
8	4,000		13,000	230,000	60,000
9	4,000		12,000		70,000
10	4,000		11,000		

as the cost savings to be derived over the estimated useful life of each system, the team is faced with choosing from among the options outlined in Table 9.

- Using a 14% cost of capital, calculate the NPV of each alternative.
- Calculate the ROI for each alternative.
- Calculate the payback period for each alternative.
- What are your conclusions?

The answers to this exercise can be found at the end of this appendix.

DATA COLLECTION EFFORTS

Planning

An important task involved in a Six Sigma project is planning and executing an effective and complete data collection effort. Whether a project team is merely fact finding or collecting data for a specific improvement effort, it is essential that the team collect and produce a valid and reliable set of numerical facts to properly understand the situation. The first thing to appreciate about collecting data is that the undertaking is not cheap. Data collection will tax employee time, data mining will tax IT assets, and data collection will demand a lot of time from the management team. To ensure a data collection effort is successful, use the following planning guidelines:

1. **Determine what you want to know**: It is important to know what the data will be used for. It is important to know if the data will be used to monitor a process, to identify the significant causes of a problem, to establish a cause and effect relationship, or to verify that a certain level of performance is being maintained.

2. **Determine how you will analyze the data**: Knowing how the data will be analyzed will determine how the data collector will gather the data. If the team is going to conduct correlation or regression analysis, the data set will need to be collected in pairs. If the team is going to conduct process capability index (Cpk) analysis or construct a histogram, then the data set may be collected in a block. If the team is going to conduct control chart analysis, then rational subgrouping techniques may be used.

3. **Determine the relevant characteristics to be analyzed**: A call center director may want to analyze first-call resolution (defectives data) and at the same time may want to determine the reasons (defects data) that contribute to the lack of first-call resolution. Knowing the characteristics of the data will empower you to collect the right data efficiently.

4. **Select the appropriate measurement technique**: The measurement technique will empower you to build the appropriate data collection plan that is repeatable and reproducible. The plan will be repeatable in that the data collector knows how to collect the data accurately over several data collection cycles. The plan will be reproducible in that different data collectors can produce data yields accurately. In order to achieve this end, the data collection plan should include a strong operational definition. Both attribute and continuous data specifications must be defined accurately; a strong operational definition will accomplish that end.

5. **Determine the time and place where the data will be collected**: Understanding the time and place where the data will be collected can be determined by the goals of the data collection effort. For example, if a call center director wants to know which shift has the best first-call resolution, then the time and place of the data col-

lection will be determined by shift and the location of the shift's effort.

6. **Decide who will collect the data and if data collection training is required.**

7. **Determine the quantity of data to be collected:** Most Six Sigma analysis data are collected in samples to understand the overall behavior of an operation. Calculating the proper sample size is discussed in the next section.

A sample data collection plan is shown in Table 10.

Calculating Sample Size

Most Six Sigma data collection efforts are inferential in nature. The effort is inferential in the sense that the Six Sigma professional will collect a sample of data from a population of operational output and draw conclusions about the entire population based on the sample data. This type of statistical sampling is not unlike political opinion polls, where pollsters survey a statistically valid sample size of opinion and draw conclusions about the opinions of an entire segment of a constituency. To ensure the validity of the conclusions drawn from samples, and the accuracy of the inferences drawn from sample data, three assumptions regarding the data must be met:

1. Samples are representative of the population.
2. Samples are independent and random.
3. The population is normally distributed.

The following sections provide the procedures for calculating a statistically valid sample size manually and with QI Macros.

Variable Data

Manual Calculation

Step 1. Determine the margin of error for the sample populations: In our example, the target value is a mean time to restore of 30 minutes. An acceptable margin of error for performance assessment is ±5 minutes.

TABLE 10. Performance Data Collection Plan for a Customer Service Call Center

Metric			Data Collection		
Metric	Type of Metric	Type of Data	Instrument	Operational Definition Procedure	Segmentation and Stratification
First-call resolution p chart for proportion of customer service calls resolved in initial contact	Quality	Discrete	Direct human observation; live or recorded with screen observations	Call survey review—direct observation. Determine if customer's issue is resolved at end of call or requires further contact. If the issue is resolved to the satisfaction of the customer, that first-call resolution is affirmed.	Calls stratified on a continuous shift. Sampled every 15 minutes—see sampling plan. Issue type categorized based on internal process function. Pareto analysis of strata.
Average speed of answer XmR chart, $\overline{X}$,S chart, Cpk	Quality	Continuous	Manpower planning and forecasting system	Supervisors will pull average speed of answer data from the manpower planning data system every 15 minutes during every hour of the operation.	Day: Continuous shift; sampled every 15-minute cycle. Month: Daily observations become a monthly subgroup.
Service level agreement % calls answered within X seconds	Quality	Discrete	Manpower planning and forecasting system	Supervisors will pull service level agreement data from the manpower planning data system every 15 minutes during every hour of the operation.	Day: Continuous shift; sampled every 15-minute cycle. Month: Daily observations become a monthly subgroup.
Occupancy/ utilization XmR chart, $\overline{X}$,S chart, Cpk	Efficiency	Continuous	Manpower planning and forecasting system	Supervisors will pull occupancy/ utilization data from the manpower planning data system every 15 minutes during every hour of the operation.	Day: Continuous shift; sampled every 15-minute cycle. Month: Daily observations become a monthly subgroup.
Average handling time XmR chart, $\overline{X}$,S chart, Cpk	Efficiency	Continuous	Manpower planning and forecasting system	Supervisors will pull average handling time data from the manpower planning data system every 15 minutes during every hour of the operation.	Day: Continuous shift; sampled every 15-minute cycle. Month: Daily observations become a monthly subgroup.
Average talk time XmR chart, $\overline{X}$,S chart, Cpk	Efficiency	Continuous	Manpower planning and forecasting system	Supervisors will pull average talk time data from the manpower planning data system every 15 minutes during every hour of the operation.	Day: Continuous shift; sampled every 15-minute cycle. Month: Daily observations become a monthly subgroup.

TABLE 10. Performance Data Collection Plan for a Customer Service Call Center (continued)

Metric	Data Collection Form	What	Data Collection		
				Sampling Plan	
			Where	When	How Many
First-call resolution	Develop with the help of QA person	First call resolved; customer service calls; agency and carrier calls	Observation of calls for both north and south coast operations	Historical calls Dates: XX/XX/XX 1 month of data	Four calls every hour, every workday for one month.
Average speed of answer	Check sheet or Excel spreadsheet—will be provided	Average speed of answer in seconds	Observation of calls for both north and south coast operations	Historical calls Dates: XX/XX/XX 1 month of data	One observation every 15 minutes during the entire workday. Each day becomes a subgroup for the monthly analysis.
Service level agreement	Check sheet or Excel spreadsheet—will be provided	Percent of incoming customer service calls that are answered within X seconds	Observation of calls for both north and south coast operations	Historical calls Dates: XX/XX/XX 1 month of data	One observation every 15 minutes during the entire workday. Each day becomes a subgroup for the monthly analysis.
Occupancy/ utilization	Check sheet or Excel spreadsheet—will be provided	Percent of time CSRs are occupied by customer interaction	Observation of calls for both north and south coast operations	Historical calls Dates: XX/XX/XX 1 month of data	One observation every 15 minutes during the entire workday. Each day becomes a subgroup for the monthly analysis.
Average handling time	Check sheet or Excel spreadsheet—will be provided	Average time for a CSR to provide and record service to an account	Observation of calls for both north and south coast operations	Historical calls Dates: XX/XX/XX 1 month of data	One observation every 15 minutes during the entire workday. Each day becomes a subgroup for the monthly analysis.
Average talk time	Check sheet or Excel spreadsheet—will be provided	Average time the CSR directly interacts with the customer over the network	Observation of calls for both north and south coast operations	Historical calls Dates: XX/XX/XX 1 month of data	One observation every 15 minutes during the entire workday. Each day becomes a subgroup for the monthly analysis.

Step 2. Determine the standard deviation: The easiest way to find the standard deviation is by analyzing historical data. Oftentimes, decision makers are faced with little historical data, which may require them to collect present or near future data. Either way, collecting a small random sample of 30 should be sufficient.

Step 3. Perform the calculation: Use the following formula from the National Institute of Standards and Technology:

$$n = \left(\frac{1.96}{\text{margin of error}} \right)^2 \times \text{stdev}^2$$

where stdev is the standard deviation. The level of confidence should reflect the judgment of the manager ($1.645 = 90\%$, $1.96 = 95\%$, $2.576 = 99\%$). Service managers should consider the risk associated with service failure and customer satisfaction. It is important to note that 1.96 in the equation provides for a 95% confidence level. This example carries an assumption that the sample mean is normally distributed and the data are sufficiently randomized and represent the population from which they were drawn. For practical purposes, the sample mean should be tested to ensure that the normal probability assumption is supported before proceeding, and the data collection plan should ensure that the data are representative of the population and are sufficiently randomized.

So, using the earlier mean time to restore example, the equation would be

$$n = \left(\frac{1.96}{5} \right) \times 6.41^2$$

which would yield a subgroup size of $n = 6$.

Calculation with QI Macros

Using the data from the example above:

1. Select **QI Macros > Anova and Analysis Tools**.
2. Select **Sample Size**.

TABLE 11. Sample Size Calculation for Variable Data

Confidence level (power)	95%	Confidence Factors	
Confidence interval	5	**Percent**	**Z**
Population (if known)		80%	1.28
		90%	1.64
Attribute Data		95%	1.96
Percent defects (50%)	50%	99%	2.58
Sample size (unknown population)	0	**Defaults**	
Sample size for known population		0.05	Confidence interval
			(precision ±5% = 0.05)
Variable Data		50%	Percent defects (attribute − 50%)
Standard deviation ([high–low]/6)	6.41	0.167	Standard deviation ([high–low]/6)
Sample size (unknown population)	6		
Sample size for known population			

3. Input data: B1, Confidence Level Select 95% > B2, Confidence Interval 5.
4. Variable Data: B11, Standard Deviation 6.41.
5. View: B12, Calculated Sample Size (Unknown Population).

The spreadsheet for the QI Macros sample size calculation is provided in Table 11.

Attribute Data

Manual Calculation

Step 1. Determine the margin of error as a percentage for the sample population: Suppose the service manager of a global telecommunications provider wants to know what percent of broadband customers are satisfied with the quality of the network services. It would be meaningful for the manager to know if that opinion is within ±3%.

Step 2. Determine the likely percent defective, q: In our example, the discrete measure is an indicator of satisfied vs. not satisfied—a 50/50 proposition.

Step 3. Determine the likely percentage of conforming outcome, p: The calculation is $p = 1.0 − q$. If $q = 0.5$, then $p = 0.5$.

Step 4. Perform the calculation: Use the following formula from the National Institute of Standards and Technology:

$$n = 1.96^2 \times \frac{(pq)}{d^2}$$

where d is the margin of error of 3%, q is the percent defective, and p is the percent conforming. Therefore:

$$n = 1.96^2 \times \frac{(0.5 \times 0.5)}{0.03^2}$$

which makes $n = 1067$, the most economical sample size.

Calculation with QI Macros

Using the data from the example above:

1. Select **QI Macros > Anova and Analysis Tools.**
2. Select **Sample Size.**
3. Input data: B1, Confidence Level Select 95% > B2, Confidence Interval .03.
4. Attribute Data: 6, Percent Defects 50%.
5. View: B7, Calculated Sample Size (Unknown Population).

The spreadsheet for the QI Macros sample size calculation is illustrated in Table 12.

Systematic Sampling

Systematic sampling frequently is used in the place of random sampling. Systematic sampling is also referred to as the Nth name selection technique. After the required sample size is produced, every Nth record is selected from the population. As long as the list from the population is sufficiently randomized, this sampling method is as good as the random sampling method. The main advantage of systematic sampling over random sampling is simplicity.

Systematic sampling can assess the performance of an operation over extended periods of time in order to get a general picture of the current

TABLE 12. Sample Size Calculation for Attribute Data

Confidence level (power)	95%	Confidence Factors	
Confidence interval	0.03	Percent	Z
Population (if known)		80%	1.28
		90%	1.64
Attribute Data		95%	1.96
Percent defects (50%)	50%	99%	2.58
Sample size (unknown population)	1067	Defaults	
Sample size for known population		0.05	Confidence interval (precision ±5% = 0.05)
Variable Data		50%	Percent defects (attribute – 50%)
Standard deviation ([high–low]/6)		0.167	Standard deviation ([high–low]/6)
Sample size (unknown population)			
Sample size for known population			

situation. Using the example of how long it takes a utility company's service technicians to complete service orders during a month, the steps for systematic sampling are as follows:

1. Decide how much data is needed. Given a confidence level of 95%, a confidence interval of 3 minutes, and a standard deviation of 6.5: monthly sample size of $n = 16$ data points to study the service technicians' service order cycle time.
2. Estimate the total number of service orders most likely to occur in the operation over the time period being evaluated (one month): $T = 160$ completed service orders per month.
3. Divide T by n to arrive at the interval of successive units included in the sample: $k = 160/16 = 10$.
4. Select the starting order and plot the time for every tenth order that follows.

Stratified Sampling

Stratified sampling is a commonly used probability method that is superior to random sampling because it reduces sampling error. A stratum is a subgroup of a population that shares one or more common characteristic(s). Examples of strata are:

Population	Stratum
High-school students	High-school seniors
Church ministries	Singles ministry
Sprinters	100-meter runners

To conduct stratified sampling, first identify the relevant strata and their representation in the population. Then conduct random sampling to select a statistically valid number of subjects from each stratum. Once done, conduct the analysis.

Block Sampling

Block sampling, also known as quota sampling, is a method designed to select units in a block of predetermined size. Block sampling is used to gain a picture of data that are time or sequence dependent. The steps for block sampling are as follows:

1. Calculate a statistically valid sample size.
2. Determine the location and time to initiate the data collection effort.
3. Take the first unit from the operation at that time and every unit that follows until you have data on *n* units.

Operational Definition

Operational definitions help to clearly define what is being measured. There are three basic elements of an operational definition: the critical-to-quality characteristic (CTQ), the instrument to be used in measuring, and the method for measuring. Each element must be clearly defined, understood, and consistently used by all data collectors. Examples of operational definitions follow.

Attribute Data

- **Characteristic (CTQ):** First-call resolution. Quality metric: The measurement of service effectiveness. If the customer's reason for calling is satisfied during the call, resolution is affirmed. *Caveat*: The reason for the customer's inquiry must be within the reasonable and customary expectations of the business-to-customer relationship.

- **Instrument:** Direct preservation of customer service calls through listening and viewing proxy screen. Direct human observation, live or recorded with screen observations.
- **Measurement method:** Call survey review—direct observation. Determine if the customer's issue is resolved at the end of the call or requires further contact. If the issue is resolved to the satisfaction of the customer, that first-call resolution is confirmed.

Variable Data

- **Characteristic (CTQ):** Average speed of answer. Quality metric: The average time it takes a customer to speak with a service representative from entering the queue to the service representative greeting.
- **Instrument:** Manpower planning and forecasting system.
- **Measurement method:** Supervisors will pull average speed of answer data from the manpower planning data system every 15 minutes during every hour of the operation. Supervisors will input the data into a spreadsheet and plot the data on a control chart for the day.

When operationally defining measures, it is vital to make certain the definition distinguishes between measuring discrete data and continuous data.

Types of Data

Data are objective information and numbers expressed as numerical fact. There are three types of data: discrete data, continuous data, and locational data. Table 13 provides definitions and examples. Discrete data and continuous data are used most often by the Six Sigma professional.

Discrete Data

Discrete data are categorical in nature. For the Six Sigma professional, discrete data are an expression of the presence or absence of the characteristic being measured. They can only be expressed as integers. Discrete measurements often are quality metrics that answer questions like:

- How may service center calls were resolved in the first customer interaction?

TABLE 13. Types of Data

Data Classification	Discrete Data	Continuous Data
Also known as	Attribute data Count data Digital data	Variable data Measurement data Analog data
Definition	■ Data that are categorical and generated by counting defects or defectives ■ Often defined by the presence or absence of an error or fault	■ Data that yield a measurement or number for each unit observed ■ Data can be divided and subdivided
Examples	First-call resolution Order form error rate Misdirected calls Rejection rate Acceptance rate Invoice error rate	Average handling time Average speed of answer Length Average cycle time Costs

- How many billing errors occurred in the last cycle?
- How many second-call service orders were completed last month?

Continuous Data

Continuous data are measurable in nature and are expressed as real numbers. These data typically are measured with some instrument or device. Continuous data often are measures of productivity, efficiency, or cost that answer questions like:

- What is the call center's average handling time?
- What is the average cycle time per completed work order?
- What is the average operating cost per customer?

Regarded as better quality data than discrete data, continuous data are more precise and a richer source of information. For example, one would know much more about how profitable a business is by looking at sales revenue per day vs. how many days a company recognized revenue.

Locational Data

Locational data answer the "where" question. Charts that utilize locational data include radar charts, precision charts, and concentration maps.

NET PRESENT VALUE EXERCISE ANSWER

In the final analysis, over the estimated useful life of the IVR, the solution will return its original cost and will generate additional savings. The NPV of this decision is greater than zero; thus this endeavor's return will be greater than its cost of capital. The company should accept the solution.

FINANCIAL IMPACT ANALYSIS EXERCISE ANSWER

Table 14 shows the NPV for each alternative using a 14% cost of capital, the ROI for each alternative, and the payback period for each alternative.

TABLE 14. Financial Impact Analysis Exercise Answer

Initial Investment	System A −$26,000	System B −$500,000	System C −$170,000	System D −$950,000	System E −$80,000
Year			Cost Savings ($)		
1	4,000	100,000	20,000	230,000	0
2	4,000	120,000	19,000	230,000	0
3	4,000	140,000	18,000	230,000	0
4	4,000	160,000	17,000	230,000	20,000
5	4,000	180,000	16,000	230,000	30,000
6	4,000	200,000	15,000	230,000	0
7	4,000		14,000	230,000	50,000
8	4,000		13,000	230,000	60,000
9	4,000		12,000		70,000
10	4,000		11,000		
Net present value	$14,000	$400,000	($15,000)	$890,000	$150,000
Return on investment	1.54	1.8	0.911764706	1.936842105	2.875
Payback period	7	4	No payback	5	7

Although system D is the most expensive, it promises the greatest return and has the best NPV. Its payback is very competitive. However, a more prudent investment seems to be system B. If there is somewhat of a constraint on capital investments, system A seems to be the best investment.

INDEX